IN
OPPOSITION
TO
CORE
CURRICULUM

Contributions to the Study of Education

Black Students in Higher Education:
Conditions and Experiences in the 1970s
Edited by *Gail E. Thomas*

The Scope of Faculty Collective Bargaining:
An Analysis of Faculty Union Agreements
at Four-Year Institutions of Higher Education
Ronald L. Johnstone

Brainpower for the Cold War:
The Sputnik Crisis
and National Defense Education Act of 1958
Barbara Barksdale Clowse

IN OPPOSITION TO CORE CURRICULUM

Alternative Models for Undergraduate Education

Edited by

James W. Hall

with Barbara L. Kevles

CONTRIBUTIONS TO THE STUDY OF EDUCATION, NUMBER 4

GREENWOOD PRESS

WESTPORT, CONNECTICUT • LONDON, ENGLAND

Library of Congress Cataloging in Publication Data
Main entry under title:

In opposition to core curriculum.

(Contributions to the study of education, ISSN
0196-707X ; no. 4)
   Bibliography: p.
   Includes index.
   1. Universities and colleges--United States--
Curricula--Planning. I. Hall, James W. II. Kevles,
Barbara L. III. Series.
LB2361.5.I5   378'.199'0973   81-8125
ISBN 0-313-22902-3 (lib. bdg.)   AACR2

Library of Congress Catalog Card Number: 81-8125
ISBN: 0-313-22902-3
ISSN: 0196-707X

First published in 1982

Greenwood Press
A division of Congressional Information Service, Inc.
88 Post Road West, Westport, Connecticut 06881

Printed in the United States of America

10 9 8 7 6 5 4 3 2 1

Education, like every other important entity of society, must be responsive to the world it serves or suffer from the constant danger of becoming static and lifeless. Its responses must be active, innovative, contemporary. And those who design education must do more than merely respond; they must develop initiatives of their own that reflect an awareness of changing necessities.

Diversity by Design, Report of the Commission on Non-Traditional Study: Samuel B. Gould, Chairman.

CONTENTS

EIGHT: CONCLUSIONS

     Atraditional Viewpoint
     James W. Hall with Barbara L. Kevles   197

     Bibliography   221

     Index   231

PREFACE

As the ninth decade of this century begins, educational institutions of higher learning are floundering in an identity crisis. Shaken by a decade of rapid changes in students, curricula, and budgets, American colleges and universities are seeking to regain the stability and clarity of the past by reassessing the questions, "What is an educated person?" and "How best can educational institutions arrive at socially and intellectually responsive curricula for today's world?" On the surface, these debates usually argue the best means to secure academic quality, as if there is an ideal rubric against which to judge all curricular aims. On a deeper level, these arguments reflect grave differences about the definition of this elusive academic grail and the mission that higher education will fulfill in the last decades of the twentieth century.

Yet the crucial issue of socially responsive curricula cannot be defined in a vacuum of abstraction. As Martin Kaplan, coauthor of the influential book *Educating for Survival* notes in his essay, "The Wrong Solution to the Right Problem," included in this volume:

> I do not think that educational issues are in fact exclusively educational issues; rather, they are—in part at least—a reflection of problems that occur on the economic, political, social, and ethical levels as well.

In response to such contemporary social ambiguities as the value of degrees in the job market, shrinking enrollments, tough competition among priorities for the tax dollar, some leading educators want to restore a core curriculum and other possibly rigid regulations of the past to foster the illusion of institutional self-confidence in an anxious and insecure world.

Advocates of a core curriculum suggest an educated person is defined by a portion of acquired knowledge the non-college graduate lacks. On the contrary, this volume argues that a specific and highly limited set of courses should not be a prescription for the educated person. First, such a definition is simply too restrictive for the many different types of students with varied backgrounds, levels of preparation, and career aspirations who fill out college applications today. In such a richly diverse society, students should be allowed to demonstrate their college-developed capacities in dozens of ways. The knowledge imparted by a core curriculum is far too unimaginative and inflexible a standard by which to assess the real talents and potential of a chronologically, economically, racially, educationally diverse college student population.

Second, the rationale of the core curriculum falls apart for even more diverse adult students. The odds are quite small that a required core introductory course will intersect with the interests or achieved level of sophistication of an adult student who has been in the work world a number of years and who probably has accumulated significant knowledge and skills.

Third, and most important, a core curriculum prevents students from achieving the highest levels of intellectual and personal maturity attainable through a college education. By denying students significant involvement in formulating or choosing their own curricula, a preselected curriculum does not allow students to confront their own career goals and to make choices, and thus, it fails to help students mature into adults capable of making considered decisions and judgments.

Other curricular designs are assessed by three recent books that have perspectives different from those of the revivalists of core. One Carnegie study, *Missions of the College Curriculum* (1977), labels many of the changes in college curricula as consumer-oriented. *The Perpetual Dream: Reform and Experiment in the*

American College by Gerald Grant and David Riesman (1978) provides an important analysis of selected alternative models by describing particular programs and their implementation. *The Modern American College* (1981), edited by Arthur W. Chickering, focuses on curricular development and its application to teaching practices in a variety of academic disciplines.

In contrast, this volume describes curricular alternatives motivated not by academic utopias or reactionary revisionism but by lasting social changes that have required colleges to serve more diverse student populations than ever before. Our writers recognize this broader intellectual and social student background and the incapacity of traditional departmental structures to respond. They propose sound educational responses to the social challenges within and without academe that maintain standards both of curricular coherence and of academic excellence. In summary, they express not only *how* new and alternative curricular approaches can be effective but also *why* they are essential for the future of higher education in America.

The essays included herein represent contributions from a group of forward-minded educators who possess experience in curricular experimentation within both traditional academic settings and innovative or external degree programs. Taking their cues from the social and educational requirements of our times, these educators stress more flexible, varied perspectives on curriculum both to meet the challenge of the new, diverse, clientele of older, part-time, and noncampus residents and the presence of pluralistic, educational values in contemporary culture.

Among the knowledgeable contributors to this collection are Martin Kaplan, former chief speech writer to Vice-President Walter F. Mondale and currently a commentator on the nationally televised CBS program, "Morning with Charles Kuralt," who illuminates the social imperatives for curricular change in the history of American education. James W. Hall, pioneer in this country's largest and most successful nontraditional degree program, together with Barbara L. Kevles, a nationally recognized magazine writer and faculty member both at New York University and The New School in New York City, explore the social conditions catalyzing the most recent curricular innovations in higher education. Warren Bryan Martin, former director of the Danforth Foundation Graduate Fellowship Program and currently scholar in residence at the Carnegie Foundation for the Advancement of Teaching, offers four alternative curricular approaches to fulfill higher education's aims.

The focus of the book then shifts from a discussion of alternative curricular theories to the application of nontraditional curricula. Dee G. Appley of the University of Massachusetts stresses student-oriented objectives combining cognitive, societal-emotional, and moral development as the desirable goals for a reformed curriculum. Former associate dean of Empire State College, State University of New York, and currently Executive Director of CLEO (Compact for Lifelong Educational Opportunities), Lois Lamdin analyzes the intellectual coherence of individually-tailored curricula for the returning older college student.

Next, several distinguished educators delve into the concepts and practice of the interdisciplinary curricular structure. Ernest A. Lynton, a recognized specialist in educational change and Commonwealth Professor at the University of Massachusetts, suggests methods to implement curricular changes within the traditional academic setting, while Charles Muscatine, a veteran professor at the University of California at Berkeley, carves out the social impetus and benefit from such reform. With diligent objectivity, Patrick J. Hill, director of the Federated Learning Communities of the State University of New York at Stony Brook, scrutinizes the operations of one contextually interdisciplinary program based in a traditional institution.

Then several writers examine the validity of nontraditional curricula for students from a disadvantaged background. John O. Stevenson, Jr., president of the National Scholarship Service and Fund for Negro Students and former dean of the Metropolitan Regional Center of Empire State College, together with this volume's co-editor, Barbara L. Kevles, delineates the advantages and disadvantages of alternative and traditional curricula for minorities. In a similar vein, John David Maguire, president of Claremont University Center and Graduate School and former president of the State University of New York campus at Old Westbury, reports on the curricular experiments to educate the disadvantaged at Old Westbury. Mary Ann Biller, Dean of Lower Hudson Regional Center, Empire State College, State University of New York, uses a new perspective to join the apparently opposing objectives of vocational and liberal arts education.

In examination of the critical issues of curricular reform, Warren Bryan Martin summarizes the two-track higher educational system of today, and Martin Kaplan wrestles with the underlying question of all curricular debates, "What Is an Educated Person?". In conclusion, James W. Hall, with Barbara L. Kevles, distills the implications for undergraduate education from the book's collected essays and offers theoretical and practical precepts for a model college education from an atraditional viewpoint.

The quest for college curricula optimally suited to today should reach beyond academe to engage those policymakers and auditors who have become increasingly influential and accountable for higher education: trustees and public boards of higher education; statewide commissions and their administrative staffs; regional accreditation teams; overseers of budgets, audits, and financial aids; and state and federal elected representatives. All of these, at one level or another, are making critical policy decisions that, taken together, will profoundly shape collegiate education in the years ahead.

This book addresses the baccalaureate curricula, including those encompassed by community or junior colleges, because it is in the undergraduate sector that most students are enrolled and because it is undergraduate education that has played the part of the neglected stepchild of institutions of higher education during the recent years of rapid campus growth and increased professionalization. This is also the province that has endured most seriously the challenges to the fundamental values of the university. The curricular changes promoted by this volume can help renew the vital purpose of this educational arena, which, after all, is the barometer of the future of American society.

By James W. Hall
With Barbara L. Kevles

Saratoga Springs, New York
December, 1980

ACKNOWLEDGMENTS

We gratefully acknowledge the support of the Danforth Foundation, Saint Louis, Missouri, and the Society for Values in Higher Education, New Haven, Connecticut, whose grants encouraged the gestation of a portion of the papers ultimately included in this volume.

We also express our deep appreciation to Karen Burg, Terri Flynn, and Diane Thompson, who over a long period of time gave invaluable assistance in the production of the book.

ABOUT THE EDITORS

James W. Hall is President of the State University of New York's highly acclaimed innovative Empire State College. He first joined the State University of New York in 1966 as Associate University Dean for Arts and Cultural Affairs and then became Assistant Vice-Chancellor for Policy and Planning. A graduate of Bucknell University, he received a M.S.M. in sacred music from Union Theological Seminary and his M.A. and Ph.D. in American Civilization from the University of Pennsylvania. He has taught at Cedar Crest College, the State University of New York at Albany, and is concurrently Professor of Social Science at Empire State College. His special research area includes American character, arts, and culture. His scholarly articles have appeared in *The Journal of Popular Culture*, *The Educational Record*, and *The Journal of Higher Education*. He is the editor of the book, *Forging the American Character*. A Danforth graduate fellow, in 1978 Hall was designated by *Change* Magazine as one of the 100 top young leaders of the American Academy. He has served on numerous national educational committees, including panels of the American Council on Education and the American Association of State Colleges and Universities. He has consulted widely in advising educational institutions on new pedagogies for higher learning. Dr. Hall is listed in *Who's Who*.

Barbara L. Kevles, collaborator with James W. Hall, President of Empire State College, in the concept and development of this book, has held the rank of Adjunct in Writing and Criticism at Empire State College, a division of the State University of New York. At the same time, Ms. Kevles has continued to teach as a faculty member of the prestigious *Writing Workshop* of The New School in New York City and as a lecturer at New York University, where she also serves as consultant to the Director of the Programs in Communication to develop specialized curricula for the adult learner. Barbara Kevles was educated at Bryn Mawr College where she received a Bachelor of Arts degree. She has for a number of years articulated a special interest in social change and related issues in medicine, politics, and education. A charter editor of *Working Woman* and a national magazine writer, she has published more than one hundred articles in numerous magazines such as *The Atlantic, The New York Times, Change* and well-known literary journals. Her critically influential interview with Pulitzer poet, "Anne Sexton: The Art of Poetry XV," first appeared in *The Paris Review* and later was anthologized in *Writers At Work IV* and *Anne Sexton: The Artist and Her Critics*. In addition, Barbara Kevles is author of the introduction to the *1981 Writer's Market* and an introductory textbook published by Writer's Digest Books, *Basic Magazine Writing*.

ABOUT THE CONTRIBUTORS

Dee G. Appley has taught for more than twenty years at a number of public and private institutions of higher education including York University in Toronto, Connecticut College for Women, and, most recently, as Professor of Psychology at the University of Massachusetts, Amherst. In addition to her departmental appointments, Dr. Appley has been involved at each of these institutions with innovative or interdisciplinary programs such as University Without Walls, Project 10, and Bachelor Degree with Individual Concentration. She has a long standing commitment both to action-research related to personal, organizational, and social change and to the place of values within this process. She has co-authored with Alvin E. Winder the book, *T-Groups and Therapy Groups in a Changing Society*. Dr. Appley together with Alvin Winder also co-edited the anniversary issue of the *Journal of Applied Behavioral Science* for the National Training Laboratory Institute.

Mary Ann Biller is Dean of the Lower Hudson Regional Learning Center of Empire State College of the State University of New York. From 1974 to 1977, Dr. Biller also directed the New Models for Career Education Project and its outgrowth, a National Conference on Career Education—both funded with grants totaling over one half million dollars provided by the Kellogg Foundation.

Prior, Dr. Biller held the post of President at Saint Thomas Aquinas College in Sparkill, New York. Dr. Biller completed her doctoral work at Saint John's University in New York City while a faculty member at Saint Thomas and later, chairperson of the college's Philosophy Department. Dr. Biller is a member of the Mid-Hudson Advisory Board of Chemical Bank and the New York State Planning Committee of the American Council on Education's National Identification Program. She has served as chairperson of college evaluation teams for the Middle States Association of Colleges and Schools as well as for its New England counterpart.

Patrick J. Hill is Associate Professor of Philosophy and Chairman of the Federated Learning Communities at the State University of New York campus at Stony Brook. Recipient of a doctorate degree from Boston University, his research has focused on philosophies of community and education with special attention to the work of John Dewey and Emanuel Mounier. An innovative educator, Dr. Hill founded the Master of Arts Program in Philosophical Perspectives to offer the older college graduate a more generalized curriculum than afforded by the traditionally narrow advanced degree or retraining program. Dr. Hill was also a founding member of the Center for the Study of Higher Education and Democratic Society as well as the organization Communitas, a network of professional academics who in papers and meetings explore relationships between a more effective liberal education and the building of academic communities. His writings have appeared in such journals as *Metaphilosophy*, *Philosophical Studies*, *Cross Currents*, and *Liberal Education*. He is a frequent consultant to colleges and universities regarding the revision of the undergraduate curriculum.

Martin Kaplan, till recently a columnist for *The Washington Star*, is now a commentator on the nationally televised CBS program, "Morning with Charles Kuralt." Previously, he served as chief speechwriter for Vice President Walter F. Mondale and, prior to that post, as executive assistant to the U.S. Commissioner of Education. Graduated summa cum laude in the field of molecular biology from Harvard University, he went as a Marshall Scholar to

Cambridge University where he received a First in English. He did his doctoral studies in Modern Thought and Literature as a Danforth graduate fellow at Stanford University. Martin Kaplan is the editor of *What Is An Educated Person?*, *The Monday Morning Imagination*, and *The Harvard Lampoon Centennial Celebration, 1876-1973*. He co-authored with E. L. Boyer *Educating for Survival*.

Lois Lamdin is Executive Director of CLEO, an organization created to serve adult educational programs for colleges in the Delaware Valley region, Dr. Lamdin received her Ph.D. in literature from the University of Pittsburgh where she also taught in her field. She then joined the faculty of Carnegie-Mellon University and, later, Hostos Community College of the City University of New York, where she held the position of chairperson of the Department of English. Subsequently, she served for five years as Associate Dean at Empire State College of the State University of New York. Her scholarly writings cover such fields as the Jewish American novel, modern American poetry, and Victorian literature. Dr. Lamdin's more recent publications include the chapter on English in Arthur Chickering's book, *The Modern American College*, and articles on the humanities and the adult student in *ADE* and *Profession '80*. She has also co-authored a CAEL monograph titled *Interpersonal Learning in an Academic Setting*. In addition, she has written on such topics as lifelong learning, the assessment of experiential learning, and nontraditional approaches to education. Currently, Dr. Lamdin is a member of the advisory board of the journal of *Alternative Higher Education*.

Ernest A. Lynton is now Commonwealth Professor at the University of Massachusetts after serving in the posts of Senior Vice President for Academic Affairs at this institution and, formerly, as founding Dean of Livingston College at the State University of New Jersey, Rutgers. Dr. Lynton was trained as a physicist at Carnegie-Mellon University where he obtained both his Bachelor of Science and Master of Science degrees. He then earned his doctorate at Yale University with a concentration in low temperature physics. In recent years, his specialty has shifted from the field of science to policy issues in higher education. Presently, he is a consultant to the Ford Foundation, Vice-Chairman of the Executive Committee of the Urban Affairs Division of the National Association of State Universities and Land Grant Colleges, and a member of the Center for Studies in Policy and the Public Interest of the University of Massachusetts.

John David Maguire has recently been elected President of the Claremont University Center and Graduate School in California after serving for over eleven years as President of the State University of New York College at Old Westbury and, prior, as Provost of Connecticut's Wesleyan University. His academic interests encompass the interdisciplinary fields of religion, literature, and psychiatry. Dr. Maguire graduated Phi Beta Kappa in philosophy from Washington and Lee University, studied as a Fulbright Scholar at the University of Edinburgh, and completed his doctoral work at Yale University. In 1967, he was one of ten recipients of the nationally awarded E. Harris Harbison Prize given by the Danforth Foundation for outstanding teaching. After the untimely death of his long-time colleague, Martin Luther King, Jr., Dr. Maguire was appointed a permanent trustee of the King Center for Social Change. An internationally respected scholar, teacher, and administrator, he delivered the 1977 William P. Fenn lectures in international education at twenty Asian universities. In 1981, Dr. Maguire finished a seven-year term as President of The Society for Values in Higher Education, a 1500-member organization of academics and professionals concerned with the ethical dimensions of their work. Dr. Maguire has entirely written or contributed to several books and authored more than thirty articles for general and specialized publications.

Warren Bryan Martin is scholar in residence at the Carnegie Foundation for the Advancement of Teaching. He was formerly Vice-President and Director of the Graduate Fellowship Program at the Danforth Foundation. Previously, he held faculty and administrative posts at such institutions as Cornell College in Iowa, University of the Pacific in California, and the University of California, Berkeley. He began his academic career as a philosophy major at Asbury College in Kentucky, then continued for a Bachelor of Divinity at Nazarene Theological Seminary in Missouri, and did his doctoral studies in church history at Boston University. Dr. Martin has actively worked to further innovation and change in the educational purposes, curricula, and governance systems of institutions of higher learning. His books on these subjects include *Conformity: Standards and Change in Higher Education, Alternative to Irrelevance*, and, in process, *A College of Character*. Dr. Martin also edited the recently issued volume, *Learning Through Teaching*. Dr. Martin has published over forty articles in such publications as *Change, Teachers College Record, The Chronicle of Higher Education*, and *The New York Times Magazine*.

Charles Muscatine is Professor of English at the University of California at Berkeley. His field of particular research is medieval literature. He has also been active in attempting to improve college curricula and, specifically, the teaching of composition. At Berkeley, he has served as Assistant Dean of the College of Letters and Science; Chairman of the Special Select Committee on Education, which produced the report, *Education at Berkeley* (1966; 2nd ed., 1968); and Director of the experimental Collegiate Seminar Program. As a member of the National Endowment for the Humanities Board of Consultants, he has served as curricular consultant for many colleges and universities.

John O. Stevenson, Jr., is President of the National Scholarship Service and Fund for Negro Students, an organization concerned with increasing minority access and participation in higher education. It serves nearly 70,000 students and 15,000 institutions annually. Prior, he was Dean of the Metropolitan Regional Center of Empire State College of the State University of New York. He received his Bachelor of Arts degree from Fordham University and, subsequently, earned his Master of Science and Ph.D. in mathematics at the Polytechnic Institute of New York. Active in a number of community-based educational projects, he serves on the Board of Advisors of Solidaridad Humana, a bilingual adult educational center on Manhattan's lower east side, and is politically active on behalf of the New York Coalition for Higher Education. A Danforth fellow, Dr. Stevenson is a member of the Board of The Society for Values in Higher Education.

ONE

ARGUMENTS AGAINST CORE CURRICULUM

1

THE WRONG SOLUTION TO THE
RIGHT PROBLEM

MARTIN KAPLAN

Ideas do not fall from the sky, which is another way of saying that any number of things are not accidental. Ideas and issues have a currency *because* of something. We live in a historical, social, economic, political, cultural context; the fact of our addressing particular issues at this moment in history has its sources.

Some time ago, I attended a conference where the topic was *core curriculum*. Several participants expressed confusion as to why, today, core curriculum should engage our attention at all. We agreed that no obvious analysis seemed available that would unravel the social, political, cultural, and intellectual forces that had driven us to find this question important. Therefore, I asked the question, "What is the problem for which core curriculum is an answer?" Or to ask otherwise, "What is the problem to which curricular reform and change are the right solutions?" I do not think that the answer to my question presupposes that the problem is educational. I do not think that educational issues are in fact

This paper was originally given as informal remarks at a conference sponsored by Empire State College of the State University of New York, The Society for Values in Higher Education, and The Danforth Foundation on the topic of "Coherence and Curriculum: Alternatives for the Future" at Rensselaerville, New York, 12-14 April 1978.

exclusively educational issues; rather, they are—in part at least—a reflection of problems that occur on the economic, political, social, and ethical levels as well. And thus, the problem to which core curriculum is a solution is not an educational problem but is a political, moral, ethical, and social problem.

To further clarify my question, I turn to historical examples in which the core curriculum (or curricular change of the kind associated with core) would seem to be a solution to some problem. The cursory review that follows is not so much a reminder of the highlights of curricular change, but rather a way to spotlight those social, political, and moral circumstances that gave rise to the notion that the curriculum needed to be changed.

Harvard President Charles Eliot's 1869 inaugural address, the *locus classicus* of the curricular debate, attempts to cut through the endless controversies as to whether language, philosophy, mathematics, or science supplies the single best mental training for students. He argues that Harvard will recognize no real antagonism between literature and science, nor consent to alternatives like mathematics or classics, science or metaphysics; instead, Harvard will have them all, and at their best. Recall that the period of Eliot's address features the rocketing of American laissez-faire capitalism, the amassing of private fortunes, the birth of great private universities, the whiff of manifest destiny. For America, it is boom time, with a hint of the world power we would become in the wake of World War I. At that moment, Harvard decides that its curriculum should also be laissez-faire, that is, responsive to individual need. Harvard has no reason to debate the content of its curricular core, only to insist that it should be as responsive as private enterprise and the entrepreneurial spirit was responsive to a world of seemingly limitless resources.

A second great moment when changing the American curriculum is seen as a solution to an as yet unnamed problem occurs in 1920. Archibald MacLeish finds the American curriculum in a state of intellectual anarchy. "There can be," he says, "no educational postulates so long as there are no generally accepted postulates of life itself. And there has been no real agreement as to the purposes and values of life since the world gave over heaven 100 years ago." MacLeish, commenting on higher education when T. S. Eliot is announcing that high culture is a shattered heap of rubble, finds that curriculum just happens to mirror that lack of intellectual and ethical consensus. And this is the precise context that gives rise to a number of extraordinary experiments that we now call the general education movement.

In Chicago, the Mortimer Adler/Robert Hutchins experiments try to invent (or, as kinder souls put it, restore) a coherence to the curriculum that can stand as a kind of countercoherence to the unanimity of the gathering European storm. Fascism, communism, and nazism are seen as coherent; these ideologies are believed to be far too strong a match for our democratic and pluralistic fuzziness. The intellectual anarchy of the American curriculum can hardly provide a competing ideology to fortify our children to go out and fight. The general education curriculum thus becomes an answer to a political and international struggle.

A second landmark in the same period is erected at Columbia University. During World War I, Columbia—for the first time at any American university as far as I know—sets up a course at the request of the Department of State. The course is called War Issues, and it proposes to explain why, after all our noble rhetoric about isolationism, we are in fact fighting. When the war ends, a Peace Issues course is born. After all, if War Issues can explain the sanctions for our bellicosity, should we not also have an ideology to explain why we are at peace and why we—an open, democratic society—deserve a rightful place on earth?

Another landmark, the great one, is the Harvard *Redbook* just after World War II. Although the *Redbook* is never adopted by Harvard, two significant points need to be made. One is that more than half of the *Redbook* focuses on the American high school curriculum, not on that of Harvard University. The Harvard section is almost an appendix to the report and is really intended to be of far lesser interest to the rest of the country. The announced purpose of the Harvard *Redbook* is to confront the fact that for the first time in American history our high schools are serving a diverse student body. Whereas American high schools had historically served the social elite, only a tiny percentage of whom went to college, suddenly high schools are the main socialization force. Given the extraordinary diversity of the student body, the immigrant population, the inklings of confrontation within our racial, cultural, and economic diversity, James Bryant Conant asks the

Harvard faculty to figure out what the country should do with the American high school. At the same time, he asks Harvard to consider its new role. Because of his commitment to diversify its student body, Harvard will, for the first time, enroll students who are more heterogeneous than ever before. The *Redbook*, therefore, is a call for a common core curriculum for the high schools.

The very first words of the *Redbook* are "The War": World War II. Conant wants, as did Columbia in World War I and as Adler/ Hutchins did in Chicago, to promote a coherent, counterrationale, countercurriculum, counterideology, countersociety to face the gathering storm in Europe. Although Harvard itself never adopts the *Redbook*, it is read as a bible, although not by those responsible for the curriculum of the American high school—that has to wait another ten years, for Conant's report on the American high school —but by countless higher educational institutions across the country, which adopt the curriculum in whole cloth as if there are no differences between the needs of their students and those of Harvard.

We come to Sir Eric Ashby. Writing in the late 1960s as a member of the Carnegie Commission, he wonders, "How can the nation be asked to raise enrollments to nine million, when there is no longer any consensus about what ought to be taught to candidates for bachelors degrees . . . ? Put bluntly," he says, "there is no convincing defensible strategy behind the undergraduate curriculum, and the more intelligent students and the more self-critical faculty know this. We ought to be disturbed that the pundits of higher education cannot themselves agree what constitutes a liberal college education." If we recall that the Carnegie Commission was not concerned primarily with the purposes of education but rather with economic issues, and especially increasing access to higher education, we see that Ashby is clearly the skunk at the tea party. By raising the issue of purposes and by claiming that the American higher education establishment has no clue what its purposes are, Ashby is a solo voice asking to what ends will institutions increase access to higher education? Admission itself will prove to be something less than magical, if after all one does not know to what one is gaining access.

A final set of perspectives is found in several quotations from a State University of New York-sponsored conference on the philosophy of the curriculum, where a number of individuals comment about what was going on in their own academic disciplines.

Gertrude Himmelfarb describes the greatest problem of historical studies as the

> nihilistic tendency ... fed by the pervasive relativism of our culture, the prevailing conviction that anything is possible and everything is permitted; that truth and falsehood, good and bad, are all in the eyes of the beholder; that in a free and democratic marketplace of ideas all ideas are equal—equally plausible, equally valid, equally true.

At this same conference, M. H. Abrams, the great literary critic, sketching the state of the humanities, admits that many see that the denial of certainty that the epistemology of humanistic inquiry entails as the prologue to radical "skepticism and relativism." Finally, Reuben Abel, another humanist and historian, says:

> A specter is haunting this discussion of the philosophy of the curriculum—the specter of nihilism. We humanists are forever embarrassed at the uncertainty of our conclusions, whereas the logicians and the mathematicians can define precisely the validity of their inferences. We can never, alas, determine absolutely the truth or falsity of any proposition about history, nor of any interpretation of literature, nor of any evaluation of art. Therefore [it is implied] anything goes! ... In the humanities, everyman can be his own historian. Any one criticism of poetry is as valid as any other.

It is not hard to read between those lines and to see that the goal of a coherent, rational core curriculum proposed by that symposium is aimed at rescuing the epistemology of those disciplines from the relativistic slough into which their chief practitioners fear to have fallen. Can it be, then, that a current problem for which the core curriculum is meant to be an answer is the shaky intellectual foundation of the humanistic disciplines? If so, this is the wrong problem, for intellectual anomie, like its educational cousin, has social, political, and moral sources.

What has been going on recently—both in higher education and in society at large? Some of the generalizations that one might make about what happened in the 1960s include a dramatic opening of opportunities of every kind in the society and a dramatic widening of principles for validating what one can do in a society. More things and more people are respected, tolerated, and considered valuable by more communities in the society than has been the case in memory. No matter at what field one happens to look, this increasing use of multivalent principles of legitimation is a central premise of the 1960s.

Contrast that perceived condition to the present. One might well point to a certain narcissism in the culture and to a sense of retraction of our social commitment to equal opportunity, to openness, to multivalent validations. America, on every issue from abortion to laetrile, appears to have shifted to the political right. Although a commonplace observation, I think it is not without substance. And if that is indeed happening in the larger society, it is equally the condition in higher education.

In the 1960s, higher education reflects extraordinary openness. The willingness to validate new patterns is vividly shown by the federal student aid and by the growth of community colleges. These conditions encourage access, diversity, and innovation. As a result, extraordinary things happen to higher education institutions in the 1960s: ferment, free electives, individualization, experimentation, new courses, new budgets, new subcommittees.

There are at least two ways to interpret these changes as they occurred at elite institutions. Some hold that what happens in the elite institutions in the 1960s is that the curriculum is seen as incomplete—not incoherent, but rather not *thorough*. It has not addressed certain social realities. Thus, for example, the ways in which the curriculum allows students to cultivate their individuality are not faulty in themselves; rather, they presume that nourishing individuality is the totality of university responsibility. Clearly, this is an incomplete picture of what a university needs to do. To make that picture more complete, one needs to focus the curriculum on those things that encourage not only independence but also interdependence; not only competition, but also cooperation; not only specialization, but also commonality; not only the university as an independent institution but also the university as part of a world to which we all belong. Those issues belong in the university curriculum as much as issues that focus on our independent selves.

There is another way to look at what has happened to the elite institutions since the 1960s. That way does not say that the curriculum of individuality and self-expression is incomplete, but rather that, on prima facie grounds, it is incoherent, it lacks an informing presence, an organizing principle; what is needed is to take those shards and discover in them, invent for them, a principle that unites them. This is the stream of thought in which the Harvard *Redbook* needs to be placed. It is certainly within the tradition that includes Adler/Hutchins worrying about the Communists, Columbia worrying about what to do with the peace, and Himmelfarb wondering about what to do when her students charge that one argument is as good as another.

It is also a stream in which the larger public seems to be swimming. Consequently, the core curriculum, from this viewpoint, becomes a genteel way to retract the social commitment of the 1960s. Is anyone still naive enough to believe that the core curriculum is simply a solution to an educational problem? We have already seen some of the reactionary social tendencies of which the core curriculum is merely an educational manifestation. The new core curriculum movement, which Harvard with its particular educational rationale has spawned, is being bought lock, stock, and barrel by other institutions, much as they bought the *Redbook*—as if the Harvard core were ideologically neutral and could provide a respectable way to wipe out the disturbing things that happened in the 1960s. One should therefore look closely at how that curriculum is meant to work.

First, the core curriculum that Harvard and, unfortunately, so many others are about to adopt or propose serves not an educational purpose but a mercantile purpose. A core curriculum constructs protective tariffs around those disciplines in which enrollments are languishing. In another mercantile sense, it gives cash value to a liberal arts degree whose worth is seen to be declining by economists and students alike. The top ten courses at Harvard in 1978, with but a few exceptions, were of the most useful professional, preprofessional kind: accounting, economics, calculus, all the premed courses one might imagine, and a couple of prelaw courses. Those are the Harvard top ten, plus a bit of excelsior thrown in so that one can get by at cocktail parties. If one compares the distribution of Harvard undergraduate elective courses with the less sanctimonious and more boldly vocational curricula of students in community colleges, one will find something of a convergence. Given that, what can increase the cash value of a Harvard degree if not the construction of a principle of liberal education that claims to be the transcendent, informing spirit of the rest of the curriculum?

Core curriculum is also an educational solution to a martial problem. The rhetoric of the Harvard report on the core curriculum hints that somehow the core curriculum is, as it was for Adler/Hutchins, Columbia, Conant, and the *Redbook*, a kind of Distant Early Warning line to protect us from the Commies and from all the other aggressive challenges that may exist in that frisky, post-OPEC Third World. The core curriculum, which contains courses sensitive to the heritage of non-Western cultures, is a way of saying that somehow we have to arm ourselves against Third World challenges. This is a martial solution to a political problem.

A third problem that the core curriculum solves is therapeutic. Somehow the core curriculum is meant to be a prescription for the moral relativism that ails us. If, by providing coherence in the curriculum today, we reassemble those shards of the culture that were blown apart in World War I, then our students will not want to commit suicide, will not enroll in record numbers in university health services because they believe that life has no meaning. The curriculum will reveal that there are reasons to be alive, reasons to go on and continue. Somehow, if the faculty can put together that kind of coherence, the curriculum will be a therapy for our anomie.

A fourth problem for which the core curriculum is a solution is evangelical. Again, as with Adler/Hutchins, some see the university as a staging area for those missionaries who can spread the word in this life. Armed with the message of a core curriculum, one can enlighten those poor individuals who did not have the benefit of a coherent eight-and-one-half course requirement. One might even declare what elements within the culture need preserving. Not only is this curative a therapeutic to ourselves as academics; it also equips us with the appropriate gospel to spread to the masses.

Although these problems are, of course, caricatures, they are nevertheless rooted in a substantive analysis of what happened in the elite institutions between the 1960s and the present, and they may be informative as to why core curriculum is such a hot topic today.

But today, another branch of institutions, differing in objectives from the elites, has entered an era in which their experimental, nontraditional higher educational institutions or programs need to establish their legitimacy. Suddenly, coherence and core curriculum are the buzz words; in the legislatures, the buzz words are like buzz saws. Soon enough these buzz words will become the criteria against which many new institutions and programs will be measured. Given that probability, shouldn't these institutions, which perhaps constitute the most vital sector of American higher education, figure out how they can establish their legitimacy on those terms? Paradoxically, these terms are set by institutions from the elite branch, that is, institutions that want to achieve vastly different goals. Nevertheless, those institutions regard themselves as the guardians of serious culture. For them, core curriculum is a fundamental notion, but it is that notion, ironically, that poses the challenge for these new institutions.

Since the battlefield is defined by coherence and core, how can new or alternative colleges engage in the contest? How can they validate alternative ways to establish curricular coherence in these institutions? And can this be done with rationales that are nonmercantile, nonmartial, nontherapeutic, and nonevangelical?

The core curriculum issue is emerging as the back-to-basics of higher education. Back-to-basics can mean different things. At best, it can mean that children should be able to read and write and count and to do just a bit more than that. This is not a particularly controversial proposition. Back-to-basics can also mean, for those who make alliances with it, a return to authoritarian rows of chairs; a dropping of child-centered strategies for elementary education; an abandonment of nontraditional means to teach reading and writing; a dropping of the arts and other "frills." As one abandons practices of the progressive school movement, the back-to-basics movement becomes back-to-the-old-authoritarianism. It is not surprising that the reactionary undertow of back-to-basics is common, nor that state legislatures across the country are passing minimal competency requirements that legitimate that movement with the public purse. Nor will it shock you if, not so long from now, public higher education will be asked not only to demonstrate that their graduates have mastered the basics but also that they have pursued a core curriculum.

Being in favor of literacy, the 3 Rs, and our children being able to read, write, and count does not necessarily mean being anti-innovation, antiliberation, or antichild-centered. Similarly, being in favor of coherence in higher education does not necessarily mean being opposed to the goals of the new nontraditional institutions. Rather, one needs to gain a purchase on the concept of coherence, to show that being in favor of coherence is coextensive with being supportive of the goals for which these nontraditional institutions stand. It is not necessary to oppose the core curriculum to be in favor of coherence. Just as it has sometimes been difficult to be a liberal anti-Communist, or at once anti-McCarthy and anti-Stalin, one can and must *support* a rationale for coherence in higher education at new institutions—and at the same time *oppose* the reactionary tendencies that underpin so many current models of coherence.

I propose two tasks that are requisite if new institutions are to succeed. The first is to unmask the ideology of the return to core curriculum by making its social, political, and ethical motivations absolutely explicit.

The second task is to define how these new institutions can establish appropriate criteria for curricular legitimacy. As consumerism sweeps our nation, we want our institutions to be accountable to the public purse. That is appropriate. It also is appropriate that our students and our legislators and ourselves want our curricula to be legitimate. But first, we must find the terrain on which to define legitimacy. Such a terrain will be different from the terrain that validates core curricula at elite institutions. Defining it will be a novel and exciting enterprise. If we succeed, we can stall in their tracks those who would retract our commitment to social openness, diversity, experiment, and access.

2

THE SOCIAL IMPERATIVES FOR CURRICULAR CHANGE IN HIGHER EDUCATION

JAMES W. HALL WITH BARBARA L. KEVLES

Contrary to sacred myth, the impulse for curricular change does not originate in ivy-wreathed missions of universities, faculty ideals of the educated person, or irrefutable logic of ivory-tower knowledge. Changes in undergraduate curriculum are generated not by the academic profession but by significant social, political, and cultural forces at work throughout society. In effect, society—not its educators—provides the impetus mirrored in the initiation of campus reform of curriculum.

Since World War II, societal forces with a grip on national priorities have forced renovations or even demolitions of requirements for two- and four-year college degrees in periods of both social stability and upheaval. In the burgeoning economy following World War II, the employment needs of expanding industry and government bureaus, the country's race to space with quantum funding of scientific research, and the dramatic growth in the number and diversity of college aspirants all exerted strong influences on undergraduate curriculum. The combined powers of government, science, and industry encouraged a core curriculum, distribution requirements, and a constricted, professionally oriented major for training well-rounded knowledgeable employees. As a result, undergraduates were offered a wider range of courses and majors, but these added offerings tended to focus on advanced level department specialties. Thus, from World War II to the mid-1960s, the power of the American undergraduate curriculum to develop a range of knowledge and broadly applicable intellectual skills diminished under the vise of vocational pressures and narrowing curricular objectives born of the social imperatives of the times.

In the domestic upheavals symbolically ushered in with the assassination of President John F. Kennedy in 1963, the required core curriculum built by societal forces in the 1950s and early 1960s collapsed under the pressures of such new political forces as the anti-Vietnam war movement, the black power movement, the feminist movement, and the changing demographic patterns of college applicants. The most pervasive changes were stimulated in part by the presence on campus of an increasingly diverse student body during the years of the anti-Vietnam protest. Representing more varied backgrounds than ever before, campus activists insisted that their studies be "relevant" to their social and ethical commitments and to their personal concerns because they viewed the college as a surrogate for the imperialistic, impersonal military-industrial-government complex. Through the influence of more participatory forms of campus governance or by the force of strikes, sit-ins, or boycotts, these activists in many cases achieved more responsive curricula by the abolishment of core requirements and, in rare cases, by the elimination of fixed majors in favor of a system of electives.

In the late 1960s and early 1970s, disillusionment with institutionalized authority also helped other national political groups gain curricular changes in higher learning.[1] Members of black power or feminist cadres sought to redress the omission of their perspectives from catalogue offerings by the alteration of existing courses or by the creation of whole new departments. Such influences significantly enriched undergraduate curricula. While advocates of participatory democracy, black power, and feminism restyled, repaired, or added to the framework of traditional curricula, experimentally oriented educators reconstructed the epistemological foundations of college curricula by radically restructuring programs or by founding new colleges. Their efforts were reinforced by the proliferating numbers of adult and part-time students and by increased pressures to reduce costs of construction and programs. And given the existing chaotic conditions prevailing in college curricula, the reformers sought new rationales by which to organize undergraduate programs. Their innovative stragegies— including such practices as off-campus experiential study; individualized, student-directed curricula; or granting credit for knowledge acquired outside traditional coursework—gave baccalaureate studies a whole fresh dimension. But whether curricular reforms were initiated by college administrators or by students' confrontation tactics (as in the late 1960s), by government grants or employment opportunities (as in the period after World War II), these reforms shared one principal characteristic: they served one or a combination of social interests—whether that "interest" was defined by business, govenment, science, race, sex, demographics, age, or political affiliation.

Today, some academics look with chagrin at the socially licensed formlessness of college curricula, which, in many instances, are only a disorganized collections of electives. They wish to rectify this deplorable state and "restore the quality of education" by reviving the core curriculum of the 1950s, but in a radically changed social environment. Although a few small colleges with homogeneous student bodies may justifiably impose a fixed core of requirements, the social imperatives of the 1980s will require the vast majority of educational institutions to serve multiple student constituencies with highly diverse curricular expectations. Thus, imposition of a core curriculum by the great bulk of today's institutions of higher learning will prove not only inappropriate but also ineffectual. Faculties must reassert their responsibility for curricular definition, but their judgments must recognize such social determinants as the diversity of student ages, economic backgrounds, race, and sex and the requirements of industry, labor, and government. In sum, these imperatives will require not a single fixed curriculum but a diversity of alternative curricula—each coherently related to students' educational objectives and life requirements while being equally responsive to the intellectual imperatives for quality and for rigorous educational standards.

A review of the symbiotic relationship in recent decades between societal stimuli and curricular change stresses that curricula must be responsive to the currents of social and cultural forces, for curricular change is but a mirror of larger movements meshed in surrounding society.

. . .

In the post-World War II prosperity, the expansion of American industry stimulated curricular change in colleges across the country. Following the end of wartime austerities, American industry faced a surge of consumer buying power, and major corporations began to plow back their record-breaking postwar profits into vast expansion programs. One industry leader, General Motors, invested as much as $1 billion to increase production to meet skyrocketing orders. In addition to expanding current distribution, American industry also used the specialized postwar technology to develop new products and services, such as mass market televisions and transcontinental telephone dial calls. To supervise these new and extended operations, American corporations suddenly needed vast numbers of educated managers, so they traveled to college campuses to sift and hire from the new crop of graduates.

During the 1950s, this corporate employment program played a significant part in helping colleges redefine their curricula. Each spring, recruiters sporting crewcuts, barwide ties, and button-down shirts would descend on ivy greens and schedule meetings with June graduates. As competition for the cream of graduating classes sharpened, this highly visible procedure became a pressure-filled operation with seniors boasting who had the most appointments.

These well-trained recruiters hunted for a new type of corporate employee: they sought graduates with business management or engineering majors or, ideally, with combinations of the two. In addition, they sought future managers who had a wide-ranging knowledge of the world and who would relate well to many kinds of people. Often, corporations expected their young executives to be active community leaders and adept party-givers in those wood-paneled, suburban "rec rooms" so popular in the fifties. Consequently, recruiters believed that the urbane, knowledgeable student would develop these essential interpersonal competencies from participating in such campus organizations as fraternities, athletic teams, and student governments and from being exposed to a liberal arts curriculum blending Western history, literature, a language usable in the European market, some sociology or psychology, and a science. Thus, new corporate hiring practices lent important support for the growth of the broad arts and science curriculum. By the mid-1950s, colleges shifting to a core of academic requirements that initiated a more diverse, less elite postwar student into the preserved wisdom of Western culture were reinforced in their aim by the new corporate employment policies that stressed the model of the well-rounded college graduate.

If the tremendous, postwar economic growth of American enterprise fostered a core of requirements for entering freshmen, so too the astronomical jump in government-financed scientific research after the Russians launched Sputnik profoundly altered the studies of upperclassmen in the same period. In the four years following the Russian launching of the first artificial earth satellite, federal expenditures to secure America's prima place in all science more than doubled to $9 billion annually, which also caused federal sums for basic research at nonprofit institutions to rise more than twofold.[2] The sharp increase in government-financed research projects on college campuses subtly influenced the scope, sequence, and curricular goals not only of science majors but also of the whole undergraduate program.

In the main, these campus-based federal projects triggered a rise in specializations among the disciplines in academe. Government-funded contracts caused major universities to employ increasing numbers of researchers who became affiliated with college faculty. In the most prestigious institutions, these scientists tended to be associated with research institutes. The major extramural grants that the scientist himself attracted gave him some independence and therefore leverage on the institution. The grant typically not only included salaries for people attached to the project and sophisticated equipment coveted by the university but also included funding for research assistants to gather and process the data. These research assistants often were graduate students attracted by the institutional reputation, a modest graduate stipend, or the almost certain guarantee of a good academic research position elsewhere upon receipt of their doctoral degrees. So the federal grants to the larger, more prestigious institutions encouraged a highly specialized approach to curriculum, a trend that, by a process of imitation and cross-pollination, filtered down to the smaller liberal arts colleges. The lesser-known colleges sought to gain the aura of the famous name institutions by likewise securing grants, new equipment, and staffs of poorly paid, graduate assistants. In addition, colleges hired scientists who recently received their doctorates from the top universities, and these specialists added a new persona to the college science department. Compared with the broadly knowledgeable faculty scientist tenured at the small colleges, these graduates of various research projects at major universities were often narrowly focused in their knowledge and equally provincial in what they could or would teach. So the development of scientific specialists, federal grants, and associated research apparatus drastically changed the focus of science curricula at small liberal arts colleges by emphasizing greater specialization within a department and more courses in these narrow specialties.

Furthermore, these scientific specialists brought a particular approach to the organization of knowledge, an approach that had a pervasive impact on the general undergraduate curriculum. Whereas faculty humanists perceived the acquisition of knowledge as interrelating themes at any given historical period, specialized scientists demanded a strong sequential approach because scientific inquiry by necessity required that the advanced level course be preceded by a more elementary one. So the scientific specialist, whereever he was, strongly influenced the organization of baccalaureate curricula structured around a fixed-departmental-based major rather than around the lateral interdisciplinary approach of faculty humanists.

In addition to constricting curricula into overspecialized, heavily concentrated majors, the hard sciences endorsed in a positive way the growth of the nubile social sciences, which, to gain wide acceptance, adopted the grant-getters' research techniques. Borrowing empiricist techniques from the hard sciences, the social sciences favored framing and testing a hypothesis over distilling conclusions from collected facts. The increasing use of statistical models and methods by psychologists, sociologists, and anthropologists further undermined the humanistic methods, which endorsed interpretive value judgments based on intuitive perceptions in favor of empirically demonstrable information.

Finally, increased government funding of basic research also led to a greater professionalization of the undergraduate curriculum, thus weakening the implied goals described on the first pages of many college catalogs. These grants, which enabled universities to hire scientific specialists, set up a process of professional cloning. The newly hired specialist at the small, regional college mimicked his professor at the major institution by communicating a style and a set of expectations in his teaching that were different from those of the "old guard" faculty at the new institution. This duplicate professor transmitted highly professional requirements to his undergraduate students and organized their curriculum so that they could qualify as lab apprentices on another funded project at the end of their senior year. As a direct result of this cloning, the undergraduate years began to lose their distinctiveness as a time to develop an understanding of self, community, and world and the intellectual abilities to use that perspective for personal and social purposes. Consequently, more and more undergraduate study was transformed into a vocational preparation to enter graduate school.

Federally financed research projects had an overwhelming impact not only on the curricular goals, structures, and offerings of academic departments but also on the faculty's perception of its pedagogical role. The research model fostered the attitude that faculty gained its greatest rewards, not from undergraduate teachings, but from designing research programs that won extramural funding for the publication of research. And to publish effective research, the grants had to support research assistants, and that meant more undergraduates had to be conscripted to do the data gathering. So the stress on self-perpetuating specialized knowledge encouraged the professionalization of undergraduate curricula and the concomitant decline of faculty qualified to teach broad undergraduate courses. The faculty member who brought in the grants and was loyal to his profession as his greatest source of recognition was applauded, while the professor who directed himself to undergraduate teaching and was loyal to one institution was cast in disfavor. In these ways, the federal funding of basic research in higher institutions of learning had unpredicted effects on undergraduate curricula. It fostered the development of specialization within departments and greater departmental offerings within those specialities, and the judgment of performance against a specific knowledge within a major rather than against a demonstration of wide comprehension of interlocking fields. It underscored the heavily concentrated major for undergraduate degrees, and, most significantly, the professionalization of undergraduate curricula via the research model machinery. Again, these forces served to shift the curricular objectives of the undergraduate years from those of broadening intellectual skills and fields to more restrictive vocational curricular objectives.

But the space program rivalry between the two superpowers was not the only social imperative encouraging the vocationally oriented, sequential college curriculum. The proliferating demand for government employees at all levels forged—with similar employment requirements from science and industry—a potent endorsement of the baccalaureate degree as the ticket to the better paying job. Consequently, the higher practical premium on the baccalaureate in the work world persuaded a larger pool of high school seniors nationwide to apply to colleges. In turn, the greater numbers of undergraduates on campus affected the curricula of institutions much as federal science projects had, but for reasons related more to administrative convenience and efficiency than to educational theory.

In the period of postwar expansion, countless government agencies, commissions, and panels were created at all levels, and these new government bodies heightened society's demand for college-trained employees. For example, the Atomic Energy Commission, established by Congress in 1946, the Office of Naval Research, also given permanent stature that same year, and the National Science Foundation, founded four years later, all required mammoth numbers of specialists and staffs. It was as if with three separate bills that brought federally coordinated scientific training and research into politically insulated institutions, the federal government in effect had founded three huge corporations with all their personnel demands.

However, science majors were not the only college graduates favored by expanding government bureaus. The demand for college-skilled manpower also occurred in the Veterans Administration, which was supervising the military's return to civilian life, in the Department of Agriculture, which had enlarged its responsibilities for price supports, and, starting in 1953, in the newly established Department of Health, Education, and Welfare. Growing bureaucratic openings for liberal arts majors continued in the mid-1960s, when the Department of Health, Education, and Welfare, spurred by President Lyndon B. Johnson's Great Society programs, burst with new agencies directed to achieve equal opportunity for the disadvantaged. In effect, the extensive government requirements for college-trained specialists, which supplemented similar employment pressures from science and industry, persuaded more high school students to opt for a four-year college program.

Significantly, the work world's impetus for postwar enrollment growth illustrates a very important historical relationship between American commerce and matriculation rates. It is axiomatic that the level of education deemed worthy of public support has historically increased commensurate with the education deemed necessary for an average citizen to function adequately in the job market. In Puritan, seventeenth-century New England, the average man learned to read, write, and calculate not only to imbibe the Bible and God's word directly but also to do good business. Throughout the nineteenth century, a high school education was considered unnecessary—even for children of the wealthy. The diploma simply was not deemed necessary for ordinary employment. But in the late nineteenth and early twentieth centuries, industrial requirements for new competencies made additional schooling essential for the average citizen. By the 1920s and 1930s, a high school diploma had become the fundamental level of education the public would support with tax dollars. After World War II, the demand for persons skilled in new technologies obliged public financing of the first two college years—and some would argue for all four years of higher education. Specifically, the new vacancies for college graduates to direct industry's development of mass markets and new products; to supervise expanded federal, state, and city bureaus; and to man the huge government programs for scientific advancement all stimulated social incentives to raise the level of education beyond what the average citizen had previously needed for a good paying job. Because of this historic interdependency between commerce and education, by 1969 the number of high school graduates entering postsecondary institutions increased threefold nationwide. With the children born during the postwar baby boom reaching college age, the larger percentages of college-bound high school seniors translated into even greater numbers of college applicants.[3] Thus, because a large block of middle-class voters identified with the goals and values of higher education, governors and state legislators, perhaps for the first time in this country's history, could justify the appropriation of substantial funds for higher education on the grounds that these institutions were fundamental to the preservation and extension of our political and economic system.

Faculty curricular committees responded to the ballooning college budgets and enrollments in mechanical ways that underlined the effects of the federally financed research projects on the content, structure, and goals of college curricula. Rather than use the extra tuition funds for experimentation, colleges simply stretched their catalog offerings by hiring more faculty with greater specializations. In addition, they stressed the regimented major as an efficient administrative method to handle the large numbers of students. Consequently, with enrollment growth, special course listings multiplied while the core of general electives diminished.

In other ways, these unprecedented student enrollments weakened the curricular benefits of introductory courses because of the way in which colleges reacted to the unwieldly class numbers. Both the established and the newly chartered colleges tended to crowd students, particularly lower division undergraduates, into large, auditorium-size lectures. Courses presented in huge lecture halls prompted students to learn by rote rather than—as in a seminar— by active analysis and distillation of conclusions. The form itself promoted passivity in the listener. Moreover, most college faculty members, employed for their specialized knowledge rather than their teaching skills, were unable to effectively use the form to inspire student dialog and spontaneous problem solving. The huge lecture courses devised to accommodate the dramatically increased enrollments served better to convey information than to sharpen students' conceptual abilities. Thus, through the implementation of these large lecture classes, the goals of learning shifted subtly from the nurturing of intellectual skills to the acquisition of knowledge. But whereas science fostered such an effect because of the discipline's approach to knowledge, the large enrollments created similar results simply as colleges sought convenient and efficient methods of instruction.

The growing numbers of college-age "postwar babies," attracted to campuses by the greater premium on the baccalaureate degree and by the more complex employment requirements, therefore, enriched course options with an increased range of advanced specialized courses, drained curriculum by diminishing the number of general core electives, reinforced the necessity for a sequentially arranged major rather than an interdisciplinary field of study, and made lower level courses information factories rather than think tanks purposing to cultivate students' critical processes.

In summary, the social imperatives of business, government, science, and new demographic patterns in the 1940s, 1950s, and early 1960s mutually supported the inauguration of an inflexible core of lecture-taught distribution requirements to fill society's need for well-rounded employees and similarly stressed a sequential approach to acquired knowledge through a single discipline major to meet the professional world's appetite for the highly trained, college-educated expert. This was the socially endorsed curriculum intact on most college campuses when President John F. Kennedy was assassinated in November 1963. And that event, which marked the beginning of a period of national domestic upheaval comprised of successive waves of political movements, reverberated on college campuses nationwide with the collapse of the curricula of the past decades.

· · ·

By the late 1960s, the preconditions for this demolition of college curriculum had been gestating, in some instances, in society for a full generation. Changes in parenting, technology, and sharp differentials in college students themselves had helped create more skepticism among college-age youths toward the prerogatives of institutionalized authority. The anti-Vietnam War movement, which in the late 1960s boldly challenged as impersonal, imperialistic, and racist the decisions of such institutions as government, large corporations, and the military, expressed the rising disillusionment with institutionalized authority felt on a national level. Amid this nationwide ferment, campus antiwar protestors linked with other student activists and successfully attacked the authority of educational institutions, now a surrogate for the unresponsive, government-military-industrial complex, by laying siege to college governance and curricula. In this same period, the whole diminished respect for institutionalized white, male supremacy provided propulsion for the black power and the feminist movements to have greater impact on college curricula than previously achieved by social changes in the law, federal programs, and influential popular literature. Thus, it occurred that the curriculum built by social forces of the more stable late 1940s, 1950s, and early 1960s blew apart under pressure of new social imperatives in this later period of domestic war.

The student rebellions against educational institutions cannot be interpreted, as some observers have suggested, as acts of willful children against surrogate parental authority. Such psychological views ignore the fact that college students of the mid-1960s emerged from a different world than previous undergraduates. Most saliently, these mid-1960s undergraduates were the first TV generation on campus and early beneficiaries of the portable paperback. These charter members of what Marshall McLuhan has called TV's "global village" grew up more informed because of television and because of the advent of more cheaply priced, easily available books. Changed patterns in parenting also contributed to the new student profile. The Victorian father who said to his child "Don't do that" was widely supplanted by more progressive parents who said, "That's a good idea. What else do you have to say?" This type of upbringing tended to foster a higher level of individualism —some would even say willfulness. The offspring of permissive parents valued self-expression over "obeying the rules." In addition to benefiting from the invention of the television, the mass-marketed paperback, and the permissive home, student activists of the mid-1960s were more socially aware and of more varied backgrounds because the social imperatives of the times propelled onto campuses larger portions of high school students who represented the less elite working class. Therefore, these students possessed both greater learning disabilities and more personalized experience with the inequalities of society. Because the "TV generation" was more politically conscious, more worldly, and more egocentric, these students took a wholly different stance toward institutionalized authority than their predecessors. The mobilization of public disillusionment with the government's involvement in the Vietnam War served to catalyze student discontent with the fallible authority educational institutions exercised through the curricular programs that influenced these students' lives.

In the late 1960s, students demonstrated against the prescribed core requirements and the concentrated departmental major, especially at state colleges and regional universities. More than their Ivy League counterparts, these regional colleges had expanded very rapidly to meet the unprecedented student demand for a college education. Acting expeditiously under tremendous enrollment pressures, these colleges had copied the elite universities' curricula, which, while perhaps suitable for the more homogeneous student body of Princeton or Harvard, did not mirror the needs of a regional student clientele, which had sharply differing preparation for college level work. Because of the discrepancies between the suitability of regional college curricula and their clientele, regional students were more likely to ask whether their courses meshed with their expectations of a college education. They questioned whether their courses should not be more relevant to their lives and postwar society, and these activists indicted the mammoth lecture courses through which that education was delivered. Thus, these undergraduates, who represented more diverse goals, more varied economic backgrounds, and often more limited formal academic capacities, found that the fixed curricula and delivery systems of many state universities and regional colleges were unresponsive to their wants and desires. Student boycotts, strikes, sit-ins, and marches forced many colleges to abolish the core and distribution requirements for an open elective system. Whereas under the earlier system of curricular requirements, a specified major and mandatory course sequence made student advisement relatively useless, the new, freer system exposed the total poverty of student academic counseling. Left to fend for themselves, students frequently chose electives because of a professor's popularity or reputation for easy grading or because class schedules prolonged their weekends. Thus, without the restraint of core requirements or effective advisement, the entry level curriculum at many colleges disintegrated into a potpourri of free choice.

Although core requirements at many regional colleges had disappeared, the required courses for departmental majors remained unassailable. Invariably, professors compromised on everything except their department requirements principally because their academic overspecialization left them ill-equipped to teach elementary or broad interdisciplinary courses. In addition, the professional world's demand for college-trained experts reinforced their unwillingness to disassemble their departmental course structures to placate student whims.

The anti-Vietnam War movement, which helped some students challenge the right of educational authority to delimit curricular requirements, motivated other students to ask even more radical questions. A minimal, but influential number doubted not only the validity of the prescribed structure and content of education but also the very purpose of the university itself. For them, the Vietnam War proved the folly of all authority and the fallibility of leaders who exercised it. These student radicals wanted proof of the worth of learning because they questioned whether knowledge itself was not the cause of the lack of freedom and the bondage of men's spirit. They also questioned whether they should allow themselves to be indoctrinated with such tools of oppression. Given the composition of universities and their links, in some cases, to the military-industrial complex, the radicals argued that it was impossible for curricula not to have a subjugating effect. Rejecting all fixed curricula—both core and departmentally based knowledge—they sought to judge learning not only by their immediate concerns but also by their social, political, and ethical commitments. Since most course descriptions did not meet radical standards, these extremists resorted to various methods to gain their way. In certain cases, they advocated the institution of forms of participatory democracy for dealing with curricular changes. This extreme political ideology cast faculty voices as one among equals, as if the right answer or method of learning could be decided by majority rule. In reality, the participatory technique permitted the stronger voices to manip- ulate the weaker so that, in effect, student radicals often sub- stituted one form of authoritarianism for another. When peaceful or violent means could not persuade colleges to eradicate tradi- tional curricula, radicals often moved to another campus more susceptible to threats of bombs, arson, or terror. Some even set up alternative educational systems called "free universities." As a result of the changed attitudes toward institutionalized authority that were fueled by the anti-war movement, curriculum as it had been on many campuses—a core, distribution requirements and a concentrated, departmentalized major—fell apart piece by piece or totally disintegrated.

In such times, the black power movement's exposure of racism in previously inviolate institutions also created a ripple effect on campuses and in college curricula. In accordance with the national movement for black rights, black students wearing afros and dashikis and carrying placards with the slogan "black is beautiful" spearheaded campus drives to redress the racist omission of the concerns of black people in curricula.

Curricular changes achieved by black students, mirroring the interests of the black power movement, had effect because of a cumulative effort by American blacks. As a consequence of the 1954 Supreme Court decision that ruled that separate, segregated schooling was inherently unequal, pace-setting middle-class blacks shifted from segregated black colleges to traditional, white- oriented universities. By the early 1960s, minority enrollments had increased noticeably at major white colleges. Yet these white colleges made no significant changes in their curricula to compen- sate for the gaping deficiencies in the ghetto education of minority students.

A decade after the Supreme Court ruling, the federal government attempted to rectify this situation by direct intervention. In 1964, with the election of President Johnson and the inception of his Great Society Program, the federal government infused major funding into Educational Opportunity Programs, among others, to assist college-bound minority students. These programs, supported by strong federal incentives, sought to raise the skills and knowledge of minority students, who suddenly had access to white institutions. Although these special curricula did not alter the racist values institutionalized in the colleges' existing courses, the social consciences of many self-defined white liberals within academe were assuaged by these programs for black undergraduates. But in reality, these special programs were delegated to the bottom of the academic pecking order and were never absorbed into the mainstream of the college curriculum. In effect, they transported the black ghetto structure to the college campus. However, these programs did place significantly more blacks on traditional white campuses just prior to the emergence of the black power movement.

Then, legitimized by the wave of protest movements, integration yielded to black separatism. Black power advocates on college campuses demanded black dormitories, representatives on faculty governance committees, and that racism be eradicated from college curricula. For example, they attacked history courses that, except for Cleopatra, the Boers, and ancient Egypt, omitted Africa; they pointed out neglect of black society, values, and culture in the study of the family. To rectify the white-biased studies, black power advocates demonstrated for and received either courses or departments devoted to black studies, which significantly enriched the range and content of undergraduate curricula. Unfortunately, black studies departments, which for a time were lively thoroughfares of intellectual exchange, are now diminishing in vitality. Previously, colleges scrambled to staff these departments, not only creating a loss at predominantly black institutions whose faculties were tapped but also occasionally at the cost of hiring lesser qualified black scholars. Today, the inability of some unqualified faculty to meet standard requirements for tenure is resulting in the gradual dismemberment of these new departments and perhaps signaling a fresh neglect of the black perspective in curriculum.

In the early 1970s, the feminist movement was another social force that produced a beneficial ripple in college curricula. Yet without the confluence of protest movements to diminish the validity of institutionalized male authority, it is questionable whether or not the feminist movement would have chipped away at societal oppression of women within and without academe. For instance, in the aftermath of World War II, society, which had depended on women's paid labor to fill its depleted work force during the war years, was content when women relinquished profitably productive careers with the war's conclusion to more fully employ their reproductive capacities. As Madison Avenue mirrored the romantic image of marrying "your college sweetheart" and the joys of suburban "family life," women fulfilled socially approved roles as the unsalaried hostess, ornament, helpmate, and self-effacing mother as the epitome of female success until, with the publication of *The Feminine Mystique*[4] in 1963 and the formation of the National Organization for Women four years later, women's rising dissatisfaction with their job as servant in society—be it homemaker, nurse, teacher, or community volunteer—became public knowledge and a political issue. So, the ensuing national movement for women's civil rights—which lobbied on such issues as women's rights to control their bodies through abortion and family planning, pay for homemakers through fairer Social Security laws, and women's rights to self-determination by equal opportunities for employment—changed social attitudes toward women and education. The smart bobbysoxer sporting a frat pin in the 1950s who wanted a degree in education for "security to fall back on" was replaced in the 1970s by the vocal campus feminist who wanted an education, a career, and her own paycheck.

As the women's movement gained greater national momentum and social acceptance, campus feminists sought to rectify the oppressive white male supremist attitudes inherent in the exclusion of women from the academic power structure and perpetuated by the omission of the woman's perspective in the body of knowledge taught on college campuses. These militant women criticized the research that omitted the view of gender from critical analysis, or the recording of history that left out the exploits and the exploitation of women as a social factor, or the scholarship of any field that did not credit women's stories or their lives or the perspective of their sex. Thus, like the black power movement, the women's movment blew a breath of fresh air into curricula through the efforts of campus feminists to supplement course syllabi with the feminist perspective or the course catalog with multidiscipline courses in women's studies.

In the late 1960s and early 1970s, the curricular protests caused by the changed attitudes toward institutionalized authority, the more diverse social and economic backgrounds of undergraduates, and the political movements of blacks and of women produced few direct curricular benefits for adult, part-time students, but they did create a receptive climate for the altering of college curricula to serve adult needs. Like blacks, older students were discriminated against in traditional colleges by being relegated to courses taught outside the mainstream of the college curriculum. In addition, the adult students' often practical motives for formal learning and academe's limited view of their learning capacities combined to make "continuing education," or so-called extension education, a low faculty priority. However, as the adult, part-time student population grew, its special needs encouraged reform-minded educators to apply nontraditional instructional modes. Simultaneously, reports by such national policy groups as the Carnegie Commission on Higher Education,[5] the Newman Task Force on Higher Education,[6] the Commission on Non-Traditional Study,[7] and others served as powerful social permits to reinforce innovations in adult education.

But until the early 1970s, working adults, housewives, the handicapped, those unable to afford campus residency could rarely find part-time adult degree programs on traditional college campuses. Colleges were willing to profit from evening classes for the working adult given by daytime faculty but were unwilling to award college credit for such programs. Most colleges believed that the daytime, eighteen- to twenty-two year-old, September-to-June campus resident was the most receptive candidate for college-level studies, and so they were reluctant, with few exceptions, to award adult students more than a diploma or certificate. A bona-fide adult college degree was hard to find.

Yet the experience of reform-minded educators contradicted theories about the ideal age, place, time of day, and length of commitment for college-level learning. In fact, many observers have noted that the most effective time to engage in broad learning is at the adult stage of life. Unlike most high school graduates, adult students bring a richer background of knowledge that gives them direction, motivation, and strong discipline in the pursuit of their studies. Although disadvantaged by rusty learning techniques and lacking in self-assurance, the adult student's basic skills frequently are much superior to those of the average undergraduate. Whereas the typical college student experiences undergraduate life as a significant period of maturation to prepare for such major adult responsibilities as first employment or marriage, the part-time, older student often is driven to formal learning typically as the result of some later life crisis—a prospective job change, a desire for promotion, or a divorce or other unsettling situation. Although faculty usually objects to what it regards as narrow adult educational goals, under specially tailored curricula these older students develop the capacity to move beyond these constricted educational goals and into broadly intellectual pursuits.

So in response to these discoveries about adult learning potential, to the rapidly growing adult student population, and to the overturning of curricular standards by campus protest movements, traditionalists and reformers within academe began to devise programs for the degree-minded older student. However, it was the exceptional campus on which a program recognized the unique adult curricular needs. In many instances, a college simply extended its basic classroom pattern and course list to provide for its adult evening classes. Where such adult degree programs were instituted, the most characteristic change was to insist that content and quality of evening classes meet daytime standards. But these programs did not customize the curriculum to the content requirements or mode of instruction most needed for effective adult learning.[8]

However, in the 1970s, with broader recognition that learning continued beyond college age, certain forward educational institutions were founded to accommodate the particular curricular requirements or the educational delivery system most efficient to serve the adult student of diverse learning levels, locations, and schedules. Such nontraditional, external degree programs undermined the premise that the acquisition of knowledge demanded that scholars and students of a certain age gather at a certain place, at certain times of day, over four successive years of study. Some external degree programs like that of Thomas A. Edison College (New Jersey), which stressed self-study through suggested bibliographies rather than faculty instruction, used the technique of examination to evaluate learning and for degrees. Where this type of program demonstrated an educational delivery system geared for the adult who by employment or family responsibility could not be affixed to a college campus, another type of adult degree program like the one established at Empire State College, State University of New York—the highly individualized university without walls—accommodated not only the logistical problems of the time- and place-bound adult student but also the curricular requirements most suitable for adult learning.[9] Such institutions as Empire State College recognized that mature adult students had most likely acquired significant bodies of knowledge and intellectual skills prior to enrollment and that this study gained outside the formal college curriculum should be awarded credit. In addition, unlike the impersonal adult evening schools, these institutions provided important academic counseling to help the unsure adult students clarify their educational goals and develop a degree program based on individualized contract study. Such institutions stressed the evolution of a coherent curriculum tailored for each adult student's knowledge, interests, and ambitions without sacrificing intellectual quality or academic standards. They believed that the core curriculum designed as basic orientation and indoctrination for a nineteen-year-old would prove too naive for an adult's experience and life requirements. Yet despite this pioneer work in the curriculum and delivery of instruction for adults, such programs as those of Empire State and Edison College remain the exceptions among institutions of higher learning today. The majority of institutions still have difficulty in recognizing that worthy college degrees may be gained without the ethos of campus life and the adherence to a fixed undergraduate curriculum.

. . .

Today, however, a new, vocal movement advocates curricular change for undergraduate studies. This movement differs from those of the recent past in that it is not propelled by social forces but is organized by those who teach and accredit college curricula. Many college faculties view with embarrassment the chaotic curricula on their campuses—in some cases, consortia of electives. They feel guilty about the faculty decisions that compromised course requirements during the protest era of the 1960s. Through these irresponsible acts, they feel that the faculty relinquished its right to control the quality of education on campuses by defining its curriculum. To reassert this important prerogative, many faculty are trying to reintroduce in a radically changed social environment the core curriculum and distribution requirements of the 1950s. Waving aside critics who condemn a core curriculum as unresponsive to the social imperatives of the times, advocates of core perceive a curriculum that is tailored to a specific social group or issue as merely catering to mercantile consumerism. For them, a curriculum that ignores the interests of a student clientele is to be admired for its integrity.

But many faculty and accreditors who espouse the reinstitution of core curricula sully their professional idealism by personal motives of convenience or self-interest. Unlike those who sincerely wish to upgrade curricular standards and the worth of a college degree, some faculty support the core to protect their jobs in liberal arts departments against the deleterious affects of economic recession and declining student enrollments. When, during the recession of the mid-1970s, liberal arts majors increasingly could not find jobs in the fields for which they had been trained, a reverse professional pull was created on college campuses. When successive freshmen classes were not conscripted to take core requirements, significant numbers turned away from a broad education in departments of history, foreign languages, and the like to more practical, job-oriented courses in law, business, engineering, health, and other professions. Some faculty who now teach in shrunken liberal arts course sections may couch their arguments for a core curriculum in eloquently altruistic terms when, in fact, they are fighting to save their paychecks by restoring thinly justified course requirements.

If some faculty see the reassembling of a core curriculum as an assertion of their professional prerogative or self-interest, state regulatory or accrediting bodies sympathize for reasons of expediency. Many accreditors prefer a uniform curricular standard so that college programs could be more easily evaluated. For instance, the contents of the college curriculum for a New York State bachelor of arts degree is broadly stated as requiring 75 percent liberal arts and science courses and not more than 25 percent professional or vocational courses. Yet some accreditors would like the state law further restricted so that the required 75 percent arts and science courses would be apportioned by certain percentages to the study of the hard sciences, mathematics, humanities, fine arts, and social sciences. Such apportionment would be a great convenience for state regulators of education. If academicians could consent, the institution of a core curriculum statewide would assuage accreditors, who prefer formulaic standards over standards of judgment for curriculum evaluation.

But one cannot reject core curriculum solely because of some advocates' motives of opportunism or convenience. Rather, its educational purpose must be judged on its own merits. Its defenders argue that core means a special curriculum designed by the faculty to be taken by all students in order to develop a weltanschauung, or world view. They say that what distinguishes a Princeton graduate from a Bucknell graduate is essentially that combination of required curriculum and special methods that differentiates one college from another. But this view seems contradicted by research that claims that the character of the graduate is determined less by a specific curriculum than by the admissions policy of an institution. When the admissions policy admits widely diverse students with no binding characteristics, the curriculum designed for a particular homogeneous student body no longer serves the needs of all the students and incites factions to push for change. Consequently, the pressures to reform the content and structure of the curriculum originate not in the faculty course structure but in the admissions policy, and that policy rather than its core of course requirements determines a college's profile. In the 1960s, colleges that did not grow much or change their clientele did not experience major curriculum upheavals or alterations of their images. However, in the same era, the rapidly growing colleges without deeply established images admitted a broad range of students. And these colleges experienced telling stresses on their curricula as they tried to serve larger numbers of more diverse students. Thus, the curricula assembled on many college campuses by certain social imperatives in the 1950s and early 1960s were blown apart in the late 1960s on campuses whose admissions policies at that time reflected very different social forces. Precisely because advocates of a core curriculum are trying to retrieve a curricular structure more suited to American society in an earlier period, this revival movement will fail in the 1980s.

. . .

The evidence of the recent past indicates that the impetus for significant changes in college curricula originates not in the faculty but in the social imperatives of the times, often reflected in college admission policies. Within that context, faculty should continue to frame the specific curricula for their colleges and to establish the standards of student performance in fulfilling that curriculum. But fundamentally, the faculty's definition of curricula—to be effective—must be made within the context of such social forces and factors as business; government; science; and student ages, sex, race, economic backgrounds and their relevancy to the times and to the admission policy of any given college.

If, at the numerous larger institutions—not at the smaller homogeneous colleges—the heterogeneous character is more a function of the institution's admissions policy and social forces than of the faculty-designed curriculum, is it logical to superimpose any single curricular approach? Given all the knowledge there is to learn, all the different careers for which people need to prepare, and the multiple backgrounds of college students today, what social value do colleges serve if they turn out people who think the same things? Ernest L. Boyer and Martin Kaplan answer this question in *Educating for Survival*,[10] in which they effectively argue that, in a nation torn in many directions, education can develop a sense of community with shared values, obligations, and social commitments. They point out that the social movements of the past decade have fractured this sense of communal values in America. In some cases, these movements have led to a highly individualistic, even narcissistic approach to education, with the resulting decline in a shared sense of community. Boyer and Kaplan say a curriculum built on a fixed, unifying base of knowledge that is responsive to key issues of the times could rectify this fractured communal value system.

We argue to the contrary. College is not the place to instill a sense of community. By the time students arrive at college, they have shared in a much more homogeneous culture than ever existed before through their exposure to television. When in American history have Americans laughed at so many of the same jokes or shared such similar political views? Through the socializing tool of television, high school students have achieved a high rate of acculturation by their freshman year at college. But more importantly, a primary purpose of elementary and secondary school is the development of a shared community value system, which Boyer and Kaplan espouse as one major purpose of the college years. To the extent that colleges during the 1950s and 1960s twisted their purposes to extend that socialization into the years of higher learning is precisely the degree to which they prolonged the adolescence of their students and the degree to which core curricula failed. For instance, the typical required freshman course in "American civilization" has tended—in the setting of auditorium-size lecture halls—to be only a detailed elaboration of work covered in earlier grades by students in secondary schools. Do college students need a fundamentally repetitious rehash of information required for a high school diploma at the college level, or should their curricula encourage maturity through a vigorous exploration of topics and methodologies growing out of their own rich curiosity and enthusiastic interests? The extent to which a preselected curriculum that purposes to socialize by inculcating a common core of knowledge does not allow students to confront their own career goals and make choices is the extent to which students are not helped to mature as decisionmaking, choice-making, judgmental adults. The extent to which a prescribed curriculum forces students to accept the wisdom of others is the extent to which students are not encouraged to develop their capacities to think independently as adults. Such a fixed, regimented curricular approach does not stimulate students to want to learn and become educated but inculcates the value of wanting to be knowledgeable or trained.

We argue against the curricular model that provides only knowledge or superficial breadth but that does not stimulate students to mature by encouraging them to make choices. We argue against an approach that may give students facts and train them to extrapolate from past cases to present cases but that does not enable them to develop these analyses into critical value judgments applicable to new situations. Such an educational approach and such a curriculum are sorely deficient. The ultimate purpose of education we say is neither socialization nor indoctrination into a community value system, but is instead to gain the capabilities by which one ultimately makes good judgments. The ultimate purpose of education is to give students the capacities to distinguish between what is good and less good, between what is better in one situation than something else in equal circumstances.

A nation whose educational system turns out technocrats steeped in encyclopedic knowledge with no ability to synthesize and make critical judgments is certainly worse off than a society whose institutions of higher learning inculcate both knowledge and the tools to use that information to make critical decisions about the self, the community, and the world. A nation's view of what, how, and why people should learn is an expression of that nation's values. And if a nation values the development of fine technicians who lack the capacities to ask questions that relate their knowledge to larger social questions, then the curriculum should, as in the Soviet Union, provide specialized knowledge through specialized institutes for specialized technological purposes.

But a curriculum that engages a student's deepest intellectual motivations and highest powers of synthesis and analysis over memorization does not require a choice between a core of requirements and chaos. Today, numerous alternative curricular approaches meet standards of academic quality and depth, such as curricula based on individualized student interests coherently organized or on principles that interrelate vocation and liberal learning or a curriculum responsive to social issues of a minority, lower economic-cultural experience, or a curriculum based on academic-human-moral development, or many others geared for particular constituencies without sacrificing quality. However, we believe a college curriculum that only inculcates knowledge, and not the means to synthesize that knowledge into new understanding, does not deserve endorsement of an institution of higher learning. Similarly, the college curriculum that does not recognize the diverse interests of a heterogeneous student clientele ignores the object lessons of the student protests of the recent past. For any curricular approach that neglects the many societal imperatives of its times can only subvert the community purposes that advocates of core curriculum so dearly cherish, for such an approach shows great disrespect for the plethora of individual values of which any society is comprised.

Notes

1. A full development of these and other forces that affected the American college may be found in Buell G. Gallagher, *Campus in Crisis* (New York: Harper & Row, 1974).

2. Daniel J. Kevles, *The Physicists: The History of a Scientific Community in Modern America* (New York: Knopf, 1978), p. 386.

3. In New York State, for example, 70.7 percent of all public and nonpublic high school graduates entered postsecondary institutions in 1970. Of these graduates, 41.5 percent matriculated at four-year colleges or universities and 24.0 percent at two-year institutions. *Distribution of High School Graduates and College-Going Rate, 1979: A Report of the University of the State of New York* (Albany, N.Y.: 1980).

4. Betty Friedan, *The Feminine Mystique* (New York: Norton, 1963).

5. A listing of Carnegie Commission Reports can be found in the bibliography for this volume.

6. See *Report on Higher Education*, Frank Newman, chairman, Task Force (Washington, D.C.: U.S. Government Printing Office, 1971).

7. See *Diversity by Design*, Report of the Commission on Non-Traditional Study: Samuel B. Gould, chairman (San Francisco: Jossey-Bass, 1972).

8. James W. Hall and Ernest G. Palola, "Curricula for Adult Learners," Paper no. 17, The Open University Conference on the Education of Adults at a Distance (Milton Keynes, U.K.: The British Open University, 1979).

9. See *Empire State College Bulletin 1978-1980* (Saratoga Springs, N.Y.: Empire State College, 1978).

10. Ernest L. Boyer and Martin Kaplan, *Educating for Survival* (New Rochelle, N.Y.: Change Magazine Press, 1977).

TWO

ALTERNATIVE CURRICULA

3

ALTERNATIVE APPROACHES TO CURRICULAR COHERENCE

WARREN BRYAN MARTIN

The current controversy about general and liberal education mainly concerns means, not ends. There is, in fact, widespread agreement about desirable outcomes, about those skills, attitudes, information, and experiences that ideally should be shared by liberally educated people. However, no such agreement exists on the means whereby these ends shall be achieved. This is why it is useful to direct attention to alternative approaches to curricular coherence.

Along the means-ends continuum—after all, means are ends in the process of becoming—it is possible to sort out four approaches to the ends sought, four clusters of conceptual and procedural means that seem to be dominating our thinking.

Amid the various and sometimes competing organizing principles for general and liberal education, what may be called *the "common fate" approach* is emerging. The emphasis in this approach is on the commonalities of the human condition, on our shared "fate," rather than on the differences and singularities in human experience.

One manifestation of this organizing principle is found in Stephen Bailey's book, *The Purpose of Education*,[1] in which the shared experience of personal and family coping, the search for meaningful work, and the expression of the "free self" are offered as organizing themes. Another variation of the common fate approach is seen in *Educating for Survival*[2] by Ernest L. Boyer and Martin Kaplan, whose emphasis is on the need to know and understand a shared and influential past, a complex present, and a challenging future and particularly to grapple with the values that underlay the past and present, as well as moral and ethical values appropriate for the future.

This concern to feature the elements of our common fate as the organizing principles for general and liberal education is, I think, a promising development. It does not require the overthrow of the subject-matter or disciplinary bastions but, rather, challenges the guardians of these fortresses to apply their subject-matter and their disciplinary methodologies to overarching problems and themes.

At a time when the practicality of general and liberal learning is questioned, the common fate approach calls for attention to issues and themes that are fundamental to the individual's life and to collective social organization, to the qualitative as well as the quantitative dimensions of human existence, to our pervasive concern for meaning in life as well as the means for its achievement.

What examples of common fate problems and themes provide the organizing principle for a core curriculum? Some of them can be stated as pairings—love and work (Freud and Weber), individualism and community (Buber), continuity and change (Marx, Einstein, and Russell), home and family (Meade, Dirkheim, and Jung). The persons mentioned in connection with these themes are selected arbitrarily. There are, no doubt, other equally important or more important persons and movements, and many of them would not have the Western perspective of nearly all of those persons listed.

Consider in more detail the pairing of home and family: these two focal points of concern—controversial yet basic, lively, and substantive—can be approached from all of the subject-matter specializations in the humanities and arts, the social and behavioral sciences, and the biological sciences. This approach does not call for other features in the disciplines to be ignored but, rather, does call for these common fate themes to reach across departmental lines and provide opportunity for the better integration of knowledge as well as its applications, so as to show the usefulness of general and liberal education for individuals and society.

Faculty would be challenged, where this pairing of home and family is made, to deal with the contemporary home and family—its breakdown, its resilience; its traditions, present variations, and future prospects. Anthropology, economics, sociology, psychology —as disciplines—can approach the home and family without strain or artificiality, and each one has solid contributions to make. The same can be said for history, literature, religion, art, and music. Biology, even applied mathematics, can be related to the theme. Environmental studies, Third World perspective and minority group orientations, urban studies, these and other cross-disciplinary approaches are relevant.

But a college curriculum need not be unified year after year by attention to the same problem/theme. After, say a three-year concentration on home and family, the faculty might vote for the common fate theme for the next period to be continuity and change —in nature, in social organizations, in science and technology, in the life of the person.

Such an organizing principle as is provided by this common fate approach gives the liberal arts curriculum distinction and character, unity and cohesiveness, application and significance relevant to the preoccupations of parents and students—self-realization, interpersonal relationships, social status, and professionally relevant skills.

This approach to general and liberal education has a special potential for creating an active and useful connection with the community at large, for bringing liberal arts colleges into working relationships with social agencies, churches, volunteer groups, labor unions, political entities, businesses, and industry. For example, if faculty members would work hard to relate their subject-matter specializations to, say, the home and family; or to subdivisions of those broad concerns, say, parent education and child-rearing skills, or home management, or the psychological, sociological, and economical connections between satisfaction in the home and effectiveness on the job; if this kind of thing could happen, the faculty would necessarily relate to community leaders and could become community leaders themselves. Skills and experiences from campus and community could be blended, and everybody would benefit. Students too could be drawn into these connections, and their study would become more purposeful.

A second approach to general and liberal education may be called *the "common tools" approach*. Rather than trying to tell people what they need to know in order to be an educated person, as is implied by the use of those content-oriented distribution requirements that are so familiar—a little history, some literature and psychology, seasoned with a dash of science—perhaps it is better to concentrate on giving students the tools, the technical equipment necessary for them to hold jobs, function as citizens, gain self-esteem, and enjoy leisure. This is what they really need to know.

Active devotees of the common tools approach include those who would characterize this part of the curriculum by its attention first to basic skills and later to advanced skills. Basic skills are defined as those of communication (reading, writing, speaking) and of computation (simple math), plus the ability to comprehend ideas of value (democracy, capitalism). Advanced skills are defined as the further development and fuller utilization of basic skills, plus others that relate to, say, the methodology of science; the place of technology; the importance of contextual thinking, criticism, and creativity. Common tools advocates would have what is usually called "general education" become a synonym for training in basic skills. They would then have "liberal education" distinguished from general education and defined in terms similar to those emphasized by the Carnegie Council: ". . . consisting of a curriculum more or less in its entirety organized around the cultural heritage of civilization and thus concentrating heavily on the humanities."[3]

Those committed to the common tools approach are less interested in liberal education, as defined above, and more interested in general education, defined as basic skills and seen as necessary preparation for mastering advanced skills.

Steven Marcus, in a provocative essay, challenged academics who do not want to get involved in basic skills instruction:

There may be a certain element of cant—or of hot air—in the perennial and current lament that *the high schools in America are not doing their job. When did they ever?* . . . I suggest that we stop bellyaching for a bit and see if we can determine what it is that we might do. One of the first things we might do is to admit that the work of higher education in America —particularly in the first two years—has varied both historically and according to what level of the system of higher education one is examining; but it has always been there. What has not always been there is the unwillingness on the part of people like ourselves to admit that this is what we are doing, and the even further unwillingness to admit that this is proper and legitimate and rewarding work for specialists in medieval literature or French history, or the logical theory of signs. If such admission is made, then a step toward demystification among ourselves will have been taken. And if this step can be followed by the acknowledgment in all good cheer and with appropriate academic irony and skepticism—that much of the work that we have to do in the first two years is the work that is not done in secondary education and will not be done in secondary education, and that it is our proper work to do, then a step away from demoralization will have been made as well.[4]

In addition to the basic tools of reading and writing and some computational skills, the adherents of the common tools approach to general and liberal education often look back with affection and appreciation to Daniel Bell's book, *The Reforming of General Education*[5] because among Bell's proposals was the idea of a "third tier" of courses.

Bell believed that general and liberal education could not stop with the year or two of undergraduate study. He proposed a set of courses at the upper-division level that would have two objectives: first, to enable students to develop a degree of sophistication about the methodological skills employed by the major disciplines, particularly those of science and of scientific technology, and, second, to draw students back into broad contact with the intellectual world when they concentrate on their major specialty.

At Columbia, Bell's proposals were never enacted—in part because of the disruptions of the student movements in the late 1960s—but those proposals have lingered in the memories of some of Bell's colleagues and still figure in curriculum debates. Even now, the Columbia Committee on General Education is conducting faculty seminars and workshops that have as their objective the establishment of so-called teaching companies—cross-disciplinary teams that integrate ways of thinking, relate professional methodologies, find the commonalities in subject-matter specializations, and eventually help students to see that people who first acquire the common tools can then develop their use of advanced tools in pursuits that are personally and socially relevant.[6]

Perhaps the main advantage of the tools approach is that it seems so practical, so full of utilitarian benefits. The disadvantage is that it can be defined too narrowly. Only about one-fourth of the hours in a week are normally spent on the job. And a majority of the jobs in America can be performed by a person with a high school education and a few weeks of on-site training. Furthermore, the same academics who dislike teaching the basic skills are favorably disposed toward teaching certain advanced skills in the subject-matter specializations—skills for which there is, alas, a limited market and early obsolescence.

The third way of looking at general and liberal education may be called *the "common ground" approach*, which is differentiated from the others in that it does not feature shared experiences, neither the experiential ones of the common fate approach—coping, working, expressing the free self—nor the shared experiences of basic and advanced skills training. It is characterized by the quest for shared assumptions that will provide a foundation for and give direction to the education of students. Shared experiences, in this case, build out of shared assumptions.

Are there themes or emphases that are or ought to be common to general and liberal education; activities, processes, that give a liberal arts college distinctiveness, even character? Devotees who cluster around the common ground approach believe that there are such characteristics. Here are several: liberal arts educators are always trying to draw students—to lure, seduce, require, or coerce students—into thinking about themselves and their world, as well as about their professional future, in a context that transcends immediate and provincial pressures. Contextual awareness, as an enrichment to judgment, is another element in liberal education, as is historical perspective that acknowledges roots and emphasizes the purposes of the task for which techniques are tools.

In this age of immediacy and pragmatism, not many people want to take the time required for contextual learning. Hence, seven out of ten degrees are in areas that are called "professionally specific." The corollary to that fact is that the recipients of these degrees have usually taken as few courses as possible outside of their major and, within the professional specialization, have given little or no attention to, say, the philosophy and ethics of law, the social psychology of medicine, the aesthetics of engineering, the ideological basis for business.

Education ought to contribute to one's capacity to earn a living. At the same time, the earning of one's living does not necessarily explain why it is worth earning—why it is worth staying alive. Education ought to help to take a person beyond living defined as work to living that combines work and leisure so as to make both worthwhile.

What else can be said in response to the question "What is the common ground for liberal and liberating education?" Here is a second assertion, and like the first, it seems to go against the grain. To be committed to liberal education means not only to think relationally and, as a corollary, to become more relativistic; it also means to develop a capacity for discrimination and, as a corollary, to run the risk of being called an elitist.

It is the confidence, some would say the arrogance, of those who think that they recognize the characteristics of the educated person, that liberal learning helps one to untangle a skein of thought and encourages development of a capacity for good judgment; that liberal learning helps persons to discriminate and, in the presence of hard options, to choose and act. And in so doing, it helps to educate an elite whose principle for leadership should be service.

To be friendly to the principle of discrimination and to the promotion of an elite, to dare to suggest that a liberal arts program should be unapologetically discriminatory and elitist, is in this time of egalitarianism at best unfashionable and at worst dangerous. And for obvious reasons. The old forms of discrimination used by the governing elite have been discredited. They are in disgrace, and to defend them is disgraceful. Obviously, then, those words must be refurbished if they are to be used.[7]

Advocates of the common ground approach argue that a liberal arts program promoting something called humane and liberating learning is not promoting ideational egalitarianism; it is not saying that everything is of equal value and that what one chooses for study from an almost infinite array of options is entirely a matter of individual preference. A liberal arts program discriminates in the best sense of that volatile word. It discriminates, for example, between culture and civilization.[8]

A liberal education not only discriminates between culture and civilization but—say those who have a common ground as the basis for curricular coherence—also discriminates between pluralism and egalitarianism. The trouble with egalitarianism is that it has become another word for standardization: standardization at the lowest common denominator. As such, it is the enemy of pluralism which allows for differentiation.

If the liberal arts college is to accept the responsibility of making such discriminations as those between culture and civilization, pluralism and egalitarianism, it follows that liberal education is essential to the preparation of leaders, to the education of a meritocratic elite.

We would do well to emphasize, or at least so say those who hold to this common ground, that people who have the advantages of the liberal arts comprise an elite, no matter their racial or ethnic origins, no matter the social class or economic status out of which they come. This elite should be made to feel comfortable with its privileges as long as it knows, and is never allowed to forget, that these privileges convey serious responsibilities, among which is the task of leadership in achieving social justice.

Liberal arts education serves best when, in those students who, like it or not, become the ruling elite, it helps to develop a sense of their own legitimacy and their responsibility to clarify their ethical, social, and political mission, thereby assuring that they will not become agents of exploitation and mere civilization but of humane achievement and true culture.

It is this sort of common ground, then, that makes the liberal arts program or institution uncommon. This uncommon institution is not an educational cafeteria; it is not characterized by undifferentiated pluralism; it is not a community of convenience. It is rather, a community of conviction, defining the limits of pluralism with shared assumptions, values, and objectives that together comprise the common ground on which the members of the community stand.

The fourth organizing principle for general and liberal education features *the uncommon individual*. Here the structural provisions for education are those that extend options and encourage variety. The curriculum puts the individual at the center—her/his needs and interests, her/his ideas and perspectives, her/his uniqueness. The uncommon individual, say advocates of this approach, is the organizing principle around which all general and liberal education should be organized.

Believers in the individualized approach are not much concerned about curricular coherence in institutional terms. They emphasize that most learning takes place outside colleges and universities and that it is the individual, usually with a mentor, who must bring coherence to these many experiences.

In such programs, most learning takes place at times and within contexts that have little to do with institutions of higher education. It can occur in settings that involve family, friends, or employers, activities that involve work or recreation. A person may learn more in such informal environments than in rigid classroom settings. It is the individual, capable of being educated in so many places and in so many different ways, who is the focal point of interest for educators, usually nontraditionalists, who adhere to this fourth organizing principle. And the fact that they are willing to credit "life experience" is their acknowledgment that learning is ongoing.

What best motivates people to learn? The evidence is overwhelming that people learn best when they are receiving information or knowledge that affects them personally. No doubt the spate of recent studies on stages of adult development—mid-career crises—are of greater interest to persons thirty-five to fifty than to others. This fact about learning, this aspect of learning theory, is so well accepted and powerful that it has drawn all sorts of ego-serving, self-actualizing activities and has become so noticeable that ours is being called "the narcissist society."[9] The next most effective learning relates to one's job or profession, particularly to its rewards and sanctions. Hence, we saw the faculty member in the university of the 1960s become more dedicated to his or her professional association or guild than to the educational institution with which that person was affiliated. That happened because the guild, then, controlled most rewards and sanctions. And the third level of impact, behind the learning that is personal and professionally important, is the learning that affects one's institutional connections. But the institution is clearly in third place. Again, educators who favor individualized learning contracts are building on this knowledge of the psychology of learning.

Why do people learn? To survive—physically and emotionally. Abraham Maslow's research emphasized attention to the lower and higher levels of life, that it is necessary for humans to assure their survival and meet their basic needs before they can move to the higher level of life with its attention to self-realization, social interaction, purpose, leisure, and pleasure. Survival first, significance second. Bread, then honor.[10]

Nevertheless, despite the ambivalence of human nature, say advocates of this fourth organizing principle with its emphasis on the uncommon individual, the college or university, through an individualized liberal arts program, can be a mechanism by which students are introduced to themselves, to interpersonal relationships, to contextual thinking, to the world—and this in a way and to a measure not otherwise possible.

Empire State College, with its learning centers scattered around the state of New York, its individualized contract learning approach to higher education, and its Center for Individualized Education, is an institutional representative of this fourth approach to general and liberal education.

This approach is radical, first, in its assumption that most of the facilities for the activities can be found in the larger community, in the society at large; second, in its confidence that faculty can become mentors and that students will accept tutelary relationships; third, in its determination to take city and country, the nation and the world as the arena for teaching and learning.

Here, then, are four prevailing if not predominant, approaches to general and liberal education: the common fate approach, with its emphasis on core experiences with which every human being must deal; the common tools approach, with its insistence that methods of inquiry and the mastery of intellectual skills are fundamental to success in a technological society; the common ground approach, or the uncommon institution approach, with its commitment to making the institutions of higher education instrumentalities for the promotion of values that can serve as the foundation upon which every program can be built; and the uncommon individual approach, with its attention to the singularity of each human being and the benefits to be derived from shaping the course of study around the needs and interests of the person in the world.

The four approaches have much in common; they do overlap. But they do contain elements that are not easily reconciled and that appear to be contradictory. These are alternative approaches to curricular coherence, and perhaps it is not necessary for one institution to try to incorporate all four of them. What is important is that each college or university weigh these options, draw from them the elements that can be used to help realize the institutions's mission, and, by so doing, develop its own expression of curricular coherence.

Notes

1. Stephen Bailey, *The Purposes of Education* (Bloomington, Ind.: Phi Delta Kappa Educational Foundation, 1976).

2. Ernest L. Boyer and Martin Kaplan, *Educating for Survival* (New Rochelle, N.Y.: Change Magazine Press, 1977).

3. Carnegie Foundation for the Advancement of Teaching, *Missions of the College Curriculum* (San Francisco: Jossey-Bass, 1977), p. 9.

4. Steven Marcus, "Some Questions in General Education Today," in *Parnassus: Essays in Honor of Jacques Barzun* (New York: Harper and Row, 1976), p. 100.

5. Daniel Bell, *The Reforming of General Education* (Garden City, N.Y.: Doubleday, 1966).

6. Robert L. Belknap and Richard Kuhns, *Tradition and Innovation: General Education and the Reintegration of the University* (New York: Columbia University Press, 1977).

7. William Arrowsmith, "Thoughts on American Culture and Civilization," *Schoolworlds '76*, p. 156.

8. Ibid.

9. Christopher Lasch, *Culture of Narcissism: American Life in an Age of Diminishing Expectations* (New York: Warner, 1979).

10. Abraham H. Maslow, *Toward a Psychology of Being*, 2nd ed. (New York: Van Nostrand Reinhold, 1968).

THREE

CURRICULA FOCUSED ON THE INDIVIDUAL STUDENT

4

HUMAN DEVELOPMENT AND CURRICULAR DESIGN

DEE G. APPLEY

To think about human development and curricular design in the framework of higher education takes us immediately to the question of what brings people to colleges and universities. Are they there to realize their own potential or to be prepared to function as citizens for the benefit of society? Are there educational objectives that can benefit the individual and society? In other words, what are the aims of higher education?

It will be helpful for us to examine with Lawrence Kohlberg and Rochelle Mayer[1] two competing educational ideologies: the romantic tradition and the cultural transmission tradition. The romantics, from Rousseau to the current deschooling advocates, believe that the discovery of the natural and the inner self is the important aim and that this is best done with no interference. The cultural transmitters look to the classical academic traditions of Western education as a means to transmit to the present generation information, rules, and values selected in the past as the main educational task. There are two versions of cultural transmission: traditional and technological; the former is concerned with having the student acquire the culture of Western man; the latter sees education as a means to vocational adaptation. Both are measured by standards set by the culture.

In a controversy over Harvard's 1978 attempt at curricular reform, we find a recent example of romantics vs. cultural transmitters. Editor Shelley G. Burtt, in an article in the *Harvard Independent*, a weekly student newspaper, attacked the proposal as unworkable and as a threat to the "right of the individual student to structure his or her education." On the other side, "Dr. Bok [President of Harvard] described the proposal as an effort to adapt the curriculum to the needs that have developed since the last major revision shortly after World War II. The new mathematical requirement, he said, reflects the spread of the use of quantitative skills in our society well beyond the fields of engineering and math."[2]

Underlying these two educational ideologies are two theories of psychological development that Kohlberg and Mayer describe as they explore "Development as the Aim of Education." For the romantics, development is a matter of maturation, and an appropriate metaphor is the development of a plant. What the environment must do is provide nourishment, but the unfolding occurs through an inevitable set of prepatterned stages. Emotional and cognitive developments are two unrelated activities. The former is inherent in the individual; the latter is based on acquired knowledge. For the cultural transmitters, the theory of psychological development can be described as associationistic-learning or environmental-contingency theory, and the appropriate metaphor is a machine. The machine model can be wax on which we etch, or a telephone switchboard or a computer, but "cognitive development is the result of guided learning and teaching," and affective development is not relevant.[3]

When we examine the epistemological components of these educational ideologies, once again we find how they are different. For the romantics, what is real (that is, what are facts and how they can be interpreted) proves to have an existential, phenomenological answer. Knowledge and reality refer to the immediate inner experience of the self. For the cultural transmitters, knowledge is that which is "objective," and experience must be culturally shared and tested.

Both the romantics and the cultural transmitters are dissatisfied with the results of present educational experience, but for different reasons. The romantics with their list of traits essentially judge the mental health of personalities; while the cultural transmitters look, in the short run, at what has been achieved on tests and, in the long run, for signs of success in the system. Yet both must be disappointed when they find the many personal and social problems that abound: drug abuse, low achievement scores, war, mental illness, disaffected workers, child abuse, unemployment, suicide, to name a few.

There is still a third educational ideology called progressivism, based on the work of John Dewey. And this time the metaphor for the learner is a philosopher or, better still, a scientist-poet. Already we can begin to feel that we are talking about *human* development. As we examine this third educational ideology, development is seen as a progression through invariant, ordered sequential stages, *but* the educational environment must actively stimulate this development by presenting resolvable but genuine problems or conflicts.[4] Interaction and dialectical process are critical components of this orientation.

This progressive ideology has as its underlying psychological theory what can be called an interactionist theory, where both affective and cognitive development are involved. There are stages in this developmental process, but each stage is a transformation. "Attainment of a higher stage presupposes attainment of the prior stage and represents a reorganization or transformation of it . . . *attainment of the next stage is a valid aim of educational experience*."[5] What is "real" is not just the individual's experience nor just the environmental problem but the relationship between this inquiring human being and this problematic situation. So progressivists would look at both internal stages and external behavior. Thus, progressivists would distinguish between *humanitarian* criteria in judging the quality of the individual's experience and *educative* criteria in judging the quality of the experience itself. Some experiences therefore can be *miseducative* as Dewey was able to see.[6] A miseducative experience would then be one that interferes with or distorts the growth of further experience. However, both freely selected and required experiences can be miseducative.

Another very important issue related to the aims of education is whether these aims should be universal or individual. The pro-

gressivist position is that we are seeking universal qualitative states
or sequences important in all individual development. This brings
us to a very important problem: the ethical values underlying
educational ideologies. It is at this point that we begin to see how
the curriculum and human development are indeed related.

Should educational aims contain values that are particular or
universal? Kohlberg and Mayer help us to confront several fallacies
in any value judgment. They define these as (1) the fallacy of value
neutrality, where values and morality are defined as *conformity* to
a particular culture; (2) the naturalistic fallacy, which defines what
ought to be as what *is*; (3) and when this fallacy is applied to human
nature by psychologists, becomes the psychologist's fallacy, which
fails to distinguish between what is desired and what is desirable;
and finally (4) the fallacy of value relativism. This forces us to take
into consideration philosophy's concern with the true, the good,
and the beautiful (epistemology, ethics, and aesthetics) to carry us
beyond these fallacies to universals.

Kohlberg and Mayer make a case for accepting the methodological nonrelativism of moral judgment as well as the methodological nonrelativism of scientific judgment. They, and I, present
for our consideration "that certain values or principles ought to be
universal and that these principles are distinct from the rules of any
given culture."[7] This is true in spite of the fact that philosophers do
not agree on the exact principles nor on the priorities among them,
but they do agree that moral evaluations ought to refer to such a
realm of principles and would indeed include such options as
"justice as fairness."[8] One of the important corollaries of this
perspective is that moral development—the development of a capacity to judge what is right—is an essential aspect of human development and is therefore an essential aim of education, including
higher education.

I am proposing, then, that we accept human development as an
aim of education and recognize our responsibilities as educators for
providing for the development of students' socioemotional and
moral, as well as cognitive, capacities. We will need to struggle with
considerations of optimal human development and ideal norms,[9]
even while we acknowledge the "bounded rationality" of human
decisions.[10]

If we accept that human development is an aim of education (and this includes cognitive, socioemotional, and moral development) and that this development is still in process when learners arrive at college, then we must indeed concern ourselves with curricular design, and we will need to understand how we will want to define curriculum. Usually, this is defined by the formal offerings at the college or university, and these offerings are usually presented through departments and majors. We will in a very short time be naturally carried to the awareness that we need a typology of learning environments that is *commensurate with the variety of learners*, and this may say something about what now happens in courses (or does not happen).

David A. Kolb and Ronald Fry[11] offer a model for *experiential learning* at the university level based on programmatic work developed out of Kurt Lewin's action/research model.[12] In the work of Kolb and Fry, we find many parallels with the work of Kohlberg and Mayer. Learning is seen as a central life task, and "how one learns becomes a major determinant of the course of [his] personal development."[13] And experiential learning is seen as describing the central process of human adaptation to the social and physical environment. Of special importance here, too, is the idea that learning, by its very nature, involves tension and a conflict-filled process.

In this framework, there are three major developmental stages in the human growth process: *acquisition* (birth to adolescence); *specialization* (which can end in mid-career); and *integration* (which develops after specialization, if it comes). During the college years, there are many pressures on the individual to choose a job and a career, and this serves to accentuate the specialization level. The accentuation process becomes the most powerful force both because the individual self-selects the environment and the environmental experiences and because the environment shapes the individual; it is an interaction between choices and socialization.

Such diverse individuals as Paulo Freire, Friedrich Schiller, and Carl Jung have commented on the destructive effects of specialization and its dehumanizing consequences. Even for many "successful" people, whose rewards come from their having contributed through their highly developed specialization, the price for having abandoned their nondominant modes (see Figure 1 and Table 1) is that they are left underdeveloped human beings. Ob-

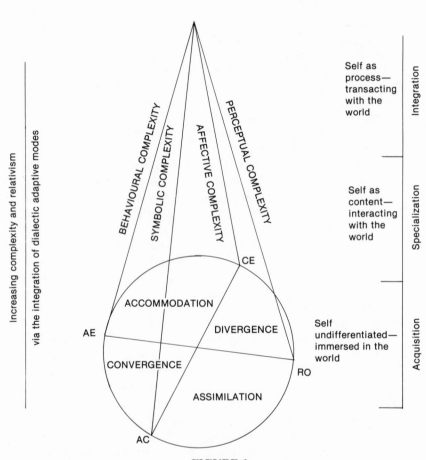

FIGURE 1
The Experiential Learning Theory of Growth
and Development

SOURCE: David A. Kolb and Ronald Fry, "Towards an Applied Theory of Experiential Learning," in *Theories of Group Processes*, edited by Cary L. Cooper (New York: John Wiley & Sons, 1975), p. 43. Reprinted by permission of John Wiley & Sons Ltd.

NOTE: AE = active experimentation   RO = reflective observation
         AC = abstract conceptualization   CE = concrete experience

TABLE 1

(1) *Affectively complex* environments are characterized by:
  (a) focus on here-and-now experiences.
  (b) legitimization of expression of feelings and emotions.
  (c) situations structured to allow ambiguity.
  (d) high degree of personalization.

(2) *Perceptually complex* environments are characterized by:
  (a) opportunities to view subject matter from different perspectives.
  (b) time to reflect, and roles (e.g., listener, observer) which allow reflection.
  (c) complexity and multiplicity of observational frameworks.

(3) *Symbolically complex* environments are characterized by:
  (a) emphasis on recall of concepts.
  (b) thinking or acting governed by rules of logic and inference.
  (c) situations structured to maximize certainty.
  (d) authorities respected as caretakers of knowledge.

(4) *Behaviorally complex* environments are characterized by:
  (a) responsibility for setting own goals.
  (b) opportunities for real risk taking.
  (c) environmental responses contingent upon self-initiated action.

SOURCE: David A. Kolb and Ronald Fry, "Towards an Applied Theory of Experiential Learning," in *Theories of Group Processes*, edited by Cary L. Cooper (New York: John Wiley & Sons, 1975), p. 54. Reprinted by permission of John Wiley & Sons Ltd.

viously, some do come to this realization and, in Jung's scheme,[14] can become "individuated" (that is, integrated) after mid-career, and we are perhaps reminded of the present interest in the mid-life crisis. This also raises the whole issue of human development and curricular design for our newest population in colleges and universities (the older student and the continuing education population) and perhaps gives us a new perspective for understanding what could be involved in designing the curriculum in the learning environment for these so-called nontraditional students.

We might ask, in passing, are there many integrated, highly developed people in the colleges and universities who can facilitate full development and be role models? And/or can specialists facilitate the development of others to more integrated levels? If only 5 percent of the adult population in the United States has reached what can be considered to be full moral development,[15] what are the implications of this for the learning environment(s) at colleges and universities? Perhaps this question can be pursued constructively by forcing us to recognize that these learning environments *are* composed of "communities of learners" after all and that both faculty and students can be transformed in the interactive process.

So if we agree that human development is an aim of higher education and we agree that students who come to college are not yet fully developed, then one way to classify learning environments is in terms of the personal growth opportunities for experiencing affective, perceptual, symbolic, and behavioral complexities as described by Kolb and Fry (see Table 1).[16]

These are four perspectives that can be viewed along two dimensions. There is an active-reflective dimension (which is dialectically related) and a concrete-abstract dimension (which is dialectically related). In addition, correlated to the active pole is the development toward greater behavioral complexity; correlated to the reflective pole is the development of increasing perceptual complexity; correlated to the concrete pole is the development of affective complexity; and correlated to the abstract dimension is the development of symbolic complexity (see Figure 1).

People need all four perspectives, and more highly developed people move toward increasing complexity along, *and integration among*, all of these dimensions. By the time an individual reaches college, he or she has a particular profile based on the equipment she or he came into the world with, past life experiences, and the demands of the present environment. Kolb and Fry have a measure called the learning style inventory based on these perspectives that yields four statistically prevalent learning styles that they call converger, diverger, assimilator, and accommodator. The converger's dominant learning abilities are abstract conceptualization and active experimentation (the learning style characteristic of many engineers); the diverger is best at concrete experience and reflective observation (the learning style characteristic of those who major in the arts and in the humanities and liberal arts); the assimilator's dominant learning abilities are abstract conceptualization and reflective observation (most often found in majors in basic sciences and mathematics; and later those in research in planning departments); and the accommodator is best at concrete experience and active experimentation (more risk taking than the other three styles, and often found in business majors).

Consciousness is the quality of human beings that is most unique, and a highly developed, highly integrated individual would be a more conscious, more aware individual. It would seem rather obvious that the more perspectives available to an individual, as compared with specialization, the more complex and conscious that individual could become.[17] Although "successful" specialists in the system are not likely to think that they are underdeveloped, I am proposing that, if we value optimal human development, perhaps we should consider as "evil" those acts or conditions that, intentionally or unintentionally, stop or impede further development.[18]

An important question that arises is: As we design the curriculum, do we ask learners for their preferences (shades of romantics), or do we prescribe compensatory experiences (shades of cultural transmission)? We might want to recall Kohlberg and Mayer's list of fallacies of judgment and remind ourselves that miseducative experiences are possible. At least we must recognize that the learner's *needs* and *desires* may not be the same. However, whether courses are prescribed or elective, an examination of the learning environments help us to recognize that the course is only a vehicle for the learning and that the content is only one part of a total "system" that includes the teacher-learner-content-in-process.

We may wish to note that experiential learning has some important implications and that we are discussing an experiential learning model. These implications include (1) the integration of the cognitive and socioemotional perspectives in learning; (2) the role of individual differences in learning styles; (3) the concept of growth and development as inherent in the experiential learning model; and (4) the necessity for a model of learning environments that is commensurate with the experiential learning process.[19] We will also need to recognize that it takes a condition of psychological safety for learners to acquire nondominant skills and constructs and to move to a more integrated stage of growth.[20]

As we begin to develop this topic, human development and curricular design, it becomes clear that the curriculum, as it is usually understood, is only a vehicle for the educational process and is not an end in itself. The learning environment is composed of teachers and learners interacting around something called courses. And certain courses are more likely to engage particular models of inquiry or perspective. The curriculum can be a dead or deadening concept if it is thought of only in terms of numbers: how many hours, how many of each kind, in what order, and so forth. Or it can be (as its etymological origin suggests) a flowing concept, a course to follow, with some boundaries, but these need not be rigidly defined.

That brings us—for a moment—to the question of interdisciplinary courses, or at least to the recognition that, if development is to be an aim of education, there needs to be some opportunity for integration. Or at least *time* for integration. Fifty-minute classes, five courses a semester or trimester, tests, papers. What about time to reflect? To see connections? To get invested; committed? We might wish to recall the four experiential learning dimensions: concrete experience, reflective observation, abstract conceptualization, and active experimentation.

Perhaps this is the place to look at how one overspecialized perspective can impede this proposed aim of education, that is, facilitating the development of more highly integrated, more highly moral, more fully educated women and men. Currently, overspecialization occurs in large part because of the importance that has been given to being "scientific." This scientific orientation prescribes a fact-filled perspective without benefit of the enrichment of the other modes that have been considered, at best, less important or, even worse, irrelevant. (Let me add quickly that I am *not* suggesting that we give up the scientific perspective, but rather give up the overspecialization of perspectives, so a humanities overspecialization is not the answer either.)

Students come to college to continue their development. Often this is stopped by "the curriculum," at least as it has been designed in many places until now. Most people never reach the levels of development that we know are possible. Progressivism is one educational ideology with aims that are more likely to provide learning environments that facilitate this continuing development. Colleges and universities could explicitly state their commitment to human development as an educational aim. We could arrive at a model that better educates free and just individuals better able to create and live in a free and just society.[21] If human development were an explicit aim of education, people in these educational communities could begin to see each other as resources for one another: that all could give and take energy (and even create energy through synergistic encounters) as they interact and collaborate via the curriculum. Enthusiasm would be a welcome addition to higher education.

My colleague, Alvin Winder, and I have been working on a theory of collaboration. We define collaboration as a relational system in which: (1) individuals in a group share mutual aspirations and a common conceptual framework; (2) the interactions among individuals are characterized by "justice as fairness"; and (3) these aspirations and conceptualizations are characterized by each individual's *consciousness* of his/her motives toward the other, by *caring* or concern for the other, and by *commitment* to work with the other over time, provided that this commitment is a matter of *choice*.[22]

For many people, what is required now is an existential "leap of faith" in order to overcome the resistance imposed by an attachment to both an habitual value system and a fear of rapid change.[23] Fortunately, a capacity for change is inherent in the human growth process and can be engaged by the necessity of adapting to crisis.[24] This engagement can be nurtured in an environment that supports faith in, and hope for, the future. Central to the development of such an environment is the presence of human caring.[25]

In exploring human development and curricular design, I have been talking about complex problems with complex solutions, about developing complex people in complex environments. It is not the collapse of institutions of higher education but the reorganization and transformation of institutions into more facilitating human environments that is needed. At the present time, it often happens that in the process of producing (or creating) knowledge, we are failing to produce (or create) fully developed, educated men and women. It has been proposed by an observer that the reason some universities are such great storehouses of knowledge is that the freshmen bring so much and the seniors take so little away.

Rather than seeing colleges and universities as storehouses of knowledge (which are dead), I suggest that we envision them instead as energy centers (which are alive). Then, paradoxically, students could leave what they brought when they came and still take away more than they brought when they came because we would be creating energy as well as knowledge in our human encounters and working together more creatively on the solutions for meaningful problems that have universal importance.[26]

Notes

1. Lawrence Kohlberg and Rochelle Mayer, "Development as the Aim of Education," *Harvard Educational Review* 42, No. 4 (November 1972): 449-94.

2. Edward B. Fiske, *The New York Times*, February 26, 1978, pp. 1, 20.

3. Kohlberg and Mayer, "Development as the Aim of Education," p. 456.

4. Ibid., p. 454.

5. Ibid., pp. 458-59, emphasis added.

6. John Dewey, *Experience and Education* (New York: Collier, 1938; rev. 1963).

7. Kohlberg and Mayer, "Development as the Aim of Education," p. 468.

8. John Rawls, *A Theory of Justice* (Cambridge: Harvard University Press, 1971).

9. Jochen Brandstadter and Klaus A. Schneewind, "Optimal Human Development: Some Implications for Psychology," *Human Development* 20 (1977): 48-64.

10. H. A. Simon, *Models of Man, Social and Rational: Mathematical*

Essays on Rational Human Behavior in a Social Setting (New York: John Wiley & Sons, 1957).

11. David A. Kolb and Ronald Fry, "Towards an Applied Theory of Experiential Learning," in *Theories of Group Processes*, ed. Cary L. Cooper (New York: John Wiley & Sons, 1975).

12. Kurt Lewin, "Group Decision and Social Change," in *Readings in Social Psychology*, ed. T. Newcomb and E. Hartley (New York: Holt, Rinehart, and Winston, 1947).

13. Kolb and Fry, "Towards an Applied Theory of Experiential Learning," p. 41.

14. Carl Jung, *Psychological Types* (London: Pantheon Books, 1923).

15. Kohlberg and Mayer, "Development as the Aim of Education," p. 486.

16. Kolb and Fry, "Towards an Applied Theory of Experiential Learning," p. 54.

17. Anne Roe, "Man's Forgotten Weapon in Nunokawa," in *Human Values and Abnormal Behavior*, ed. D. Walter (Chicago: Scott, Foresman and Company, 1965), and E. F. Schumacher, *A Guide for the Perplexed* (New York: Harper and Row, 1977).

18. Jan M. Howard and Robert H. Somers, "Resisting Institutional Evil from Within," in *Sanctions for Evil*, ed. Nevitt Sanford and Craig Comstock (San Francisco: Jossey-Bass, 1971).

19. Kolb and Fry, "Towards an Applied Theory of Experiential Learning," p. 34.

20. Dee G. Appley and Alvin E. Winder, *T-Groups and Therapy Groups in a Changing Society* (San Francisco: Jossey-Bass, 1973); C. Argyris, "Dangers in Applying Results from Experimental Social Psychology," *American Psychologist* 30, No. 4 (April 1975): 469-85; and A. H. Maslow, *Motivation and Personality*, 2nd ed. (New York: Harper and Row, 1970).

21. Gardner Murphy, "Human Nature of the Future in Nunokawa," in *Human Values and Abnormal Behavior*, ed. D. Walter (Chicago: Scott, Foresman and Company, 1965), and Eric Trist, "Action Research and Adaptive Planning," in *Experimenting with Organizational Life*, ed. A. W. Clark (New York: Plenum Press, 1976).

22. Dee G. Appley and Alvin E. Winder, "An Evolving Definition of Collaboration and Some Implications for the Work Setting," *Journal of Applied Behavioral Science* 8, No. 3 (August 1977): 279-91.

23. Dee G. Appley, "Anxiety and the Human Condition," *Journal of Canadian Association of University Student Services* 1, No. 1 (1966): 23-31.

24. Arnold Toynbee, *Change and Habit: The Challenge of Our Time* (New York: Oxford University Press, 1966).

25. Dee G. Appley and Alvin E. Winder, eds., "Collaboration in Work Settings," *Journal of Applied Behavioral Science* 8, No. 3 (August 1977): 261-464, and M. Mayeroff, *On Caring* (New York: Harper and Row, 1971).

26. For an expanded version of this essay, see Dee G. Appley, "Human Development and Higher Education," Unpublished conference paper, Conference on Coherence and Curriculum: Alternatives for the Future, Sponsored by Empire State College of the State University of New York, The Society for Values in Higher Education, and The Danforth Foundation, Rensselaerville, New York, 12-14 April 1978.

5

CURRICULAR COHERENCE AND THE INDIVIDUAL STUDENT

LOIS LAMDIN

In the opening chapter of James Joyce's *Portrait of the Artist as a Young Man*, the young hero writes on the flyleaf of his geography book:

Stephen Dedalus

Class of Elements

Clongowes Wood College

Sallins

County Kildare

Ireland

Europe

The World

The Universe

The reader experiences the shock of recognition—how many of us have doodled something similar in our earliest attempts to establish ourselves in relation to a larger world. This common experience of childhood, this attempt to define the self, to locate that self in its connections with the universe, through varying degrees from the familiar to the unknown, this early attempt to create order, this is the basis for all education.

Indeed, education is the theme of Joyce's novel: the education of the young artist, his search for self as he moves from the purely sensory world of early childhood to the social world of family, friends, and community; the education of his sexual, political, religious, and intellectual selves, from the fact-oriented world of his primary education through the abstraction-dominated world of the church and the university; and finally, the imaginative flight of the creative artist seeking "silence, exile and cunning." Stephen Dedalus' education, both formal and informal, is a continuum that possesses a final coherence. On the assumption that such a holistic approach is both desirable and attainable in undergraduate education, I shall suggest in this paper practical ways to foster and implement coherence, ways that flow from the student's perception of his needs rather than from the institution's planning and perception of those needs.*

The subject is being addressed in an economy of belt tightening and a return not only to fundamentals but, I fear, also to fundamentalism. It is a climate in which every press release brings further news of institutions returning to core curricula, required sequences, distribution requirements; in other words, of reductions rather than expansions of student options.

Those of us who make our living in the academic marketplace are well aware of the ups and downs of that market, and we hedge our bets accordingly. We try to keep our perspective, recognizing the inevitability of the pendulum's continuing swing, but we are not immune to the fashions of the time. Our posture, depending on the degree of commitment we have at any moment to the reigning philosophy of that moment, ranges from welcoming to defensive to hostile.

As the pendulum swings, the vocabulary of academia also changes. Certain words that have been soiled by promiscuous use become the academic equivalent of obscenities. Words like "relevance" and "individualized" lose their meaning, become contaminated by their ubiquity. Yet these words refer to functional realities and will be resurrected, unblushingly, for this paper.

"Relevance," for example, although sullied by the rhetoric of

---

*Because of the awkwardness of the his/her construction, I have recently been using the female pronoun to denote the anonymous individual. In this paper it is "his" turn.

the 1960s, is probably the most appropriate word to describe the basis of our educational thinking. Education *must* be relevant: it must have implications for the four-fifths of a person's life that is spent outside of formal schooling; it must make clear the connections between history and tomorrow's headlines, between economic theory and the debate in Congress over tax credits, between literature and life and death. We have, in our self-consciousness, coupled "relevance" with "easy"; we do not wish to teach toward "easy relevance," as though this were an intellectual crime on a scale with matricide.

If "relevance" means that the life of the mind and the life of external experience are intimately and indissolubly connected and that nothing that touches the one leaves the other unchanged, then we realize that the ideal curriculum *is* relevant. It has implications for the rest of the person's life. What better way to ensure its relevance than to give the student who will go through a program a strong hand in designing it.

"Individualized" is another word that has been besmirched by overuse. The term "individualized education" has been used indiscriminately to describe and excuse all sorts of innovations and aberrations, and the good is becoming tainted with the shoddy. Yet the basic concept is crucial. We must respond to the individual's needs and requirements if educational planning is to make sense. And it is that kind of sense that adds up to the third word I wish to discuss—"coherence."

Curricular coherence in the individualized degree program comes out of a design in which all the parts are in some relationship to one another, and the sum of those parts is a whole that directly addresses the particular student's academic, career, and personal goals and objectives. The organizing principle of the curriculum may be in terms of the disciplinary subject matters addressed, or it may be on the basis of methodologies, or it may be thematic or problem-centered or any number of other organizing frameworks. Certainly, coherence may take many forms and may derive from different structures, but it has to do with wholeness or connectedness, with patterns, with logical sequences. It is opposed to fragmentation, transience, the collection of purely arbitrary elements.

The first perspective of coherence may be based on the Platonic view that there exists some ideal body of knowledge or set of abilities that is universally recognized as defining the educated person. Most general education curricula proceed as though this were true; the coherence of these curricula is posited to result from contact with the best that has been thought and said in the Western world (it is basically a chauvinistic model), or through prescribed courses in the major disciplines, or through the development of a set of measurable competencies (the mechanistic version of the model).

The second perspective of coherence may derive from the institutional model, that image of itself and of its students that the institution has chosen to project. Whether expressed through cooperative education, or Great Books, or behavioral objectives, or the primacy of handicrafts, or concepts of social justice, or bilingualism, these institutional models represent an idiosyncratic vision of education and are clearly designed to serve special needs and interests.

The third perspective takes its thrust for coherence directly from the student, deriving its integrity from the fidelity with which the curriculum emerges from and serves the individual's needs. It takes into account academic aspirations, career objectives, the personal need to make life meaningful. It pays heed to the student's life situation, his age, his learning style, the socioeconomic pressures under which he exists. It may also take into account what he already knows. The patterns that emerge are various and possibly even eccentric, but they can be shown to have an inherent logic and external and internal patterns that derive from the nature of the areas studied, their structures of meaning, and the interrelatedness of the components.

All of us have probably dealt comfortably with one or more of these perspectives; the ideal, the institutional, and the individual, and indeed, they frequently and comfortably intersect in any given student's curriculum. In practice, methodology has ranged from (1) the totally prescribed curriculum to (2) the choose-two-from-column-A-and-three-from-column-B approach to general education to (3) four years of complete license. College bulletins, those masterpieces of wishful prose, flounder in an uneasy rhetoric that contains echoes of everyone from Plato to John

Dewey to Ivan Ilich to Carl Rogers. In an effort to reconcile the ideal, the institution, and the individual, Podunk U. ends up sounding pretty much like Princeton or the anonymous rhetorician that, I suspect, is responsible for all college catalog prose.

But just as the ideal, the institutional, and the individual models are not necessarily dialectically opposed, they are also not necessarily conjunctive. The ideal curriculum can and should be responsive to the ideal of the educated person, to the institution's sense of its own mission, and to the individual's needs and desires, but emphasis on the latter, even if occasionally sinning against the first two, will result in an incomparably richer experience for the student and, if evidence to date is valid, for the faculty that provides the educational opportunities in which the individual options are exercised.

Let us proceed from the preexisting curriculum, the one composed of "thou shalts" and prescribed "majors," and prerequisites and distribution requirements and go on to the truly individual curriculum that emerges organically in response to the individual student's situation and that has a connectedness that is unique to that student.

Designing a curriculum, like writing a novel or planning a garden, represents a series of choices. The roads not taken are as much a part of the outcome as those the student travels. In the individualized curriculum, the choices are made by the student, not by the curriculum committee or the department chairperson or the state board of education. They represent the student's intimate knowledge of his strengths, weaknesses, likes, dislikes, needs, goals, and sometimes prejudices. However, in order that the choices be meaningful and that the result be coherent, the student must:

1.   know the options, know what he is selecting and rejecting and why;

2.   receive adequate advisement from a faculty person with rich background in education but no personal or ideological axe to grind;

3.   have the freedom to include in his program not only

current course offerings but also other educational experiences when these are appropriate;

4.   be able to articulate clearly how his program addresses his needs and why he thinks it is academically valid.

1. The first of these preconditions, that *the student must know the options*, is basic to degree program planning, but it may mean that planning will have to proceed in stages. The college freshman may not be sufficiently knowledgeable about the range of choices available to him and should be encouraged to study a variety of disciplines to discover their characteristic ideas and modes and what each may hold for him. This broad study of the disciplines might proceed conventionally through a year or more of introductory courses, or it might be approached through a study of educational theories and philosophies specifically designed to make available the kinds of structures and meanings inherent in different academic areas.

The next stage, when the student is ready to focus on an area of concentration and those studies that support and complement the concentration, involves more choices. Some of the issues at stake include the need to define for any concentration or major: (a) the major issues addressed by the discipline; (b) the methodology and specific terminologies appropriate to the discipline; (c) its history; and (d) its relevance to other areas of concern. Questions of sequential logic, of distribution, of breadth and depth, of integration through interdisciplinary study, of modes of inquiry, all these must be addressed and choices made.

Thorough career exploration may be necessary for some students in order that their choices be made on a realistic basis; for others, a searching examination of graduate school possibilities and prerequisites may be necessary. Students should also be encouraged to engage in introspection to discover their real as opposed to socially assumed objectives, their personal affinities, intellectual biases, cognitive strengths and weaknesses.

Frequently, the truly coherent curriculum does not emerge all at once as a result of deliberate creation, but evolves slowly as one interest leads to another, as connections are made, as learning opportunities arise. Sometimes the student, and his adviser, must learn to live for a time with ambiguity. But if such degree program planning is a time-consuming process, it is also an educationally meaningful one and might be considered as potentially credit bearing, depending on the kinds of learning involved.

2. *Student advisement* is crucial in designing the individualized degree program, particularly in this age of cultural affluence, when the range of choices is bewildering. Indeed, truly coherent undergraduate curricula are rare not because of lack of institutional commitment to the ideal but because of lack of adequate advising. The most thoughtful, philosophically sound institutional policies can be frustrated by the assistant professor who is annoyed that he must take a few hours from his research to talk to sophomores. The sophomores, in turn, have been conditioned to see the advisement process in limited terms. The adviser, by common consent, is one who makes certain you take all the required courses and signs your registration card without a hassle. At most, he may suggest another semester of German or tell you that the new man in macroeconomics is reputed to be pretty good. Further decisions may be made by the student on the basis of what time of day the course is given, who else is taking it, the length of the reading list, the professor's grading habits, his sign of the zodiac. Such limited advisement may suffice in colleges where the patterns are set and the options limited. The student who "takes" (the common verb is revealing) freshman English, one each of the behavioral and social sciences, a physical science or math, possibly a language, and a major sequence determined by the individual department may not have a coherent program, but he is probably not going to get into too much trouble either. However, in colleges that have made a commitment to individualization, lack of thoughtful advising can be disastrous and can lead directly to the macrame, kayaking, and folk festival management syndrome that has become the butt of traditionalists' humor.

Since curricular coherence is to a large extent dependent on the wisdom and good sense of the adviser, it is crucial that institutions committed to individualized curricula devote resources to faculty development in advising skills. Ideally, advisers should understand the conceptual bases of individualization and should have the flexibility, sensitivity, imagination, and willingness to implement them. This is far from a simple set of skills.

Let us assume, for example, that it is universally acknowledged to be desirable to study history, to understand chronology, and to know that the world did not begin with one's birth. Let us further assume that the adviser and his advisee agree that it would be useful to understand historical process, to learn about the evaluation of primary data, and to gain a sense of the influence of the past on the present and of its implications for the future.

Although the history major might want to begin with a broad-scale survey of Western civilization, which would provide a frame in which to set his later studies, the student of English literature might prefer a course in English history, which would set him straight on the intellectual and political movements reflected in the works of Chaucer, Shakespeare, Milton, and Swift, and the business major might wish to study in depth the Industrial Revolution. These choices represent not a watering down of content but a meaningful selectivity that would make vivid for the student historical meanings and methodology. However, they presuppose an adviser capable of setting forth such options.

It becomes obvious that these same faculty members who become skilled advisers will also develop a new way of looking at the courses they teach, a new flexibility that will encourage them to structure their syllabi in such a way as to allow for "give" as different students come to the materials of the course from different directions and for different reasons.

3. The possibility of including *diverse learning experiences* in the degree program is also crucial if we are truly to address the needs of the individual. In the literature of the novel of education, it is never presumed that education takes place solely or even predominantly in the classroom. I began this paper with a quote from Joyce's *Portrait* in which the hero's education is affected not only by the school and university but also by the church, the barroom, the brothel, and the family dinner table. Similarly, Rousseau's *Emile*, Henry Brooke's *The Fool of Quality*, Voltaire's *Candide*, and Henry Adams's *The Education of Henry Adams* make it clear that experience goes hand in hand with, if it does not take precedence over, formal education in determining the shape of a person's life. It is well to cultivate a certain humility about the limitations of any one academic institution so that we may admit to the curriculum those enriching experiences outside our formal purview. Creative

flexibility in encouraging independent study, cross registration, work-study arrangements, peer teaching, travel, the assessment of prior learning, and so on can contribute to the holistic coherence of the individual student's degree program, making those vital connections between study and life.

4. For the student who has become knowledgeable about the range of options available to him, who has planned his program with the help of a wise adviser, and who has been encouraged to think creatively about incorporating into his curriculum experiences from outside the classroom, one thing yet remains to ensure the coherence of the resultant degree program: his *ability to articulate that coherence.* As a precondition to curriculum approval, the student must be challenged to demonstrate the validity of his program. The articulation should be in terms of the student's own stated goals and how the particular degree program addresses those goals. Frequently, what looks like a hodgepodge of unrelated elements may in fact have an underlying logic, but that logic must be stated, the connectedness of the various elements explained, the overall design made clear.

The student who has designed his own curriculum has been forced to think about himself in relation to his studies. The crucial, often painful series of choices he has made have stamped their imprint on the program in such a way that it is likely to be more meaningful than the most artfully designed, institutionally derived program. Because it is the student's own curriculum, he has a stronger commitment to its success.

Four very different students' degree programs may serve as examples of the kinds of coherence that may emerge when the student's needs are considered of primary importance. The first of these was achieved within a conventional set of institutional resources and expectations, whereas in the other three the student was encouraged to look beyond the classroom to field and work experiences, travel, study at nonaccredited institutions, and so forth. All four are idiosyncratic to a degree but academically defensible, and each is clearly a product of unique needs, aspirations, learning styles, biases, opportunities, and affinities.

The first is that of a young woman studying in a state university, essentially adviserless, although a faculty person was designated to sign her course list each semester. The university required a junior field exam and senior project, but beyond that, students were free to choose from a fairly standard menu of departmental offerings. This young woman, Joan A., had at an early age become interested in literature and was a fairly sophisticated reader by the time she graduated from high school. She planned to go on to study comparative literature in graduate school.

For Joan A., the beginning of each college semester was a period of high adventure in which she sat in on as many classes as she could, looked over reading lists, compared professorial styles, saw how connections might be made among various subjects and modes, and then, and only then, completed her registration. Certainly, the resultant degree program (see Figure 2) had coherence. The relationships between her major and the other fields of inquiry are clear. The ties between literature and linguistics, literature and philosophy, literature and psychology are standard, although not always apparent in conventional curricula. Moreover, the foreign languages are directly tied to her interest in comparative literature. One might question the program's breadth; there is no math or science. However, she had come in with advanced placement status in chemistry and calculus. Moreover, it could be argued that the empirical methods of linguistics, logic, sociology, and anthropology had served to further her development in that direction. There is also a certain arbitrary quality to the selection of courses in her major, literature. She could have studied different periods or major figures or genres, but in fact, that is true of any major. And when questioned as to why she had declined to take a background introduction to English literature, she insisted, quite reasonably, that her eleventh-grade survey had given her the necessary sense of the panorama of the centuries.

What is most interesting in this program are the relationships among some of the areas. For instance, the student's focus on the nineteenth century is supported by three literature courses: the European novel, the British novel, and romantic poetry. Its philosophical foundations are explored through a nineteenth-century philosophy course. The courses in the epic, myth and symbol, and New Testament prepared her for the plentiful literary allusions typical of the period. The nineteenth century's emerging interest in the individual and the creative process is buttressed by the philos-

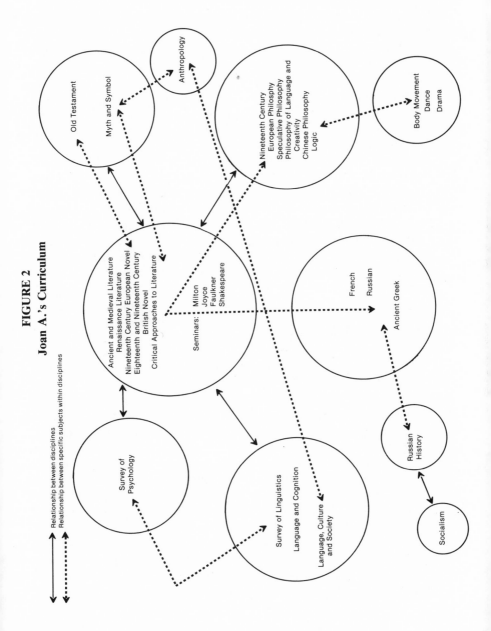

FIGURE 2

Joan A.'s Curriculum

→ Relationship between disciplines
⇢ Relationship between specific subjects within disciplines

Old Testament

Myth and Symbol

Anthropology

Nineteenth Century
European Philosphy
Speculative Philosophy
Philosophy of Language and
Creativity
Chinese Philosophy
Logic

Body Movement
Dance
Drama

Ancient and Medieval Literature
Renaissance Literature
Nineteenth Century European Novel
Eighteenth and Nineteenth Century
British Novel
Critical Approaches to Literature

Seminars: Milton
Joyce
Faulkner
Shakespeare

French
Russian

Ancient Greek

Survey of
Psychology

Survey of Linguistics
Language and Cognition

Language, Culture
and Society

Russian
History

Socialism

ophy of language and creativity as well as by introductory psychology; even the study of socialism can be shown to have a connectedness with the political climate of the century.

There are other connections, some obvious, some not. The series of courses in body movement, dance, and drama came directly out of Chinese philosophy, with its emphasis on the oneness of body and mind. Russian language and history satisfied a curiosity to learn more about the world of Dostoevski and Tolstoy. Such diversified, mutually enriching studies could take place almost anywhere, but rarely do. They may be eccentric, but they certainly speak to the student's emerging interests and chart her intellectual growth. Therein lies the program's strength.

The second degree program is that of a young man, Jim B., who had dropped out of high school during his junior year to hitchhike to California, along the way becoming interested in the life of the Indians in the West. Then, after completing his senior year of high school, he had taken off again, this time to travel the counter-culture paths in Europe and Asia. During the ensuing years, he became interested in photography and financed his travel by getting odd jobs taking pictures of tourists or doing commercial photography on a catch-as-catch-can basis. He also arranged his itineraries, when possible, to include archaeological sites and visits to underdeveloped countries, including a year spent among primitive tribes in Asia, where he washed dishes, carried supplies, and eventually took photographs for an anthropological team.

When Jim finally decided he could only further his emerging interests by getting a degree, he was twenty-seven years old, wary of academia, but passionately committed to learning more about the world. Building on his interests and knowledge of primitive people and photography, his adviser helped him put together a program in which his experientially derived learning was evaluated and assessed to serve as a basis for more sophisticated and theoretical studies. Thus, he studied introductory anthropology and archaeology, which made more meaningful the knowledge he already had of the practice of fieldwork. Studies of the origins of human society, of art and society, of knowledge and power enriched his understanding of culture. His knowledge of jazz and folk music led him to do specialized work in the rhythmic components of various tribal modes, and he also studied folk culture through sculpture and painting. He took workshops in advanced photographic techniques, including kallitype process and practical photochemistry so that in his fieldwork he did not have to be dependent on laboratory facilities. He also studied film and did an extensive project on photographing children, which he accompanied with readings in child development and field experience as a counselor to children in an institutional setting. Historical studies grew organically out of his interest in the past; zoology out of his desire to be better able to identify human and animal remains.

Most important, as the ties between anthropology and photography became clearer, Jim realized that his initial goal of graduate school was false to his own sense of himself. Although bright, he knew he did not wish to give up the following five or six years to further study; for him, a dissertation would have been a special kind of torture. Fortunately, he also realized that the ties between anthropology and photography were even stronger than he had first suspected, and ultimately, he focused on preparing himself to be a professional photographer with expertise sufficient to ensure his being hired by anthropological and archaeological expeditions.

At present, Jim is preparing his gear for his final project, an expedition with a group from the University of Washington to the Alaskan wilderness. And this time he will not be doing the dishes or carrying anything but his own camera and equipment. The coherence of Jim's program was not created; it was there in the range of his interests and was enabled to emerge by sensitive counseling in an institutional environment that respected his individuality.

The third student whose degree program is represented as an example of coherence is that by-now familiar phenomenon; the woman of forty-plus who is returning to college to get the education that earlier circumstances had denied her. This woman, Rebecca C., already had two years of a rather traditional potpourri of courses in literature, history, languages, science, anthropology, psychology, and the arts. She had touched all the bases; distribution was not her problem. However, in the years since college, she had done volunteer and later professional work in a prestigious national organization devoted to equality of all peoples. Quite sophisticated learnings were identified and assessed in human and community relations; the use of media; program planning, development, and implementation; and fund raising on a national and international scale. Obviously, Rebecca was already functioning in a professional role at what might be considered a graduate level, and initially, both she and her adviser were confronted with the problem of designing a program that complemented her previous learnings but that was still recognizably an undergraduate program. As a result, they moved into an area that touched on a future ambition she had never previously voiced. She was interested in higher education and hoped eventually to get a job doing development and public relations for a university. Thus, her learning contracts (for no courses were readily available in these subjects) dealt, through independent study, with the history and emerging philosophies of higher education in Europe and the United States, with innovative and nontraditional education, with adult development and the adult learner, and with cross-cultural views of the role of education in society.

These three examples, one classically academic and two career-oriented (although radically different), probably constitute a loaded deck. None of the three students could be considered a tabula rasa when first arriving at college; all had significant academic or practical experience on which to build and rather clearly defined goals. However, the fourth degree program to be discussed is that of a young woman, Sarah D., who arrived at college with fairly conventional notions of what she would study and absolutely no idea why. She had taken a first semester at a community college and thought it appropriate to go on to take the second half of composition, American history, music appreciation, and so on, but she showed no great enthusiasm. After a few meetings with her adviser, she revealed that her life had been dominated by the unspoken presence of recent history. She was the child of her father's second marriage, his first wife and three children having perished in Nazi Germany. Unwilling to subject his new family or himself to his memories, he refused ever to talk about the past. Sarah's curiosity became the basis for a thematic design for her degree program that focused on the holocaust, approaching it from every possible perspective in an attempt to make sense of it. She read the literature of the holocaust and wrote about it; she not only studied recent German history but also traced its roots to ancient and modern European history. She studied psychology, starting with the recent studies of the psychology of the survivor and going on to developmental, existential, and humanistic psychology. She studied theology, sociology, genetic theory, anything and everything that might shed light on the aberration of history that led to Auschwitz. Paradoxically, as she went into greater and greater depth, her study became broader; she discovered how the web of knowledge, no matter how lightly it is touched, vibrates in every strand.

In designing and implementing their degree programs, each of these four students created a coherence that grew organically from their own goals and interests. Each gained an invaluable sense that knowledge is a vital part of the current reality and that their education connected them with the world.

Although it would be philosophically satisfying to think of the individual's curriculum as a pure product of that individual's personal, academic, and career needs, such is rarely the case. Any curriculum is crucially affected by the institution that sponsors that curriculum: its locus, structure, resources, and educational ideology. Similarly, when advisers are involved, the adviser's own whims, ideologies, and personal interactions with the student play a determining role, as do the student's whims, biases, prejudices, and learning styles. Moreover, the role of chance, fortuitous or otherwise, must be acknowledged. Temporal circumstances and learning opportunities may significantly alter the shape of a curriculum, the paths winding away from the initial stimulus are various and provocative.

However, if we can think of the individual as the primary impetus for the design of the degree program, and if we can help that individual achieve a coherence that truly addresses his needs, not only of the moment, but also in terms of serving him for the rest of his life, we can consider the task of education well begun.

FOUR

THE INTERDISCIPLINARY
APPROACH TO
COLLEGE CURRICULA

6

A CURRICULUM FOR
TOMORROW'S WORLD

ERNEST A. LYNTON

A college or university that decides to deal head on with the issue of the nature of general education and the coherence of the curriculum assumes a substantial responsibility. It is something that must be done well if it is to be done at all.

An essential condition for the successful development of any coherent undergraduate curricular model is that a substantial proportion of the faculty be interested in the matter. It must be willing to devote to it a considerable amount of time and energy. It also must consider the achievement of these educational goals to be as important as its customary insistence on the quality in the disciplinary major.

I stress this so much because I believe very strongly that general education courses must be given first call on the time of the best faculty. Their development must elicit the interest and the participation of a large proportion of the faculty. Finally, the enterprise as a whole must be seen as a principal priority of the institution.

During the 1960s, a major cause for student dissatisfaction with the curriculum was general education courses, especially surveys. We as educators were passing off fake coinage. The students were protesting the endless sections of dreary courses taught by uninterested and ill-prepared teaching assistants. All too often, we entrusted to them what the rhetoric of our catalogs and speeches falsely proclaimed as the principal features of undergraduate education.[1]

We must guard against giving future students similar cause for protest. My basic point, therefore, is this: whatever conclusion we reach within our institutions with regard to the core curriculum for tomorrow's world—whether there evolves a single or a multisided dogma, whether pertinent courses are required or elective, whether we favor for the curriculum the hourglass model, pyramid, or capstone—whatever the shape and content of the enterprise, it must in every sense have first call on the institution's resources. Whoever is in charge—dean, provost, director—must have the budgetary resources as well as the authority to ensure adequate faculty contribution from all appropriate departments. Senior faculty members must be centrally involved, both as role models for their younger colleagues and because the content of core curriculum is the most difficult teaching assignment. The faculty reward system must also reflect the importance of the enterprise. Too familiar is the example of special nondepartmental courses and programs carried voluntarily by faculty who later are denied tenure because too much of their time was devoted to such activities.[2]

An educational institution could take the position—and indeed many of them do—that it has neither the resources nor the faculty interest to devote substantial attention to anything other than the quality of the disciplinary major and perhaps to an insistence on some basic skills. Well and good: that at least is being honest about institutional limitations. But the institution cannot and must not launch a venture that purports to achieve coherence in the curriculum or that intends to meet some general objectives for liberal education and then place this at the periphery of its enterprise by involving just a handful of faculty with a minimum of resources for the task. By doing such a job badly, the institution transmits to its students the inescapable message that the whole matter is really of little importance. Such a message is more antithetical to the purposes of education than a frank admission that the institution is unable or unwilling to strive for the ideal.

The question goes beyond that of material resources. A substantial fraction of the faculty must reach a high degree of consensus about the intrinsic importance of the enterprise and about the validity of their institution's particular approach. I am not very optimistic about the likelihood of reaching such a consensus even in a relatively small and homogeneous institution with a few thousand students. It becomes exponentially more difficult in our major universities with many thousands of students and hundreds of faculty of great variety of background and interest.

This inevitably suggests a pluralistic approach to the problem. It would seem appropriate to find ways to encourage the development of a variety of models within a single medium-size or large institution, each model reflecting the shared ideas—and ideals—of some group of faculty. How then can this be brought about?

A basic requirement is to go beyond glittering generalities in defining the desired results of the curricular reform. A scholarly faculty uses rigor and objectivity in dealing with educational issues in its own discipline. Its attention and commitment to general educational issues can be engaged only if it can be equally specific and concrete.

A first step, therefore, is to define with some degree of specificity the basic educational goals to be achieved through the general curriculum. The ends must be defined before the means can be developed.

A great many potential objectives can be stated for undergraduate education. Each educator could draw up—and most probably have—a personal list of potential educational goals. One such list might be the following:

1. acquaintance with several and mastery of at least one method of inquiry; understanding of techniques of reason and analysis.

2. an understanding of languages: one's own, foreign, that of computers.

3. an understanding of contemporary issues and their historical, social, political, and economic background.

4. an understanding of relationships between people and people, between people and nature, and between people and their occupations.

Haverford College postulates a different set:[3]

—learning to write the English language competently.

—learning about the natural world.

—engaging in quantitative or symbolic analysis.

—studying history.

—speaking and writing a foreign language at some reasonable level.

—examining the nature of being and of value.

—examining the subject of humans and the societies they form.

Both lists are cited to show how many different ways the complex and interrelated goals of education can be pursued. Others would use different wording, would have fewer or more goals, would disagree with some, and would emphasize others. That last point is of vital importance: as one looks at this or at any other list, it becomes clear that choices need to be made and that priorities need to be set.

Any group of faculty or administrators embarking on a discussion of the core curriculum and related issues must first define its own set of educational goals and objectives. It would do this with sufficient specificity and with an adequate ordering of priorities so that this can be translated with clarity and reasonable precision into curricular terms.

This can best be done by clustering the large number of potential objectives into a smaller number of principal goals. At a 1976 conference on the role of the humanities in undergraduate education held at the Albany campus of the State University of New York, Frank Pipkin of Harvard University suggested that all the various individual lists of objectives could be grouped into three major categories or clusters:

1.   The goal of *developing the intellect and the qualities of mind*: effective thinking, discrimination of values and aesthetic sense, mastery of methods of inquiry, understanding one or more subjects in depth.

2. The goal of *acculturation*: the knowledge and appreciation of our common heritage, some acquaintance with the great ideas and books of the past, some mastery of the body of knowledge presumed to be shared by all educated persons, a reasonable breadth of exposure to a range of disciplines and of human experience.

3. The goal of *socialization*: the ability to place an issue or a problem into a proper contextual framework, the development of a sense of citizenship and of civil responsibility, the knowledge and the critical thought needed to participate in communal decision making in a free society.

These three principal categories can be described in many different ways. But whatever the specific choice of words, this triad provides a highly useful taxonomy of general education. It constitutes an excellent starting point for the kind of discussion necessary within an institution commiting itself to the exploration of educational aims and the possibilities of a coherent core curriculum. Obviously, some overlap among these categories exists, and they are not entirely mutually exclusive. But one must begin by choosing one as the principal institutional priority. If a given faculty were to agree on acculturation as the primary objective, then it would stress required or recommended survey courses focusing on the common heritage and the shared body of knowledge. If, on the other hand, the foremost goal were the contextual one of socialization, a range of courses dealing with the social, political, and economic framework of contemporary society would be emphasized. To one or the other of these basic components of a general curriculum can then be added further required or elective items that would help to achieve the secondary objectives. But success is not possible with a buckshot approach that tries to attain all the goals that can possibly be defined for undergraduate education.

I will now venture some personal preferences regarding the aims of education that will then lead me to some sweeping generalizations regarding core curriculum.

Ernest L. Boyer and Martin Kaplan in their discussion of *Educating for Survival*[4] stress four basic premises: that we all share a common heritage, confront the challenges of the present, make the future, and make ethical choices. These premises determine educational goals. My own approach is very similar, except that I focus on two principal issues to which general education should address itself. The first of these is part of Boyer and Kaplan's own list of objectives. The second, on the other hand, is quite different. Before describing these particular and highly idiosyncratic choices, I should say that they both fall into the broad category that Pipkin called socialization and that I prefer to label contextual.

I am firmly convinced that the most important hallmark of an educated person is the ability to place issues and events and individuals in a historical as well as a contemporary context: the ability to view the instant flash picture of individual experience and perception both synchronically against a background of understanding the principal aspects of the contemporary world and diachronically by having some appreciation of historical antecedents.

Within the broad category of contextual or socializing objectives for education, I would single out two principal directions. One is the great and steadily growing need for informed decisionmaking on the part of the individual. In my mind, this is of vital importance for the near future. For all the obvious reasons that have been discussed repeatedly in newspapers and learned articles and books, we have recently seen a rather remarkable change from the imperial presidency to a much more populist mode of government. At the national level, Congress has regained much of its power, particularly regarding policy issues. Increased congressional power implies greater influence on the part of more than 500 individual members of the House and the Senate, and they in turn are much more susceptible and responsive to the opinions and pressures exerted by their local constituencies. In principle, therefore, the direct influence of the individual man and woman on the street, of the individual tendril among the grass roots, is today much greater than it has been for many decades, and it is likely to remain that way for some years to come.

If that is the case and, even more, if this situation persists for much longer, then the individual's exercise of his discriminating judgment, his ability to judge issues on their merits rather than on their emotional content, his ability as well as willingness to distinguish fact from fiction, propaganda from reasoned argument, becomes of enormous importance. An informed public does influence decisionmaking on such issues as nuclear power and other environmental problems, on many social concerns, and on the general conduct of government.

I have expressed myself more positively than is usual for me. My emphasis on the ability to judge issues and to make decisions is not derived from a utopian vision of the revival of a latter-day Athens in which a Pericles would listen to and be guided by the views of an informed citizenry. Rather, I have a great fear of what could happen if education were to fail and mob rule were to dictate congressional action by unrestrained, uninformed, emotional outpourings. I am cynical enough to believe in the latter as a real danger; I am optimistic enough to think that the worst excesses can be avoided by education.

I am likely to face more argument on what I see as the second specter looming in the future. Here I differ fundamentally with Boyer and Kaplan. Where they see contemporary society as increasingly fragmented, I am alarmed by a growing trend toward homogenization. That is most apparent, of course, in our mode of living: more and more, we all eat the same mass-produced convenience foods and shop in the same chain stores. When we travel, we stay in hotels and motels so much out of the same mold that there is no way of telling, once inside, that we have driven or flown hundreds of miles. More and more, our opinions are formed by the same syndicated columns, the same national news weeklies, the same network anchormen.

Boyer and Kaplan state that we are fragmented in one sense: that there is no feeling of community and of shared experience. We are all isolated atoms with little sense of the overall structure. What to me makes this totally unbearable is that increasingly we are all becoming *identical* isolated atoms, formed in the same mold, holding the same opinions, eating and reading and wearing the same things, and increasingly distrusting any display of difference.

I would, therefore, place very near the top of my list of educational objectives whatever can be done to counteract this homogenization of the individual. I would do all that is possible to bring about not just the *acceptance* of difference but indeed the *celebra-*

tion of difference. I would foster the realization that the strength, the richness, and the excitement of our society and its culture depend to a very large extent on internal heterogeneity and on the ability to remain cohesive by becoming a rich mixture of many distinct ingredients, rather than a shapeless and bland melt in which all differences have been homogenized.

How is any set of priorities established by an institution and its faculty to be achieved? The traditional approach tackles this in terms of some combination of distribution requirements, core curriculum, comprehensive examination, and what have you: a set of educational devices and activities that are viewed as quite distinct from the course of study leading to the major. However, a very different approach is at least worth trying and may be more likely to succeed. I now come back full circle to my original point: faculty commitment, involvement, and interest are of paramount importance if educational objectives are to be successfully achieved by the institution. Frankly, I am pessimistic about the traditional "general education" approach in most institutions because of at least three factors: first, the sheer size of most institutions and the difficulty of engaging the involvement of any appreciable fraction of the faculty; second, the understandable identification of most faculty members with their own discipline and department, not with their institution; and third, an increasing portion of our students pursuing their education in other than the traditional, continuous four-year pattern. Moreover, our younger undergraduate students tend to move between school and work and many change institutions once or twice during their careers. Even our most traditional institutions are enrolling a growing fraction of older and nontraditional students. As a result, distribution requirements and a coherent core curriculum for the institution as a whole become increasingly problematical.

These same contemporary trends pose problems as well for the undergraduate major. We are just beginning to learn that we can no longer think of the entering freshman as a tabula rasa ready to be imprinted by a predetermined package of courses through which he or she moves without interruption from the beginning to the end.

Instead, we are beginning to learn from pioneering institutions like Empire State College, the University Without Walls, and the University of Massachusetts College of Public and Community Service. We are recognizing the need to fashion coherence out of the kaleidoscope of prior experience and to add to this new skills and bodies of knowledge. We are beginning to see, within the area of specialization, that the purpose of the formal educational process provided by the institution is to make explicit the learning acquired from prior experience and then to combine this with additional materials and methodologies to achieve a new degree of coherence through a new depth of understanding.

Let me propose that we take the approach one step farther and include in the degree requirements for the major that which is needed to achieve the particular general educational objectives of the institution. Instead of viewing a coherent curriculum for general or liberal education as something separate from and parallel to the departmental major, why not extend the definition and context of the latter to include both educational objectives?

What I am suggesting is that we try to achieve coherence in undergraduate education by fusing into an *extended major* general educational objectives with specific disciplinary ones. Let us assume that an institution or some unit within it has discussed the aims of general education and has agreed on some set of priorities. We should then insist that each department determine what areas of study added to the disciplinary requirements achieve the general educational aims as defined. The emphasis should be placed on the coherence of an extended and inclusive major. The major should no longer be narrowly defined as being merely the acquisition of skills and methodology identified with a given discipline but should include as well whatever is needed to integrate that particular knowledge and those particular professional skills and activities into broader educational objectives.

The approach, in my opinion, would work equally well with an acculturating as well as with a socializing or contextual definition of education. Take, as example, an *extended major* in French literature. The contextual approach would insist on including a considerable number of courses in French history and in contemporary French society, together with appropriate cross-cultural and comparative courses. The acculturating mode would juxtapose

French literary, philosophical, and artistic achievements with those of other countries and cultures. In science or in professional areas, it is equally possible to develop extended curricula to achieve any of the principal objectives of general education.

I believe that it is better to place the responsibility for that integration at the departmental level than to separate disciplinary and general educational objectives, as is currently fashionable. An extended major is likely to achieve the necessary degree of faculty interest and commitment and also to evoke more student enthusiasm.[5]

In a traditional institution, with traditional young students committed to a four-year sequence, the extended major could be defined by adding a number of cognate extradepartmental courses to those required for the major. But even under these traditional circumstances, the greatest coherence is likely to come about if each student fashions an individualized package with the help and overview of a good adviser. Such flexibility becomes increasingly important as the background, preparation, age, and educational continuity of the students become more varied.

This then leads to an interesting conclusion. Not only can educational coherence be achieved in a nontraditional, individualized educational mode, such as that of Empire State College or the University Without Walls through the concept of an extended major. These institutions, in fact, can accomplish this better than most traditional ones because they know how to fashion a coherent curriculum through the interaction of a mentor and the individual student.

We can therefore look to these institutions once again to take the lead and to show us how to fashion a coherent, integrated curriculum through the notion of an extended major.

Notes

1. A great many books have been written about the student unrest of the 1960s. While most focus on the political, social, and organizational issues that triggered student activism, they also indicate that student dissatisfaction with the curriculum and with undergraduate teaching was a major underlying cause. Compare, for example, Neil Smelser, ''Berkeley in Crisis

and Change," in *Academic Transformation*, ed. David Riesman and Verne A. Stadtman (New York: McGraw-Hill, 1973).

2. For a brief but incisive discussion of institutional and organizational factors affecting general education, compare, for example, Daniel Bell, *The Reforming of General Education* (New York: Columbia University Press, 1966), pp. 63-68. Compare also, Christopher Jencks and David Riesman, *The Academic Revolution* (Garden City, N.Y.: Doubleday, 1968), pp. 498 ff.

3. Internal memorandum, Haverford College, 1976.

4. Ernest L. Boyer and Martin Kaplan, *Educating for Survival* (New Rochelle, N.Y.: Change Magazine Press, 1977).

5. In proposing the development of an extended major, I am, in a sense, also arguing against the growing specialization of the subject matter major that has occurred during the past twenty-five years. During that period, a transformation has often taken place from a liberal undergraduate education with an area of concentration into a quasi-professional curriculum designed to prepare individuals for graduate work. Within this context, the idea of an extended major is not new, but rather a return to earlier educational models. Lawrence Vasey, in his introductory chapter to *Content and Curriculum*, ed. Carl Kaysen (New York: McGraw-Hill, 1973), describes the transformation of the major subject system during this century. He refers to "group major" as an old-fashioned term for interdisciplinary majors with some resemblance to my extended major.

7

TOWARD A NEW CURRICULUM

CHARLES MUSCATINE

In thinking about the prospects for a new undergraduate curriculum, it is probably wise to distinguish between the short term and the long, for in the short term the prospects are poor. Although many faculties have come out recently with "new" curricula, save some minor improvements, few are much different from the curricula abandoned by the same faculties in the 1960s, now reinstituted with more righteousness than imagination. Plans such as Harvard's contain a few innovations, but we will have to wait some years to see whether the proposed new courses stay new in practice or turn out—as is likely—to be the old ones rewarmed and served up under new names. The new Berkeley curriculum is not far from the lowest common denominator: a brokerage among the facilities at hand rather than a fresh plan for the future.

On large university campuses, the faculties are behaving as expected. Few faculty members are recruited for an interest in curriculum, and it speaks well for deans at places such as Harvard and Berkeley that any change has come about at all. After all, no tenured member of the Harvard faculty remains who was not appointed to tenure by the Conant plan, and a faculty chosen for subject-matter expertise in national and international competition cannot be expected to take an automatic interest in the undergraduate curriculum. For them, there is a world elsewhere. At Berkeley, with some 35 percent tenured faculty and only light recruitment these days, the prospect is the same.

In this context, the short-term possibilities for curricular change are few: keep tinkering with and tightening the old machinery, as at Harvard or Berkeley, and give the oddballs that happen to exist in these institutions some room to move around. Give some room to pluralism. Harvard and Berkeley should have, alongside the omnibus curriculum, some unconventional options for the future. This is an elementary matter of self-interest: for there are ample signs that the public is not going to continue indefinitely to respect and support the faculties and the curricula as they are now constituted. Indeed, neither was designed for the sort of world that tomorrow's may be.

An effective new curriculum will be based on a full awareness of the stunning diversity of teachers and students and on the futility of trying to formulate elaborate traditional "educational aims" for such a group. At Berkeley, for instance, we have students from established middle-class families, brought up with music, art, ideas, and books, who take learning for granted; others, just off the boat or from the barrio, ambitious to learn; yet others, from endless California suburbs, consumers of television and wide tires, do not know why they are in college at all. Some faculty trace their roles back to Socrates or Newton; others regard themselves primarily as gentlefolk and amateurs; yet others resonate most sympathetically with the real estate business or the chemical industry. To agree on common educational aims for all, one would indeed have to retreat to a small number of irreducible virtues, and that is not a bad idea. Most of the long lists I have seen are redundant, and many are fatuous, little more than thinly clad social elitism. More often than not, they make absurd (and thus damaging) claims for the short period of study that we normally have to offer: *"Educated* person?" *"Mastery* of a method of inquiry?" *"Understanding* of contemporary issues?" All we usually have, let us remember, is 120 semester-hours in the lives of some remarkably healthy and mobile types!

But even if we had a short list of agreed-on aims, do we know how to get there? My own feeling is that we do not, that what innovators best can do for us right now is to conduct first a rigorous stock taking and then a vigorous investigation of the three fields that seem to me to matter most in terms of tomorrow's curriculum: learning theory and human development; the modes of thought (or the operations of the mind); and the major future problems of human civilization.

It is in some concatenation or balance of these three elements that we will find the new curriculum.

An emphasis on learning theory and human development responds to the imperative need to start where the student is, to respect individual differences in background and temperament.[1] An emphasis on the modes of thought, or on the operations of the mind, in this scheme, responds to the ever more rapid obsolescence of information, of subject matter. It anticipates that the *how* of learning will need to become more important in relation to the *what* than it is now. An emphasis on *problems* of human culture tips the balance in favor of a curriculum focused on what Ernest Lynton has called in his essay in this volume "informed decisionmaking." The notion is powerful and integrative. It keeps intellectual activity—the dealing with information and ideas—at the center of the curriculum, while insisting on the ultimate importance of value judgments. It proclaims a role for the individual but calls for the social responsibility on which civilized society depends. While it does not enforce the primacy of any particular social or cultural tradition, it favors cosmopolitanism and discourages insularity. Its major axiom is fundamentally political, but one that we can widely agree on: democracy depends on the ability of individuals (in Lynton's words) "to judge issues and to make decisions."

A curriculum based on future problems, on recent advances in learning theory, and on a fresh insight into the structure of knowledge may very well not look much like the old curriculum at all. If a single criticism can be made of the so-called new curricula that are now being adopted, it is that they automatically preserve features of the traditional system that may in the future need to be radically modified, if not abolished altogether. I am referring to such institutions as the department, the departmental major, and even the "course" as we know it.

The academic department has long been a very powerful and

successful implement, and for certain purposes, it may last forever. It is certainly a convenient administrative device, especially worthy when peer-group judgments are concerned. The question is, which peer-group? The department gets its authority, presumably, from the integrity of the field it represents. Departments are truly and effectively representative of the interests of academic fields. The educational weakness of departments comes from this same source, not only in the familiar parochialism generated by academic fields, but also in the weakness of the concept of academic field itself where undergraduate (I do not say graduate) education is concerned. How many fundamental intellectual disciplines are there, and how many departments represent fundamental intellectual disciplines as opposed to special subject matters and special collections of jargon? I cannot answer the question, but raising it will do. The student of the future will need to recognize, analyze, and resolve social prolems, but will he or she find anything intellectually indispensable in the Department of Sociology? of Anthropology? of Economics? The student will need to read with accuracy and sensitivity; is this need best to be fulfilled through a monopoly of a Department of English? The student will have to study research techniques, the handling of information and evidence, the operation of logic, the nature of value systems, the forms of fair persuasion: which departments are best for this?[2] To put it another way, while most departments deal with some of these disciplines, none is responsible to the student for them.

A curriculum responsible to the student for a coherent *general* education will very likely have to turn away from the academic department altogether. And even the academic departmental major is not beyond question. Its current justification is that the student should learn at least one thing in depth. But what is the student learning in depth?[3] The academic fields are by their nature abstractions. The English major abstracts from the rich complex of the history of culture just the long, thin thread of the literature of one language. From the physical world, the Physics and Zoology majors make the same kinds of abstractions—excellent for professional scholars because they are so intellectually manageable. By the same token, they are so much removed from reality. While I would not recommend that students not be given a whiff of the beauties of abstraction and its cognate expertise, for "depth," perhaps something deep in the way of reality would be even more beneficial. If the curriculum is to point toward real problems and keep the student in some realistic contact with the prospects for his or her own future, perhaps true depth will be found in problematics—in interdisciplinary studies rather than in the old "major."

Using the same postulates, the same questions can be asked about courses, and, God knows, about units, credit hours, contact hours, and of course the role of the faculty. The faculty that will attend to what can be learned about human development, about mental operations, and about major problems of civilization will be a new breed. It will be a faculty newly interested in the connections between research and the needs of the culture, that is, between scholarship and students. It will find time for research and time for teaching to be less of an issue. Our ideal faculty hybrid in the long term will still be a researcher and a writer. However, the new faculty member will not exploit the "disinterestedness" of research as a license for private antiquarianism at public expense, will not be content with learning that never escapes its coterie origins, will not indulge in the kind of arrogance that dismisses as "popularization" any attempt to turn specialist research to public benefit—a process that is in the first place the only justification for public support of narrow research expertise. What I am suggesting is that, seen this way, a continuous interest in curriculum will not be an incidental trait but will become central to our professional character.

Curricular reform in the long term will be resisted by very powerful forces, not the least of which are the virtues of the old curriculum itself.

The old curriculum makes possible easy and flexible record-keeping for a transient student body. A unit earned in Maine has easy currency in California.

The old curriculum is very convenient for research-oriented faculties in particular, for it assumes that before students can be expected to think and question for themselves they must be grounded in the "disciplines." The "disciplines" (by which is usually meant not disciplines but specific bodies of information, each having its own operating jargon) always require introductions, and since introductory courses are not on the frontiers of research, their teaching can be safely entrusted to inferiors and assistants, freeing the regular or senior faculty for "advanced" teaching with graduate students, far from the less profitable contact with inexperienced minds.

The cost benefit of using lower paid assistants is obvious; another cost benefit is that, since every one needs the same introduction, the introductory courses can be large.

Although the knowledge-retention rate among graduating students may be disappointingly low and much college-acquired information may soon become obsolete, the system evidently is effective in socializing for the job market and for a tranquil society. The present system guarantees that the graduate has spent four years doing a great variety of arbitrarily assigned jobs with a certain minimum of efficiency and reliability. The graduate has kept up to 1,800 scheduled appointments in class, or done work (or created the appearance of having done work) equivalent to 60 percent of that required in class. The graduate has been trained to anticipate the wishes of superiors, to memorize their views, and to be able to repeat them on short notice. College has taught toleration of boredom and, through the examination system, acceptance of periodic crisis. Through the grading system, it has taught habituation to competition and the risks and benefits of bargaining and cheating.

Through the device of courses and units, students learn to divide their time and attention: to manage five things at a time, and then in ten or fifteen weeks—after the crisis—to manage five other things at a time. Those who find this experience spiritually or intellectually intolerable, or those who lose their health or their wits, are soon weeded out. Survival is keyed to a complacent consumption of courses. Recent statistics at Berkeley show that a good majority of graduating seniors are satisfied with their college education,[4] and our student ratings of courses have never been higher.

This is not a system inherently designed to train powerful thinkers, but there have been and there continue to be some conspicuous pedagogical successes. In any case, intelligence cannot be stamped out completely; some powerful thinkers do get though the system. Borne on the departmental major system, trained in abstract disciplines by disciplinary experts, many of these become disciplinary experts in turn. They remain on the campus, safely kept from too unsettling contacts with the needs of the culture. Bolstered by reassuring conceptions of scholarly disinterestedness and the free pursuit of truth, hedged about by the cult of expertise, they have every reason to be content with things as they are.

With the students pleased and the faculties content with themselves, *do* we want to change anything? The foregoing description may be something of a caricature, but it will remind us of what we are up against and how deep may be the conservatism, both within and outside the colleges, that stands ready to resist change.

The present system *is* a marvel of short-term convenience; in the long term, it is a hindrance to education for democracy and for individual initiative. Its design promotes memorization in place of thought and imagination: passive acceptance in place of questioning and contribution; superficial consumerism in place of persevering with a problem in depth. It propagates the dangerous myth that civic and moral judgment must finally give way to technical expertise. It fails notably to habituate the student to functioning in the process of informed decisionmaking that is the ideal of our form of government and essential to our conduct of business.

Although we most likely could not survive a whole society of independent, creative thinkers, we surely need more than we have. We are already beginning to hear "respectable" academic voices pronouncing democracy a failure. I think that the public, by and large, wants democracy and individual initiative and is insufficiently aware to what extent our college curricula and faculties presently impede its wish. If this is so, then one of the most delicate and difficult tasks we have is to make public the critique of the present system. This critique should be designed to marshal public support, in the short term, for creative pluralism and, in the long term, for a new curriculum. Our critique should at the same time be responsible to what is good in what we have and to what is likely to remain good. A curriculum devoted to the problems of the future will always have a new future ahead of it and will always need to be reformed, and reinformed, by the results of research, even specialist research.

Notes

1. On student development, a fundamental study of cognitive factors is William G. Perry, Jr., *Forms of Intellectual and Ethical Development in*

the College Years (New York: Holt, Rinehart and Winston, 1970); on affective and motivational factors, an early but still pertinent work is Joseph Katz and Nevitt Sanford, "The Curriculum in the Perspective of the Theory of Personality Development," in *The American College*, ed. A. Sanford (New York: John Wiley & Sons, 1962), pp. 418-44. See also Joseph Katz et al., *No Time for Youth: Growth and Constraint in College Students* (San Francisco: Jossey-Bass, 1968); Paul A. Heist, *The Creative College Student: An Unmet Challenge* (San Francisco: Jossey-Bass, 1968); and Arthur W. Chickering, *Education and Identity* (San Francisco: Jossey-Bass, 1969). A survey of theories is collected in Lee Knefelcamp, Carole Widick, and Clyde A. Parker, eds., *Applying New Developmental Findings*, New Directions for Students Services, no. 4 (San Francisco: Jossey-Bass, 1978).

2. An interesting attack on the problem, still relevant despite its setting in the political commotion of the late 1960s, is Norman Birnbaum, "The Arbitrary Disciplines," *Change* (July-August 1969), pp. 10-21. See also Arthur Levine and John Weingart, "Alternatives to Departments," in *Reform of Undergraduate Education*, ed. Arthur Levine and John Weingart (San Francisco: Jossey-Bass, 1973), pp. 75-95; and Dean E. McHenry et al., *Academic Departments* (San Francisco: Jossey-Bass, 1977).

3. Thus, in the "Provisional Report" by the Harvard College Faculty "Task Force on Concentrations," (n.p.: n.p., July, 1976), pp. 4-5, it is said "We believe that no student should graduate without gaining control of a coherent and substantial body of knowledge and the disciplines and techniques that have been developed to organize and extend it. It is not enough to master a collection of facts; students should be able to apply what they have learned constructively and independently. Furthermore, the knowledge, perspective, and proficiency they gain should be sufficiently extensive and widely applicable to have lasting value in varying and unpredictable circumstances." But as I argue below, there is in fact no necessary connection between most departmental majors and the goals of intellectual independence and lasting value. Nevertheless, the major is widely considered one of higher education's manifest successes. A convenient summary of the subject will be found in Arthur Levine, *Handbook on Undergraduate Curriculum* (San Francisco: Jossey-Bass, 1978), pp. 28-53.

4. Austin C. Frank, *The 1975 Seniors at Berkeley* (Berkeley: University of California Office of Student Affairs Research, 1976). Questionnaires were sent to 3,500 graduating seniors. Replies were received from 577. Of these, 80 percent expressed satisfaction with their total college experience.

8

COMMUNITIES OF LEARNERS: CURRICULUM AS THE INFRASTRUCTURE OF ACADEMIC COMMUNITIES

PATRICK J. HILL

At Stony Brook, the downstate center of the State University of New York, a novel approach to undergraduate education emerged in 1976: the Federated Learning Communities (FLC). Its total approach represented a structural break with curricular rationale and organization of the past. In effect, FLC created a new medium or environment for undergraduate education within a traditional university.

The emergence of FLC was preceded by a highly critical institutional self-study.[1] A summary of the undergraduate section of that self-study, entitled "The Eclipse of the Academic Community," provides a useful introduction to the rationale of FLC's complex structure.[2] This study explains the diminished vitality in undergraduate education in terms of three phenomena: the mismatched expectations of faculty and our new, traditional campus students as to the nature of undergraduate education, the atomization of the curriculum, and the resulting "privatized" character of academic experience.

MISMATCHED EXPECTATIONS

Students and faculty bring very different expectations into the undergraduate classroom.[3] The hopes of many of our current undergraduates, at least the traditional eighteen- to twenty-two year-olds, focus on four major areas: (1) a link between their studies and postcollege careers; (2) the acquisition of insights applicable for the understanding of their personal lives and the great and pressing issues of our time; (3) faculty responsiveness to their ideas in face-to-face learning situations; and (4) initiative or outreach on the part of the faculty to arouse interest and motivate study. In brief, the students expect an academic community responsive to their presence.[4] Faculty, by way of contrast, often expect: (1) a considerable overlap of their specialized professional life with their teaching activities; (2) a predisposition of at least the good students toward the worth of the faculty's activities and interests; and (3) that scholarly and well-organized presentations in the classroom of some version of their professional research constitute the greatest part of their responsibilities as teachers.

Needless to say, at least some of these conflicting expectations are going to be frustrated. A small number of programs in the curricula of most American colleges lead students to a definable career. In addition, faculty often conduct classes in ways that eliminate a student's exploration of personal values or life's basic truth, for example, by dismissing questions as unmanageable, by referring them to other departments, or by offering answers that are "only" probable or partial. Further, faculty-student exchanges are hampered by cultural differences about the value of reading, gratification postponement, or the worth of the vocation dedicated to inquiry. The gradual frustration of student and faculty expectations leads to a lessened enthusiasm for coursework, mutual withdrawal from energetic classroom work and communication, and finally minimal cooperation in fulfilling course obligations. For many students, original motivations to find career and personal direction through courses and dynamic exchanges in a community of learners are lost in the unresponsive academic environment of many college campuses. For many faculty, teaching becomes boring, or it focuses on smaller and smaller numbers of responsive students.

ATOMIZATION OF THE CURRICULUM

The contemporary curriculum frustrates the expectations of undergraduates and their faculty in other more subtle ways. The staggeringly comprehensive curriculum bewilders the unfocused or searching undergraduate. In small colleges, there are often twenty different majors, and two or three times that number are offered in large universities. Minimal distribution requirements at best expose the student to still more options, and the centrifugal proliferation of specialized courses in those disciplines (for example, philosophy or history) that traditionally have addressed the fundamental or shared dimensions of being human further undermines possibilities in the curriculum for addressing student expectations.[5] This bewildering array of options tells many young undergraduates that all courses are equally important or unimportant.

However, the sheer number of courses and options is not the only or even the primary source of the curriculum's frustration of student and faculty expectations. More significant is the *atomized* nature of the curriculum, that is, the absence of obvious and meaningful relationships or interaction among the numerous courses. Aside from departmental sequences (mostly in the natural sciences), each course stands virtually on its own. Little or no use is made of the material from one course by others. The student is deprived of any curricular support system that might reinforce the importance of what is being discussed in that single course. Where occasional overlap occurs, it is frequently undercut by the unique interpretations endemic to creative faculty members. The student is left with no interpretation of the educational enterprise other than that each faculty member is "doing his or her own thing." The student may not be far from wrong. In effect, all intellectual endeavor reduces de facto to matters of taste. Such a reduction is self-defeating and destructive to the possibility of students taking ideas seriously and using them to understand themselves, others, or their environment.[6]

Although television's consumer orientation has often been blamed as the reason students reduce intellectual matters to judgments of taste, little attention has been paid to how much college curricula reinforce the value of taste as supreme. There is nearly a total absence of required comparisons or integration of courses presumed by the curriculum. While professors will almost automatically ask that students compare or contrast ideas within their course, almost nothing in the undergraduate experience forces students to compare or contrast courses, disciplines, or ideas from separate courses. Each course (in some cases, the department itself) is hermetically sealed. Such rigid divisions encourage the view that the life of the mind is not an objectively based and meaningful activity, but rather is a consumer-oriented performance on the part of individualized, idiosyncratic professors. Such is the apparent meaning of the atomistic undergraduate curriculum for the academically unfocused undergraduate.

The atomized curriculum, it should be noted, is not *necessarily* productive of an incoherent education. It should be remembered that we are describing the personally unfocused young student who lacks an academic heritage and who constitutes perhaps 50 percent of today's undergraduate population. For the more mature student with academic focus and rich life experiences on which to draw, the abundance of courses in the curriculum can be a great resource and an opportunity for a coherent education. Indeed, what might appear to an outsider as a set of incoherent courses is often quite coherent to the focused student. A course on Goethe, one on economic development, a third in elementary Spanish, a fourth on basic ecology, and a fifth on urban planning make abundant sense to one planning to work in Third World cities and interested in the dynamic of humanity's attempt to model nature to its own purposes. How the situation of such adult learners relates to that of the younger adult, and what implications that relation has for understanding the sources of coherence in the curriculum will be explored below.

PRIVATIZATION OF ACADEMIC EXPERIENCE

Ultimately, the mismatched expectations of faculty and students within the context of an expanding and atomized curriculum results in "privatization" of academic experience: not only is experience individualized, but it also is unshared and unpublic. Almost all essential dimensions of a vital academic community, in addition to shared expectations and minimal interactions, are undermined. Shared experiences are at a minimum in academia. It is rare for students to interact after having read the same book, prepared for the same exam, or taken the same course. There is no sense of working together toward a common goal. The possibility of a common intellectual language is lessened so that highly creative work by faculty within a single discipline is likely unintelligible to the student body at large and to many faculty colleagues. Finally, the minimal condition of academic community, that is, faculty-student contact, is largely undermined as each party utilizes the absence of structure to pursue private ends. Although most of the disciplines being taught at our universities understand human growth in terms of interaction with a challenging environment and would endorse John Dewey's judgment that "no man and no mind was ever emancipated merely by being left alone," the actual organization of the curriculum and of extracurricular activities endorses the discredited view of human growth as an autodigestive unfolding of innate potential.

What response on the part of the institution would properly overcome the mismatched expectations of faculty and students, the atomization of the curriculum, and the consequently privatized academic experience? It was a difficult, delicate, and fundamentally philosophical task. Which, if any, student and faculty expectations were to be encouraged? In what form, what proportion? Clearly, the students' expectation that it was faculty's responsibility to motivate them was not to be wholly encouraged. But what of the students' desire for face-to-face contact with faculty members in an intellectual community? Was that viable or outdated? Were faculty preferences for specialization rather than holistic inquiry to be tolerated?

My own thinking about contemplated reforms was considerably influenced by the parallels I saw between the city and the university. In one American tradition spanning Thomas Jefferson to Ralph Borsodi, urban life is described in basically negative terms of impersonality, anonymity, rootlessness, and overchoice. To these thinkers, the gemeinschaften of bygone days or projected utopian communities are the only human alternatives to the moral, social, and aesthetic grossness of the modern city. In another tradition, represented by thinkers like Dewey, Richard Sennett, John McDermott, and Harvey Cox, the city is the imperfect realization of the central values of modernity, namely, individual freedom, mobility, plurality, democracy, and specialized function.[7] The passing of the homogeneous, agriculturally based society of past centuries lamented by the antiurbanites is viewed by these thinkers as a release from the cloying bondage of small, confining, monolithic communities. What in modern cities strikes antiurban thinkers as rootless and impersonal appears to the prourbanites as opportunity for free movement among diverse life-styles and the potential to select from a wealth of options those promising the most growth.

What is to be learned from each tradition? From the antiurbanites we learn of the flaws in the organization of our large-scale institutions, flaws so fundamental as to deprive the citizen of the support systems and the incentive for the humane realization of the values we associate with modernity. From the prourbanites, we learn that the alternative is not a return to preindustrial communities based on only holistic human relationships and homogeneous values. Individual freedom, plurality, anonymity, mobility, specialization—these all are values worth preserving. So in the most general terms, both city and university are charged with the task of creating new structures of association. This new social organization would make readily available the benefits of human association without deprecating the aforementioned modern values. With reference to higher education, our major malaise stems not from excessive specialization, a plethora of courses, or unlimited student freedom but rather from social atomism: the lack of vital interaction among specialized courses and the absence of support, guidance, and preparation for the intelligent use of freedom in a pluralistic setting. With the invaluable assistance of a major grant from the Fund for the Improvement of Post-Secondary Education, this institutional diagnosis led to the creation of the Federated Learning Communities at Stony Brook.

The Federated Learning Communities

The depth and the nature of the problems described above, along with the sensitivity to modern values, warranted experimentation with new structures. The structures of FLC are essentially new modes of academic community, new bases for disciplinary and human relationships, for vital dialog and communal inquiry, for invention, for sharing and support in the process of learning. Professional educators will recognize one or another of the modes as having been tried elsewhere, but the configuration of all these elements in a total structure, we believe, represents a new medium of undergraduate education. The exposition of FLC will be organized around the program's four curricular innovations:

FEDERATION OF DISCIPLINARY COURSES

First, we decided to address the social atomism of university life by the federation of thematically overlapping but disciplinary diverse courses into an integrated semester.

The question of *what* to federate was as important as the decision to federate. Two critical choices were made, both of which can be seen as consistent with the general guidelines described above. The first choice was to federate already existing courses (or at least already existing interests) of the Stony Brook faculty. A new academic community was thus built on routine or everyday activities of both faculty and students. To have done otherwise, most flagrantly through the creation of small and specially designed interdisciplinary courses, would have run the risk of psychological and institutional marginality and would have created a refuge for the students, a warm and holistic nest disconnected from the mainstream of the university and thus from many of the values of modernity.

The second choice on what to federate was made with an eye to the value of plurality. The idea of federation might have been used within just one or two divisions of the university. But the central concern to bring the plural disciplines and ideologies of the university into communication and to introduce students to that dialog necessitated that FLC draw on the three traditional divisions of the university and on as many majors as possible. FLC thus attempted to become a *microcosm* of the resources of the university.

The third choice as to what to federate was made with an eye to the students' expectation that their college education would contribute to their understanding of the great and pressing issues of our time. This decision seemed at first to exclude several departments, but ways were found to include history, Stony Brooks's period-oriented literature departments, and the natural sciences in all of the first five FLC programs. Thus, despite the focus on "relevant" contemporary issues, the students could be introduced to the value of historical and literary understanding.

From the standpoint of the faculty, federation takes the form of a weekly seminar wherein individuals explore each other's disciplines, develop a passing recognition of the basic vocabulary and concerns of one's federated colleagues, and, most importantly, search out overlapping and mutually implicatory material that would keep the courses in relation with one another. The act of federation diminishes the autonomy of the individual courses. The diminishment is for the most part voluntary and results from unanticipated and somewhat uncontrollable consequences of genuine dialog.

From the standpoint of the students, the most immediate impact of federation is that a thematically coherent group of three courses from different disciplines becomes the unit of education, rather than individuated courses or sequentially spread departmental progressions. Two consecutive semesters with six different disciplines constitute the heart of an FLC program. Figure 3 illustrates the FLC program on "Technology, Values, and Society," which federates philosophy, history, and engineering courses in its first semester and chemistry, sociology, and literature in its second.

The act of federation makes the course come alive for the students. The disciplines are no longer experienced as arbitrary dissections of the world but are experienced as complementary perspectives or a shared problem. In those FLC semesters that worked the best, the courses not only raised but addressed continually from week to week the themes of the program. One course frequently took the lead in this respect, implicating the others and forcing response. A good deal of confusion resulted from differing ideological and disciplinary perspectives, but the confusion was focused and manageable. Great difficulty remained, of course, for both faculty and students to effect a shared, even a personal integration of the thematic material. But the students experienced from week to week the real interaction of the disciplines and their own growing sophistication in understanding the thematic problem.

Another less obvious implication of federation is the creation of multiple authority figures. More often than not, the multiple professorial authority figures support and complement one another. They are all obviously committed to the value of inquiry, to the importance of the program's thematic focus, and to a whole range of specific values and thinkers. Infrequently, but significantly, the

FIGURE 3

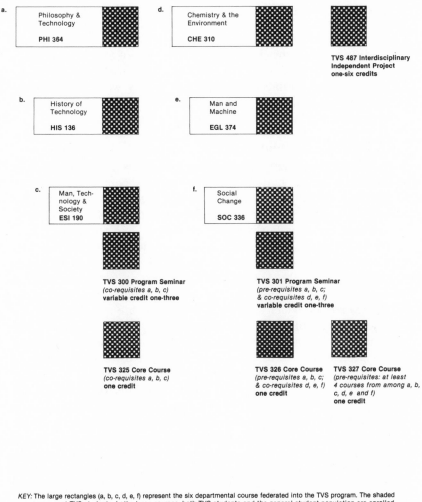

a. Philosophy & Technology
PHI 364

d. Chemistry & the Environment
CHE 310

TVS 487 Interdisciplinary Independent Project
one-six credits

b. History of Technology
HIS 136

e. Man and Machine
EGL 374

c. Man, Technology & Society
ESI 190

f. Social Change
SOC 336

TVS 300 Program Seminar
(co-requisites a, b, c)
variable credit one-three

TVS 301 Program Seminar
(pre-requisites a, b, c;
& co-requisites d, e, f)
variable credit one-three

TVS 325 Core Course
(co-requisites a, b, c)
one credit

TVS 326 Core Course
(pre-requisites a, b, c;
& co-requisites d, e, f)
one credit

TVS 327 Core Course
(pre-requisites: at least
4 courses from among a, b,
c, d, e and f)
one credit

KEY: The large rectangles (a, b, c, d, e, f) represent the six departmental course federated into the TVS program. The shaded areas represent TVS students. In the large courses, both TVS students and the general student population are enrolled. The smaller squares represent the unique components of the TVS program: the Program Seminar taught by the Master Learner, the team-taught Core Course, and the Interdisciplinary Study Project. In these courses, only TVS students may enroll.

multiple authority figures come into conflict. A professor dismisses a question about the ethical or developmental significance of the Chinese social experiment only to have a question returned in the next class buttressed with the authority of a professor teaching another of the federated courses. Or a professor distributes a Monsanto pamphlet on the role of chemicals in everyday life, which excites a federated colleague to write a refutation and to request it be distributed to the class. The students cannot avoid refashioning their view of expertise. With the assistance of the pressures of a pluralistic community, they live day to day with the ambiguity obviously appropriate to the situation. There are no unquestioned experts on whom they can rely to remove the ambiguity.[8]

PROGRAM SEMINAR

The second structural innovation of FLC is a Meta Seminar or Program Seminar built on the three federated courses. Registration for the Program Seminar lists the three federated courses as absolute corequisites. The Program Seminar, sometimes called the Meta Seminar, requires fairly heavy writing and participation, but no reading material not already assigned in the three federated courses. The Program Seminar is like the traditional discussion session but with three rather than one course as its academic base.

The Program Seminar is an open or a reflective space in the curriculum in which time and assistance are provided for the student to think about the relationships among the parts that constitute the rest of his or her education and to define a personal perspective relative to those parts. What is discussed in the Program Seminar is for the most part determined by the enrolled students, whose questions and difficulties about relating the three federated courses constitute the agenda. A few examples illustrate the nature and academic purpose of the Program Seminar. In the program on World Hunger, the federated courses in economics and ecology at different times during the semester discussed the problem of exploitation. The contrasting accounts, inspired by different disciplinary and ideological perspectives, were brought up for discussion in the Program Seminar. And the philosophy course with its Kantian perspective was utilized to explore the differences. The discussion was relayed back to the professors and resulted in a modification of a final exam to allow students to draw on their multicurricular perspectives.

A glance at Figure 3 might crystallize the manner in which the Program Seminar creates the possibility of shared academic experience. While there might be 300 or 400 students enrolled in the federated course, the Program Seminar has an upper limit of 40 students with multiple sections when necessary. The Program Seminar, because of its comparative smallness and its rigid corequisite structure, becomes an academic center wherein people who share academic experience become known to one another. In the ordinary course of registration patterns, a dozen students might register for two or three of the federated courses. But without the Program Seminar as an academic center, those students would not know that they were in the same courses nor would they have the opportunity or the assistance to tap the educational resources of intelligent dialog. Those resources, termed by my colleague, Charles Hoffmann, as FLC's "multiplier effect," are highly appreciated by the students, who regard their student community as an academic resource quite as valuable as that of the faculty. Higher education, with respect to graduate education, has acknowledged for some time that much of what students learn comes from other students. In undergraduate education, for a host of reasons, the academic resources of a student community have for the most part gone untapped.

In terms of curricular organization, the Program Seminar functions mainly to provide the opportunity for public reflection on the shared academic experience of the federated courses. In pedagogical terms, the Program Seminar has two additional functions. First, the Seminar encourages students to utilize the disciplinary resources of courses and the interdisciplinary resources of community to develop their own ideas and perspectives on the content of the federated course materials. The assignments always demand that students attempt to do something their teachers have not done, that is, to bring the resources of the federated disciplinary courses into interdisciplinary relation around a subtheme of the students' choice.

Second, the Program Seminar functions as a reliable cybernetic mechanism. Far too much of our teaching proceeds without any feedback or on the basis of highly selective feedback through exams or the comments of a handful of interested students. In the Program Seminar, one monitors weekly and over long-term periods the impact of lectures and assignments through the responses of a large subset of students with differing interests and abilities. How this happens will be apparent when the third of FLC's structural innovations is described.

THE MASTER LEARNER AND MUMFORD FELLOW

The two structural reforms just described address squarely the problem of the atomized curriculum and the privatized character of academic experience. Several things were yet to be addressed for a positive thrust toward the building of community. First, it was foreseen that the centrifugal pressures within the lives of the teachers and students would prove stronger than the structural imposition of a federated curriculum and the Program Seminar. Second, the problem of the mismatched educational expectations of faculty and undergraduates was not yet addressed. And third, nothing was yet provided in the way of support and guidance for students to utilize freedom intelligently in a pluralistic setting. These remaining problems were addressed by the creation of a new type of teaching professional, the Master Learner and the Mumford Fellow.

Who and what are the Master Learners? The Master Learners are faculty members at Stony Brook who have earned the respect of the faculty as both scholars and teachers and who have earned that same respect from students. They are "masters" in the sense that they have mastered at least one discipline and subject matter and in the sense that they have over time won the respect of both students and colleagues as better-than-average teachers. The Mumford Fellows are graduate students who are well along in pursuit of a doctorate in a discipline different from that of the Master Learner and who show unusual promise as teachers. Depending on previous experience and readiness, the Mumford Fellow comes in time to share collegially all the tasks of the Master Learner enumerated below. The diverse disciplinary background, pedagogical skills, intellectual resources and personalities of the Master Learner and the Mumford Fellow interact differently with the faculty and students of different programs to make impossible rigid definitions of their respective responsibilities. What is said below of Master Learners is true of the collegial team of Master Learner and Mumford Fellow.[9]

The Master Learners are called learners because their chief task is to become students again in a thematic area in which they, at the outset, possess no expertise. Although their academic resources and ages prevent them from fully returning to the role of student, they engage in all of the activities of undergraduate students. The Master Learners actually take the six federated courses and the Core Course in the same manner as the program's students do. They are in class every day, they take notes, they take exams, do term papers (yes, usually at the last minute), and are graded. While engaged in the role of full-time student, the Master Learners are relieved from all their normal teaching duties. The only teaching they do during this period is in the aforementioned Program Seminar. Obviously, since the Master Learners are learning from the same sources and at the same time as the students in the Program Seminar, the "teaching" of the Program Seminar cannot be of the sort appropriate to the disciplinary classroom wherein they are acknowledged masters.

The role of the Master Learners is exceedingly complex and ambiguous. While they are essentially community builders, for the purposes of this essay it will be useful to distinguish five different dimensions of their role.

1. The Master Learners are interpreters or mediators. They explain the expectations of students to the faculty and the expectations of faculty to the students. The Master Learners, more importantly, assist faculty and students in seeing values in those expectations that might otherwise not be perceived. Understandably, some students and some faculty often see the Master Learners in partisan terms. The students expect an advocate or ombudsman; the faculty expects an unquestioned reinforcement of its objectives. Although in time the experience of again being students influenced the Master Learners of the first five programs significantly to modify their own teaching styles and goals, such partisanship or preconception at the outset of a program would make the Master Learners incapable of functioning as mediators.

2. The Master Learners are participant observers or diagnosticians of the educational process. As a function of being in the classroom every day and interacting frequently with forty students over a twelve- to eighteen-month association, the Master Learners are in a unique and enviable position to report what works and what does not work. The first three Master Learners, for example, all agreed that the assignments given to Stony Brook undergraduates constituted an educationally dysfunctional workload. In order to survive, students had to devise criteria for the significance of presented material and assignments other than the ones animating the courses.

3. On the basis of this daily and long-term observation, the Master Learners function as feedback mechanisms to the faculty regarding the effectiveness of their teaching. The feedback, it should be stressed, is not "merely" collegial feedback. Nor is it "merely" a more detailed version of a student evaluation. On the basis of their extraordinary knowledge of the program's students, the Master Learners are able to differentiate responses. A spontaneous teaching style, for example, engages one sort of good student but leaves another sort of good student confused and disappointed. Further, Master Learners know how intelligent particular students are, what effort has been invested, and the difficulties of students who for one reason or another invest little effort in the course.

The particular means of feedback employed by each Master Learner has varied. Many times direct feedback has resulted in a redoing of a lecture, a modification of an exam, or a change in the course material. On at least two occasions, early intervention averted serious pedagogical errors. Some Master Learners have attempted week-to-week feedback sessions. Regardless of the variety, each faculty participant receives at the end of the semester a lengthy and detailed report containing commentary and evaluation of a quantity and quality not likely to be matched in the rest of that person's teaching career.

4. The Master Learners are community builders and the embodied resistances to the centrifugal pressure in the lives of faculty and students. Aside from the aforementioned mediation of the diverse expectations of faculty and students, the Master Learners also are intellectual mediators. Learning the language of the diverse

disciplines they are studying, they circulate a weekly report to the faculty. They grope toward a "dejargonized" common language and assist the faculty at seeing connections amid their work. At the Program Seminar, the Master Learners likewise forge a language intelligible to the multidisciplinary participants, and they place students with similar interests in touch with each other. Finally, on the basis of superior knowledge of the interests of the federated faculty and of the university, Master Learners assist the program's students in locating faculty resources in support of their developing interests.

5. The Master Learners are role models for the students. To greater and lesser degrees, they embody all the values of the university: love of learning, the process of inquiry, and the importance of discipline; and more particularly a host of assumed habits unfamiliar to our students, like an empirical orientation to the reading of newspapers and relating them to coursework.

Outside evaluations describe the impact of the Master Learners on students in terms of their being "good authority figures." A parental or judgmental role remains, but the situation of shared experience, or, as some would say, "shared suffering," creates uncommon pedagogical opportunities. The students' awareness of intellectual strengths and weaknesses and of personal focus seems to grow by leaps and bounds in interaction with this trusted figure. And to some extent, varying with program and personnel, that authority is transferrable to the federated teachers.[10]

THE CORE COURSE

The fourth structural innovation in FLC is an inadequately titled "Core Course." The Core Course, team-taught by all six federated faculty, is the place wherein the most sustained attention is given both to the theme of the program and to the nature and inter-relationship of the federated disciplines. The Core Course meets once a month for three hours over a three-semester span.

The faculty initiate and attempt to exemplify the process of interdisciplinary inquiry in the Core Course. At the start of the third FLC program in "Technology, Values, and Society," the topic of "Rock Music" was chosen, and the federated faculty led the discussion by means of leading questions from each of their disciplines. The sociologist spoke of the structure of power in the music industry; the philosopher, of different patterns of sound in classical and rock music; the literary person, of the cultural significance of rock festivals. In similar sessions, the students are thus led away from the fundamental misconception engendered by the atomized curriculum, that is, that disciplines differ only by subject matter.

Perpetuating such faculty-initiated and -dominated inquiry over the three semesters, however, could have defeated an essential purpose of the Core Course. From the start, it was recognized and intended that student exposure to the study of a single theme in light of six disciplines would *over time* create an opportunity for a changed relationship with individual faculty, who would be still fairly well locked into the perspective of one or two disciplines. The Core Course is the locus of the changing faculty/student relationship because it is the place where the weaknesses of specialized inquiry and the strengths of multidisciplinary inquiry are most visible and where the experiences of students, or at least good students, place them at some advantage over the faculty. Put in less adversarial terms, the Core Course offers the opportunity for a dialog between disciplinary and interdisciplinary paradigms with the students, better than the faculty, representing the strength of interdisciplinary inquiry. The students thus become resources for the further education of the faculty. Over time, they, more or less smoothly, assume responsibility for teaching the Core Course with considerable assistance from the Master Learners and the federated faculty.

The pedagogic *goal* of the Core Course is quite clear: the passage of FLC students from passive learners in poorly understood disciplinary courses of an atomized curriculum to active learners utilizing and presenting disciplinary resources in interdisciplinary inquiries that they themselves conduct. That goal, as will be admitted and explored presently, is difficult to attain; the value of the goal, it will be argued in the next section, justifies the effort to attain it.[11]

The FLC Experience

Coherence is a property of the interrelationship between individual focus and the courses of the curriculum. In the general education movement, emphasis is on the courses as the source of coherence, that is, through a combination of courses that address the range of human experience or of Western heritage. In Empire State College and in many adult-centered learning programs, the emphasis is properly on individually generated focus. FLC is philosophically midway between these two approaches. It recognizes that most eighteen- to twenty-two-year-old students lack the experience and the opportunity to generate the personal focus and hence the curricular coherence possible for adult learners. FLC creates such opportunities for focused coherence by opening up engaging space within the curriculum in which students become active and cooperative learners in the academic/social communities built on top of that shared curricular experience.

In order to understand how this cluster of curricular innovations functions as the infrastructure of academic community, let us follow some students through the experience of the total FLC environment during an idealized time period. Forty FLC students are enrolled in an engineering course in contemporary technology, a history of technology course, and a philosophy of technology course. The forty FLC students comprise a subset of total enrollment in these three courses that ranges from eighty to 400 students. One day in the engineering class, the professor attacks the myth of the "technological fix" and makes the startling claim that technology has never solved a social problem without creating negative side effects. The non-FLC students dutifully record the professor's claim and file it with other notes to be reread at exam time. Four FLC students, majors from biochemistry, literature, philosophy, and sociology, discuss the claim as they walk toward their history course. In the history course, again with all forty students present, one of the FLC students asks the history professor's opinion. The professor refers to chapters in their assigned text wherein counterclaims might be found. Later in the day, the professor of philosophy also is consulted, and he suggests that the concept of "solution" be examined before the claim can be considered. During the lunch break, several students meet with the Master Learner and the Mumford Fellow. The automobile is discussed as a possible contradiction to the professor's claim and dismissed because of its pollution. The airplane is dismissed because of its energy consumption and its military application.

Suggestions come rapidly but are shot down by one or another member. Musical and medical technology, for example, electric guitars or eyeglasses, seem like promising examples. The Master Learner suggests that at the next Program Seminar the engineer's claim be discussed in light of the other two courses. Each person is to come prepared with two examples, one that makes the engineer's claim seem strongest and one that makes it seem weakest. In the intervening days, students try out examples on their friends and teachers. At the Program Seminar, the Master Learner leads a brief plenary session examining the engineer's claims to be sure that all are aware of its meaning. Then the seminar breaks into four groups, and each student tests the refined examples he or she has brought. According to plan, the groups report back to a plenary session, where the most promising examples from each group are discussed. For some, the claim seems strained with respect to developments like eyeglasses, but to others, the claim is now seen as a shorthand way of reminding ourselves that there will always be side effects of any technological development.

A computer science major drops in to see the Master Learner. She confesses that she is having difficulty keeping up with the reading in the history course. The Master Learner reveals a similar difficulty that he and other students are having and promises to talk to the professor. In the meantime, he shares his own method of sorting out the most important passages. Conversation turns to her major and its relationship to the insights of their philosophy course. She decides that she would like to do her Program Seminar paper on the history of the computer in education with special attention to its influences on society and on human self-esteem.

In a campus pub, four FLC students are relaxing after a long day of classes. Two are commuter students who report that before FLC their highest priority was to get off campus the minute classes were over. The conversation switches back and forth between a party they are planning and an upcoming Core Course meeting for which they have responsibility. The topic of nuclear energy, a front-page preoccupation at the moment, comes up. A physics major in the group, well informed on the subject, defends the risk involved as preferable to the known alternative. He rejects some naive assumptions of the theater major about solar energy. The sociology major challenges him on the basis of their history course. He cites the maldistribution of the benefits involved. A literature major, not previously concerned with the issue, is asked his opinion and hesitatingly formulates some questions that no one can answer. As the bartender calls for the last round, they agree to consult with the faculty about some disputed facts and to talk with the Mumford Fellow about making energy a topic of a future Core Course. Conversation returns to the upcoming party as the bartender shoos them out the door.

As can be seen, the academic-social community created by FLC's curricular structures brings all the diverse components of a learning situation—students, professors, and their courses—into vital, engaging relationships. The superior vitality of the FLC experience, I imagine, would not be contested by many. Past experience with interdisciplinary and processively oriented programs, however, would lead many to wonder if academic quality were not being sacrificed for vitality. A brief consideration of these legitimate concerns will conclude this section of the essay. FLC in its structure is somewhat immune from criticisms of typical interdisciplinary programs because the programs and credit structures are solidly based on six, already existing disciplinary courses. And when successful, FLC communicates the message to students that disciplines have important and irreplaceable strengths not offset by their weaknesses in areas requiring interdisciplinary inquiry.

But FLC also is obviously interdisciplinary and process oriented, most importantly in its Program Seminars and Core Courses. How can the academic quality of these enterprises be defended? These are legitimate concerns worth exploring.

Let us postpone temporarily the question of process-oriented learning and concentrate first on interdisciplinary inquiry. At the outset, it can be conceded that, if interdisciplinary activities are measured by the same standard of excellence as is appropriate to a discipline-based traditional course, the interdisciplinary activity would be found inferior. Students in a course on "The Greek Mind" cannot develop the understanding or the appropriate sense of sophistication that would be generated in separate courses on Greek philosophy, Greek drama, Greek art, Greek history, and so forth. Professors of such interdisciplinary courses cannot help but suffer in their capacity to keep up with and understand the latest research in all these fields. To repeat: judged by departmental standards, the courses cannot help but be thought inferior and the students, poorly trained.

The standards of the departments, however, are two-edged swords. If one allows what I think is scarcely deniable, that is, that the disciplines themselves have different standards of excellence, the problem becomes more complex. Some, to be sure, will defend a single standard of excellence and will say, for example, that however much we might employ or enjoy the insights of literature and art, the bottom line is the objective or behaviorally measurable evidence collected by social scientists. When the novelist or the philosopher objects to the imposition of an inappropriate standard and characterizes the social sciences as inhumane, then the problem of plural standards must be faced. Existing disciplinary standards, understandably, are either individualistic or the products of unheterogeneous communities. Not only for the sake of inter-disciplinary inquiry but also to provide a legitimate intellectual foundation for assembling all the disciplines within a university, we need a meta-discipline, a mode of intellectual mediation appropriate to the various and conflicting disciplines and perspectives. Future ages, I believe, will be astonished that we were not concerned to develop one from the outset.

Even if this need were granted, however, as many will not do, the objection would be raised that the very notion of a standard of excellence for interdisciplinary inquiry makes no sense. Excellence cannot be achieved in interdisciplinary studies because no goal for the activity exists. Interdisciplinary activity is essentially "wishy-washy." A useful metaphor will reply to this forceful objection: a pianist or a cellist in solo performance is rightly judged by standards of excellence appropriate to a single instrument. In a symphonic performance, however, different criteria are relevant. The different criteria in no sense dilute the standards of musical excellence appropriate to solo performance, but they certainly demand additional skills, for example, the capacity to play responsively, and they may require a modification of interpretation and style (not to mention temperament).

From the standpoint of the disciplines, the recurring faults of interdisciplinary studies are superficiality and lack of standards. From the standpoint of interdisciplinary studies, the recurring fault of disciplinary studies and a fortiori unfederated disciplinary studies, is mistaking a partial viewpoint for a more inclusive one. Whatever the disciplinary rigor, students are miseducated if they believe (say) that the benefits and drawbacks of the introduction of formula feeding in the Third World are to be understood solely with reference to the effect on the labor force. Interdisciplinary excellence is judged both in terms of movement toward more inclusive understanding in terms of the awareness of specifiable complexities of interacting variables. One criterion of the existence of such a movement is the transformations of disciplinary understandings of given situations.

Let it be granted that there are standards of excellence appropriate to interdisciplinary inquiry. That might conceivably justify some kind of interdisciplinary course, but what would justify the learner-led Program Seminar or the team-taught Core Course? Here indeed additional justification is required. As admitted before, end-products would undoubtedly be of a more scholarly sort if appropriately skilled faculty conducted and controlled the inquiry from beginning to end. Four considerations outweigh this theoretical point, however. One is the aforementioned fundamental value of assisting young people to move from passive and purposeless students to focused and self-initiating learners with knowledge of and respect for the disciplinary resources of the university. That value is surely worth some small three- to six-credit space in the 120-credit curriculum of our colleges. Second, just as disciplinary standards are inappropriate to interdisciplinary inquiries, product-focused standards are inappropriate to those that are process-focused. The Program Seminar and the Core Course immerse students in the activity of thinking rather than in the results of lengthy thought processes. In the metaphor of my colleague Lawrence Slobodkin, the Program Seminar and the Core Course are "the kitchen of the intellect." As students are miseducated to identify partial viewpoints with inclusive ones, so too they are miseducated (and often repulsed) if they never participate in or witness ideas taking shape. The kitchen is filled with unwashed pots and dirty water and unused scallion tops as the Program Seminar and the Core Course are filled with false starts, detours, dead ends, and conflicts. As one who knows nothing of the kitchen and sees only the beautifully garnished roast at the candlelit table is ignorant, so too is the one who lives in abstraction from the process that leads to fruitful hypotheses, insights, and variable hypotheses. Third, there is no more reason to say that criteria of excellence cannot be specified for process-oriented inquiries than for interdisciplinary inquiries. Directions in the first Program Seminar informed students: "Your grade in the Program Seminar is a measure of your use of the learning opportunities presented to all of us through the federated courses, the Program Seminar, the Core Course and the comparatively intensive feedback provided to you. . . . Our focus is the process of learning, not the conclusions." Fourth, and perhaps most controversially, the faculty is not now in a position to teach courses on World Hunger or on Technology, Values, and Society in the breadth of the perspectives incorporated in an FLC program. Nor is it likely to be for some time, given the resistance to this type of learning described in the concluding section of this essay. Perhaps some day the faculty, or at least the Master Learners and Mumford Fellows, will be. But for the time being, the utilization of students in a sequence of federated courses as resources for the education of faculty and students is an alternative with considerable positive side effects.

It is obvious, I hope, despite the strong defense of the academic legitimacy of FLC-like education, that the entire university is not being urged to restructure in the shape of FLC. FLC, to be sure, implicates the present devitalized structure of the present curriculum. As said before, FLC attempts to insert a transitional, microcosmic experience in the curriculum to enable students to move toward an understanding and appreciation of the academic and social utility of the university.

All students, to be sure, do not need an FLC-like experience. But some of the goals of FLC might frame the character of generally educated persons. Such persons have mastered one discipline and understand its strengths and weaknesses, most particularly the partiality of its viewpoint. They have moved from passivity to active moral commitment in a relativistic world. They have immersed themselves in a communal, interdisciplinary study of one problem of social magnitude and have learned thereby the value—indeed the necessity—of seeking many and diverse perspectives. They have developed skills in understanding and in integrating these diverse perspectives. They have mastered the systems of access to these perspectives. They will themselves be able to conduct with their fellows and to contribute their own expertise to subsequent social issues as the need arises in their lives. Tolerance of ambiguity, empathic understanding, awareness of one's own partiality, openness to growth through dialog in plural communities—all these things have become part of their instinctive responses to each novel situation they encounter.

Resistance

At this writing, FLC is finishing its sixth program and is recycling two of its early programs. The resistance to novel ideas that characterized Stony Brook's initial responses to FLC—a long and painful story—has gradually softened: the presence of colleagues in one's classroom is now accepted; FLC has developed a base in Ammann College, one of the campus's many residential halls; programmatic spin-offs are occurring rapidly; and FLC faculty are being looked to for leadership in curricular and pedagogical matters. However, the gradual acceptance of FLC into the mainstream of Stony Brook activities has misled many outside observers (and many prospective participants) to underestimate the demands of an FLC program. The initial attractiveness, indeed the romantic appeal, of a community of scholars blinds many to the intellectual and psychological costs of participation. The closing pages of this essay will enumerate several of these costs.

1. Both students and faculty experience FLC as a fishbowl, as a near total environment. The benefits of anonymity, in other words, are lost. The students, merely because they are known by other students and by the faculty and a fortiori because their potential and ability are known, often feel subtly pressured to take assignments far more seriously than they might otherwise.

The faculty is under an equally demanding pressure. Two of their colleagues observe their teaching on good days and on bad. Those colleagues are monitoring the effectiveness of their teaching through frequent interaction with "their" students. Practices and foibles of many years standing are suddenly subject to comparative scrutiny. And finally, the faculty must attempt to learn in the public situation of the Core Course with students, many of whom will surpass them in knowledge of several of the disciplinary perspectives of the program's thematic.

2. FLC is a high-feedback system. While almost everyone, students and faculty, professes to desire honest feedback concerning performance, it is probably truer to say that what they want is mostly positive feedback. A good deal of positive feedback does exist in an FLC community, concentrated more in student-student relations than anywhere else, but a good deal of unexpected negative feedback also exists. The negative feedback, for the most part, originates in the diversity of the FLC community.

3. Students consistently single out that diversity as the community's major educational asset. But the faculty, for a host of reasons, reacts very differently. The lived reality of attempting interdisciplinary dialog under current conditions often involves a jungle of private languages, conflicting paradigms, unshared ideologies, and endlessly questionable value judgments. When the unprepared explorers discover that reality, when they discover that even their own long-standing assumptions and value judgments about matters intellectual and pedagogical are publicly questioned, then all sorts of forces counterproductive to the creation of academic community can be let loose. The single most destructive force is what I call epistemological triage, the undermining of the creation of community by judgments (often not voiced) concerning the comparative worth of the disciplines in a program and in a university. Some disciplines (most often those in one's own division) are really worth studying; others are merely useful; and a third set is not worth serious study (nor worth retaining in any university in time of retrenchment).[12]

This triaging on the part of the faculty can occur as well with reference to negative feedback from students. Despite the legitimization of the feedback through the Master Learner's endorsement, the faculty still can dismiss that feedback and decide that only upper-division majors are able to assess the worth of their teaching. In the absence of a clear institutional message to the contrary, one that would say that we must all learn to communicate better with wider audiences, the feedback will likely not be acted on.

4. FLC is a process-oriented community. Its programs are not able to deliver prepackaged understanding of the great issues they address. Many students cannot cope with the phenomenon of their teachers disagreeing or of a Core Course meeting that produces no "answer." Success for many students throughout their lives was gained by writing down the teacher's view and regurgitating it at the appointed time. Ingenious schemes will be devised to avoid making up one's own mind, for example, by deciding that for whatever reason only one professor can be unquestioningly believed. The nature of the community and of the problems being studied, however, will not easily tolerate such avoidance.

The faculty, too, for reasons discussed earlier, also resists the process. It is as comfortable as are the students with the more manageable analyses. It often judges the worth of the inquiry by familiar disciplinary standards and finds it seriously wanting.

In partial summary of the intellectual and psychological resistances of faculty and students to FLC, it might be observed that the members do genuinely desire to escape the isolation of their privatized lives but that they expect the community that they join to respond to them on their terms. Despite extensive orientation, nothing in their previous experience has prepared them for life in a multiperspective, high-feedback, and open environment. As the new members' experience in FLC brings them to realize that the community has business other than praising their ideas or providing a warm refuge from an impersonal and unappreciative university, then real opportunities for growth are present.

While preferring to end on the hopeful notes, we would be misleading if those notes of hope drown out the critique of current practices embodied in the FLC experiment. The discontent of much of the student body, especially the eighteen- to twenty-two-year-olds, did not disappear with the end of the Vietnam war. There is profound alienation with the role assigned to youth in our society, and the years in college are not experienced as an exception to or an oasis in an unresponsive adult-centered milieu. As unsuccessful and utopian as were many of the reforms in higher education in the late

1960s and early 1970s, they were at least responsive to the depths of alienation of so many of our young people. The same thing can be said about FLC: whatever the ultimate judgment on its success and on its contribution to higher education, its evolving structures at least address the psychologically dissatisfying and epistemologically inadequate means by which we in higher education currently attempt to initiate the young to our most treasured and fundamental values.

Notes

1. The first report of the Institutional Self-Study was called *Stony Brook in Transition* (Stony Brook, 1974). Written by a twenty-three-person Steering Committee chaired by Academic Vice-President Sidney Gelber, the entire Self-Study drew on the resources of over one hundred faculty, students, and administrators.

2. This was one of several follow-up reports to the Institutional Self-Study. Written by the author of the present essay, it drew on contributions from many other Stony Brook colleagues, notably, Bruce Bashford, Alice Bernstein, James Bess, Steve Cole, Ken Feldman, Sidney Gelber, Norman Goodman, Joseph Katz, Robert Marcus, Joan Moos, Frank Myers, Paul Newlin, Rhoda Selvin, John Thorpe, and Martin Timin.

3. The concept of mismatched expectations was first employed in a seminal way by R. D. Laing et al., in *Interpersonal Perception* (London: Tavistock Publications, 1966). I elaborated the concept and applied it to higher education in my essay, "The Incomplete Revolution: A Reassessment of Recent Reforms in Higher Education," *Cross Currents*, 24, no. 4 (Winter 1975): 423-43. In those pages, the description of the mismatch of faculty and student expectations is more complete, especially with respect to the expectations of the faculty than is possible in the present study. And the findings of the Stony Brook study are placed in larger perspective, particularly with reference to the very different situation of adult learners.

4. The expectations for academic community, it will be recognized, as well as those for illumination of personal and social direction are quite continuous with, if not identical to, the values that were articulated in the student movement of the 1960s, that is, freedom, relevance, and participation. Together, these three values constituted at once a demand for the inclusion of the students in a face-to-face or participatory democratic community and at the same time a profound question of the legitimacy of the authority and the rules by which their lives were currently governed.

For a host of reasons, economic ones perhaps being primary, the educational vision of the student movement has few defenses in the 1970s and in the dawning 1980s. But the academic expectations of the new students have not changed greatly, despite the recognition of most about the current impracticality of the vision.

5. Four departments, namely, philosophy, history, literature, and political science, might reasonably be thought to be charged with addressing the central or shared dimensions of being human. In a study called "The Eclipse of Academic Community," we studied those four departments at Stony Brook, UCLA, Santa Barbara, and Stanford and found that the total number of undergraduate courses offered by these four departments averaged 447! Even if we were to eliminate the courses that these departments assign upper-level numbers as rough guidelines to the entering student, there were still staggering numbers of courses remaining. At Stony Brook, where the situation has changed remarkably in this regard since 1975, there were 282 different undergraduate courses at the freshman and sophomore level in those four departments.

The casual observer might feel that the departmental major provides a coherent course of study. However, many departmental majors require (and often only suggest) roughly fifteen or fewer courses that must be taken. And the fifteen courses are very often not *specified*, but left to the students's choice from among grouped courses. Further, the departmental major has a *professional* coherence that is synonymous with educational coherence only for the minority who are bound for graduate school. Finally, regardless of its coherence or incoherence, departmental majors provide direction for roughly one quarter of the students' choices, time, and energy.

6. As a function of this reduction, students expect that what is educationally significant will effect an immediate, positive reaction or, in their language, a "turn-on." They do not feel, as they would not feel in sampling the unusual taste of artichokes for the first time or in being introduced to someone else's idiosyncratic friend, that it behooves them to work at it until they find out why something that does not impress them is highly regarded by others. Significance, in the atomistic university, in other words, is a function only of what can be interpersonally generated. Hence, the importance that student evaluations of teaching place on the *enthusiasm* of the teacher. The crisis of teaching in higher education is thus similar to the collapse of family life in America (where the problem is termed "nuclearization"). In both cases, larger social systems in which the unit operates provide little sustenance and external support from which a meeting can draw strength and meaning.

7. See John Dewey, *The Public and Its Problems* (Chicago: The Swallow Press, 1927); Richard Sennett, *The Uses of Disorder* (New York: Vintage Books, 1970), and *The Fall of Public Man* (New York: Vintage Books, 1978); Harvey Cox, *The Secular City* (New York: MacMillan, 1965); and John McDermott *The Culture of Experience* (New York: New York University Press, 1979).

8. Faculty in FLC programs have become increasingly less shy about the alleged privacy of their colleagues' classrooms. The first group relied exclusively on circulated notes to keep informed of their colleagues' lectures. The second group began rotating visits. And the third, in an incident described above, several times got drawn into debate with a colleague.

9. The persons filling the Master Learner role have been Patrick Hill (philosophy), Charles Hoffman (economics), Marshall Spector (philosophy), Arnold Strassenburg (physics), and Marjorie Miller (philosophy). The Mumford Fellows have been Jennifer Randisi (English), Steven Olsen, (English), and Thomas Thorp (philosophy). Three persons, Susan Bordo (philosophy), Lynne Mitchnick (sociology), and Juliet Papadakos (English), have served in both roles.

10. The new roles of Master Learner and Mumford Fellow, perhaps for reasons of more obvious novelty, have attracted more attention than the cluster of structural innovations that together constitute the FLC program. While the Master Learner and the Mumford Fellow are undeniably the central figures in an FLC program, the abstraction of the roles from the total curricular environment or infrastructure of FLC badly misinterprets the program and belittles philosophically the role of shared experience. Without the creation of the conditions wherein shared experience is possible, the Master Learner and Mumford Fellow could not operate. And their roles would be reduced to that of gimmicks.

11. A fifth structural innovation, not particularly germane to the focus of this anthology, is a "cycle of differentiated responsibilities." All of the activities of participating faculty (other than the Master Learner and Mumford Fellow) are undertaken as overloads by the faculty. In the semester following completion of a program, the faculty is given a reduced course load to compensate for their overload involvement in FLC.

12. The term "triage" was first widely used by medical personnel in military situations. Given their limited resources, they immediately divided the wounded into three categories: (1) those who would likely recover with little or no care; (2) those who would likely die even with extensive care; and (3) those for whom medical assistance might produce signficiant results.

FIVE

CURRICULA FOR
THE DISADVANTAGED

9

DISADVANTAGED STUDENTS AND CURRICULA IN HIGHER EDUCATION

JOHN O. STEVENSON, JR., WITH BARBARA L. KEVLES

What does a *traditional* curriculum in a traditional institution of higher education offer to a disadvantaged student? Or what can a curriculum in a nontraditional institution offer to a lower income minority student? These questions call for a broader than usual definition of curriculum. Most educators say that a curriculum is a course of study, specified in advance, involving one or more disciplines and leading to a goal specified in advance: a degree, the completion of major requirements, or a certificate of competency. Years of teaching and administrating in a variety of educational settings indicate that a curriculum is simply the totality of experiences a student will have at a particular school. This definition includes the notion of courses of study but also something more. And it is the "something more" that will allow us to answer the two questions posed at the beginning of this essay.

To answer these questions, we will juxtapose curricular opportunities for the lower income student at two contrasting institutions—City University of New York (CUNY) and Empire State College. The choice of CUNY is apt. The City University of New York began in 1834 with the avowed mission of educating the children of the city's working-class and immigrant parents. Wave after wave of poor ethnics came to the "poor man's Harvard" to learn English (as a second language), to acquire study skills unknown in their native culture, to earn degrees that would enable them to find work in the New York area and to prove their merit at Harvard's graduate and professional schools and at other programs of equal merit. As CUNY grew and new campuses emerged in various parts of New York City, this realpolitik mission continued and created a "curriculum" that was more than a course of study.

When immigrants from a particular ethnic group enrolled in CUNY, they most often choose the school nearest to or even in their neighborhood. They found that for the most part their classmates and teachers were not too different from them. Perhaps the dean of faculty had immigrated a generation before. The ward leaders, assembly men, and union stewards all spoke the same language, and that language could influence who was the president of the school. Thus, the political reality of the community surrounding the various CUNY branches had an impact on the total experience of the students in the school. In a sense, the communities' politics were part of the students' experience and thus an integral part of their "curriculum."

In 1969, City College was located in black Harlem. In the spring of that year, a militant segment of City College's black students seized the west campus, precisely because the college was not theirs. Quite appropriately, they claimed that the "curriculum " was irrelevant to them.[1]

CUNY reacted in an unforeseen way. The university had intended to inaugurate an open admission program in 1975. This was in anticipation of the projected enrollment decline of the 1970s. If CUNY moved the schedule up, the push would solve two problems at once. An open admissions policy would placate the blacks and increase enrollment. Many protested that such a move would "darken" the university's curriculum and its academic standards. In a masterful piece of statistical legerdemain, the Chancellor's Office of CUNY showed that 70 percent of the potential beneficiaries of open admissions would be white ethnics.[2] White ethnics, however, ignored this statistical prediction and continued to graduate from high school and go to work or to private sectarian colleges. And so legions of underprepared and poor minority students poured into CUNY and did what their counterparts had done before: created the environment that also became part of the "curriculum" and so marked the schools as theirs. In effect, certain senior and community colleges became predominantly minority institutions. As a matter of fact, York College's mission defined it to be the lynchpin of the economic redevelopment of black South Jamaica. And as percentages of minority faculty increased by almost 100 percent and blacks and Hispanics took their places on the CUNY Council of Presidents, a "curriculum" was emerging that addressed the real politics of the City of New York.

But did the courses of study change? Well, no and yes. CUNY colleges still offered reading and writing courses for students whose native language was not English; it still ran courses to study the cultural realities of its predominant student body; students still found career-oriented courses much to their liking; preparation for graduate study still went on. Some differences observed were that a goodly number of students *and* faculty (and even a dean and president or two or three) spoke Spanish or French or Chinese or could "get down" in the street argot of the present ghettos, or in general were black, brown, or yellow. So the complexion of the "curriculum" and its locus of power changed, although the course curriculum did not.

But curriculum may even be the experience that a student clientele creates for itself. Certainly minority faculty and students at CUNY worked together to accomplish that—at least for a while. And the experience was often poignantly successful.

At this time, John Stevenson was teaching a remedial course in basic arithmetic that met six hours a week for one credit. Dr. Stevenson remembers that among his first students at York College was B., a Vietnam veteran, a black man who had suffered severe physical and emotional disabilities as a result of his experience in Southeast Asia. These difficulties prevented him from pursuing his career choice, law enforcement and police work. Not only was the course difficult for him, but he had trouble speaking and writing coherently.

But at York that year, many students had similar problems and most were black. And of course, B's instructor was black. So B. and his classmates worked cooperatively in and out of class trying to make sense of their course work. Dr. Stevenson met with B., often in his spare time, to work specifically on mathematics. The student earned a "B" for doggedness, but Dr. Stevenson was not sanguine. Several years later, Dr. Stevenson met B. in midtown Manhattan and discovered that he had become a CPA with one of the "Big Eight" firms. His success was due not so much to his teacher or the course but to the colloborative experience he had had at York. At least for a time, an institution belonged to him, was for him, formed by him and his needs. The curriculum was the course content *and* the experience of the peer support of his fellow students and faculty—that collaborative effort so distinctive of black culture—that also was an essential "curriculum" for him.

But a political difference then made a difference to the curricula of succeeding minority students. Outside the colleges of CUNY, the real political structure was still white and still thought of the university as theirs. By 1974, the minority population of CUNY exceeded the total enrollment at the four CUNY university centers and at Cornell. In the middle of that academic year, CUNY was a predominantly minority institution. Then the budget crunch hit, and by 1978, CUNY's student body was only 35 percent minority, and black faculty were being fired at twice the rate of white faculty.[3] How? The university imposed tuition, reimposed entrance requirements, and mandated a testing program to determine eligibility to move from the sophomore to the junior year. As minority enrollments decreased under these enforced requirements, the curriculum as peer collaboration disappeared from the CUNY "curriculum" for minority students.

But CUNY remains a traditional institution in course structure too. One would look for nontraditional institutions, perhaps, to be able better to respond to the needs of minority students, to be more flexible in allowing minority students to *define* what their experience will be.

Empire State College is the newest unit of the State University of New York. It was created to provide access to higher education for those students, minority and white, for whom the traditional college and its setting are inappropriate. Empire allows, even requires, students to design their own degree requirements, which members of the faculty supervise, evaluate, and approve. Rather than attending classes, students work independently with faculty members in completing learning activities outlined in "contracts." In addition, credit may be earned for college-level learning acquired from life experience. Since none of these processes needs a campus, Empire State can be located anywhere in the State of New York. In fact, the college has thirty-four locations in the state. Its sites include freestanding rental quarters, offices in state agencies, libraries, space in other colleges, and facilities in community organization headquarters.

One of these organizations is the Bedford-Stuyvesant Restoration Corporation. "Restoration," as it is called, is located in the largest black community in America, the Bedford-Stuyvesant section of Brooklyn, New York. Restoration is a brain child of Bobby Kennedy, among others, and enjoys the support of New York's foundations. Seeded by Carnegie Corporation money, the Bed-Stuy Unit, operating under the aegis of the larger Metropolitan Regional Center of Empire State, has a student population that is almost wholly black, so this is a good place to look for what non-traditional curricula may offer minority students.

The case of L. serves as a good example from which to generalize.[4] L. was raised in the rural South. Her family's financial status did not enable her to attend college. Instead, she found work as a nurse's aide, and over the next seventeen years, she was involved in various health-related jobs. Finally, she advanced to a low-paying supervisory position in a New York City health complex. As a single parent, L. needed to work full time. But available in-service and continuing education courses did not serve her needs. "I couldn't get the [training] I needed at night. . . . Being head of household, I couldn't give up my job and attend day classes."

L.'s first Empire State contract introduced her to general administration and to comprehensive community health planning along with fieldwork internships at two different health centers. While completing this study, L. and her mentor became aware that she needed to address weaknesses in research techniques. Her next contract then focused specifically on management with applications to two more health care agencies. Both L. and her mentor agreed that during this study her ability to focus her research improved.

Personnel management became the topic of her third contract. Within its scope, L. was clearly in charge of her learning—interviewing personnel directors of her choice and submitting critical analyses of their operations from a broad spectrum of concerns.

L. went on to study psychology, logic, statistics. While awaiting the Empire State evaluation of her work for the BA, she enrolled in a program to become a registered nurse with the intent of pursuing a master's degree in Health Care Administration.

She spoke about her experience in Empire State: "It's the kind of education you can't get at a traditional school—the kind of instruction you get from your mentor, the material you have to research and be responsible for, the different people you meet —I'm well prepared."

Initially, L. had voiced some concern about being able to "get over" at Empire State. It was so different and required so much more work than other places did. Resources for additional academic and counseling support were painfully thin.[5] L. found that she had to prepare her Degree Program and prepare her request for advanced standing pretty much by herself. Her claim that she is now "well prepared" testifies to the intellectual progress she felt she made.

L.'s colleagues at the Bed-Stuy Unit express pretty much the same feelings. They feel that they have made enormous progress in attaining personal goals: degrees, job advancement, graduate school, personal satisfaction. They view Empire State as being wholly responsible for this. Most say that but for Empire State their goals would have been unmet.

So again what impact did the Empire State curriculum have on them? In a real sense, none. The school simply stayed out of their way but was ready to help them to develop their own talent and goals. It provided a context in which they could realize themselves as individuals and as learners. Of course, that is a rather courageous thing to do inasmuch as it involves the student and school in a dialog that has no script; in which needs, goals, and achievements may develop in startling juxtaposition; and in which the stakes are the student's future life, career, and study styles.

But one of the curious facts about Bed-Stuy students is the degree to which they ascribe their success to Empire State, rather than to their own efforts. It is important to speculate about the reasons for this in order to evaluate the curriculum for them. The

Bedford-Stuyvesant Unit Evaluation found that students enrolled in the Unit "generally *perceive* themselves as having higher abilities in leadership . . . and *lower* academic abilities . . . than other people their age." Preliminary unpublished studies by Dr. Rudolph A. Cain, the unit's coordinator, show that perceptions by students within the Unit of their own academic abilities still lag significantly behind their documented academic achievements. Other Empire State students treat an enhanced self-esteem as often a more important result of their curricular experience than the product of their academic study. Why?

Student self-perception often derives from community values. In Bed-Stuy, survival requires cooperation, collaboration, and a communication style that is highly verbal and group oriented. By contrast, Empire State is a highly individualistic place, stressing self-determination and self-definition and relying on highly articulate written communications to conduct its business. Empire State's academic values contrast dramatically with how people conduct business in Bed-Stuy.[6] Thus, its curriculum is focused entirely on the academic content of student work and does not address notions of the students' broader political experiences and community values. Furthermore, the values implied by the Bed-Stuy students' academic success—independence, individualism, written communication—may be ones they have difficulty accepting. This may well account for their reluctance to see themselves as academically successful (even though they are) and for their transferring responsibility for their success to the college. While Empire State students own their degrees in unprecedented ways, students do not often feel they own the institution. For minority students who see collective action and institution building as ways to survive America's racism, the lack of a school to own may be profound.

Open admissions at CUNY gave minority students an institution to own. While open admissions and free tuition were in place at CUNY, minorities were able to exercise an unprecedented hegemony over the university, and this led to a curriculum that was indeed responsive to minority students. After all, they created it by their presence. But that hegemony was short lived.

Empire State as a nontraditional school should be able to be quite responsive to minority students. That turns out to be true in ways that deny some very important values that minority groups hold—especially the values of collective struggle and peer support. And so perhaps CUNY allowed minority students to accept as real and to utilize their nonwritten, verbally oriented, collective cultural experience; whereas Empire State forces minority students to reject the strength of their own collective efforts in an attempt to have them become literate, independent, self-reliant learners.

With the current diminished presence of minorities in CUNY, no longer is it possible for minority students in the university to have a collective curricular experience. On the other hand, the Empire State curriculum, while denying the very possibility of a collective curricular experience, at least leaves its minority students with skills they may find useful in the larger society. In a way, *any* curriculum may provide a minority student only the ability to take what the curriculum offers.

Notes

1. It is important to remember that admission to CUNY units was then based on having an academic diploma and a high school average higher than the cut-offs set by the individual units. CUNY's cut off in 1969 was a 90 percent average. Without belaboring the quality of high school life in New York City, it was extremely unlikely that minority students would qualify for CUNY. As a matter of fact, most went to high schools that awarded general diplomas.

At present, the university once again has entrance requirements. Moreover, students must now pass proficiency exams in order to move from the sophomore to the junior year. These facts coupled with the imposition of tuition had a disastrous effect on minority enrollment. One last item is worthy of interest: the 1980 freshman year of City College was composed of well over 50 percent minority students.

2. This statistic was reported to the public by the then CUNY Vice-Chancellors Timothy Healy and Joseph Meng. It was verified for the author by members of the present vice-chancellor's staff.

3. These statistics are drawn from CUNY staff and student profiles of those years published by CUNY.

4. *Bedford-Stuyvesant Unit Evaluation*, Empire State College Research Series (Saratoga Springs, N.Y.: Empire State College Office of Research and Evaluation, 1977).

5. Two faculty served forty-five students at a time. Some tutorial

resources were available, but the philosophy of Empire State College implied that students accomplish their work pretty much on their own. This caused difficulties for students who had problems developing necessary skills. By contrast, CUNY's SEEK program provides special instruction, tutoring, counseling, and stipends in addition to regular coursework and programs available at the respective colleges.

6. As a matter of fact, Hispanic students at the college's lower east side unit indicated a positive distaste for independent study unless it was founded on a great deal of group interaction in the form of a seminar setting. They were simply not willing to function in the absence of their peers. As a matter of fact, a study done by the Southern Regional Educational Board and reported in *The Chronicle of Higher Education* for August 25, 1980, shows that Hispanics are making increasingly better use of traditional higher education than blacks. While the number of blacks enrolled in full-time undergraduate study rose by 2.1 percent in the period 1976-78, the number of Hispanics rose by 13 percent.

10

THE DISADVANTAGED STUDENT AND THE UNDERGRADUATE CURRICULUM

JOHN DAVID MAGUIRE

It is common these days to hear that the majority of American college students, compared with previous generations of under-graduates, are disadvantaged. Such comments, I believe, stretch the notion of "disadvantage" in a way that distorts its most accurate use. In essence, disadvantaged students are those who have suffered poverty, too little money, a deficit of books, overcrowded apartments, prejudice, and wretched schools. The principal sources of their disadvantage are economic, social, and historical.[1]

I presume that the disadvantaged college student seeks the same goals as the advantaged student: literacy; facility with concepts, words, numbers; an awareness of one's origins; liberation from narrow perspectives; the ability to think; intellectual knowledge; and skills. And the challenge of this essay is to suggest some reasons why disadvantaged college students do not achieve these goals and an approach to curricula that might help disadvantaged students attain these advantages.

It should be clear that my observations, strictures, and sugges-

This chapter is reprinted in an altered version with permission from *Liberal Education*, Vol. 66, No. 1 (Spring, 1980). Copyright by the Association of American Colleges, 1818 R. Street, N.W., Washington, D.C. 20009.

tions about "the disadvantaged adult learner" come from years of working with such students.[2] My most sustained engagement has taken place for nearly a decade at the State University of New York's College at Old Westbury—SUNY's next-to-newest (some would say "most turbulent") campus. I intend to describe the "curriculum for the disadvantaged" at Old Westbury as a paradigm with wider implications. The conundrum that we have faced at Old Westbury—the challenge facing every institution that takes disadvantaged students seriously—is how to devise a curriculum that continues to widen those students' world, enhance their competencies, and embolden them to action in that world.

First a word about the institution. The average age of its 2,700 students is twenty-eight; 60 percent come from families with less than $7,000 a year income; 36 percent are black; 14 percent Hispanic; and more than 50 percent are women. Each entering student takes a skills diagnostic examination. As a result, nearly 40 percent of each year's entering class is assigned to intensive work in either basic reading, writing, or computation, and about 18 percent of all instruction takes place in remediation or developing basic skills. Certification of competency in all three areas—reading, writing, mathematics—is required before students can enter the junior year. Some students, barely meeting the norm for college entrance preparedness, enroll in introductory courses that are especially designed to include major attention to skills development at the same time that the student is commencing the subject.

We find that the more that remediation can be integrated with the introduction to a particular subject matter and its methods, the more engaged the student becomes. When skills development is isolated from college-level subject matter, the more the sense of inadequacy and second-class citizenship is reinforced. Thus, we seek to relate remediation directly to introductory courses and to view it as part of a much broader educational undertaking.

Beyond the courses themselves, the college has six academic tutors to provide small group tutorials and to train about 200 mostly upper-division students to serve as peer tutors. The disadvantaged student must actually "duck or hide" (to quote one staff member) to avoid being immersed in these skills development activities. These trained peer tutors as well as counselors work with skills-deficient students individually or in small groups in the fields represented in every lower division course. The counseling center offers cognition-oriented, skills-building workshops.

We find that initially disadvantaged students require significant support, particularly supplementary academic support, outside the classroom. A variety have therefore been provided. The most effective support has been a "blocked course of studies" in which a group of students with similar deficiencies in skills pursues an identical course of study with the academic tutors, as well as with the regular instructor, attending class sessions and continuing the work of the class in tutorials that follow immediately, using the same materials, amplifying elements in that field. The key to academic success for the disadvantaged and their most effective avenue to other parts of the curriculum is immersion in repeated drills. We find that there is no substitute for steady drills—daily exercises in writing short essays, solving mathematical problems, and working on reading and language skills. And when colleges refuse to acknowledge the disadvantaged student's deficiency in basic skills and take steps to remedy this deficiency at the *outset* of the college experience, these students are sentenced to academic failure or to only minimal academic achievement.

Attrition at Old Westbury is higher among disadvantaged students than among those possessing adequate skills. Although one-third of the students leave because this still small college fails to provide the diversity of specialization these students seek, studies show that poor academic performance accounts for only 35 percent of the "stop outs." Another 30 percent leave because of some life or family crisis: financial, ill health, domestic conflict.

After a decade, we are most certain about one axiom: there is no single, magical approach to the teaching of students, disadvantaged or otherwise. Nevertheless, we have some convictions about curricula for the disadvantaged.

Unlike most colleges, Old Westbury's curriculum is organized by theme, having taken as its organizing principle in 1970 the "exploration of the riddle of human justice." Not surprisingly, a large amount of its educational effort goes into tracing out the implications of a cultivated commitment to social justice and social responsibility. Almost every course seeks at sometime to relate its subject matter to a wider social and historical context. Repeatedly, the issue of personal responsibility as citizen, as social actor, is addressed, and efforts are made in a variety of settings—not just in philosophy—to show that it is possible, indeed imperative, to think systematically about such issues as justice, obligation, responsibility, citizenship, and friendship. A premium is placed on producing graduates who will have the self-awareness, the self-confidence, and the intellectual and practical skills to be effective agents of social change.

Of the nonskills instruction, about 40 percent of the college's programs and courses are interdisciplinary, organized around either themes, problems, areas of the world, or historical periods. About 30 percent are disciplinary—fields such as biology, mathematics, psychology, sociology—and about 30 percent are career or preprofessional—business and management, urban and regional studies, early childhood education, community health, computer and information sciences. Disadvantaged students distribute themselves fairly evenly among the three types of programs.

Because the interdisciplinary programs came first in the college's development and still represent the largest portion of the curriculum, their approach strongly influences and suffuses both the disciplinary and the career programs. Even our disciplinary programs and especially our preprofessional and career programs are intimately related to interdisciplinary programs, and all students do a significant work in cognate interdisciplinary courses and fields. The conviction that perpetuates this practice is that excessive specialization and narrow careerism represent a kind of premature closure, that students will likely have multiple careers during their lifetimes, and that global understanding should be the primary goal of the undergraduate curriculum, not the inculcation of a particular technique. The faculty believes, to be sure, in mastery, but not of a narrow, one-track, readily obsolescent type.[3] Disadvantaged students are too often equipped with "employable skills" by colleges that forget that the major vocational jobs in terms of executive responsibility and earning power may because of new technological developments disappear by this century's end.[4]

The conviction that a broad preparation—and the practices that flow from it—is paramount may also account for how little Old

Westbury is concerned with a common core curriculum and the greater premium it places on intellectual activities of varied sorts *shared* by various groups. The faculty recognizes the need for curricular integration. But if posed the hard choice, the faculty would argue that the primary need is not so much for the integration of a student's courses with one another but course integration with an eye to change—through all one is learning and experiencing at the college—the inequities and social injustice of the larger world in which the student lives and must act as a responsible citizen.[5]

Thus, in discussions one constantly hears calls for the broad rather than the narrow curriculum, for diversity rather than singularity, for the many rather than the one. The issue of combining and balancing dominates. How can we simultaneously impart empowering skills; introduce the student to distinct and distinguishable methods; confront the student with—yea immerse him in—a variety of perspectives, theories, points of view; guide some integrative combination of these elements; and instill a lifetime commitment to social responsibility? The challenge of achieving this kind of coherence has been more consuming at Old Westbury than has been the struggle over particular *contents* of the curriculum.

The college's greatest failures have occurred precisely when one of these elements momentarily dominated the others, when someone or some small group was momentarily convinced that it had found *the* way, *the* perspective, *the* truth (and we all became, for the time being, like Sherwood Anderson's grotesques, who confuse part of something with the whole). We fail precisely when—even for the moment—we give up wrestling with relating.

By emphasizing approaches to the curriculum, I do not mean to play down the crucial character of academic program content. With the needs of disadvantaged students directly in mind, the faculty has designed a structure for the curriculum that, in addition to providing for instruction in communicative and computational skills, had three basic components.

The first is the requirement that all students fulfill an *academic major* whether oriented toward career and professional studies or toward the more traditional liberal arts. Such new majors as urban

and regional studies, environmental science, and media and communications have recently been introduced. This expansion has had
the secondary effect of increasing the range of elective options open
to students in other fields.

The second component provides for and requires the development of a *practical skill* or competency, which is perceived as being
a proper part of general education and as rejecting the traditional
dichotomy between academic learning and practical experience and
ability. Therefore, all students, by the time they graduate, must
have developed some specific skill or competency that, in combination with their major, is relevant to getting a job, continuing in
professional or graduate school, or surviving in and changing a
community or workplace. For example, a student might choose to
master a foreign language, computer skills, journalism, graphic
design, organization techniques, skills in communication and
teaching, or basic administration or accounting. These skills may
be obtained through course work, internships, field placements,
independent studies, or a combination of these. The goal is, in any
case, that students should develop clearly identifiable and rigor-
ously definable new skills.

Two concerns lay behind the introduction of the third component—*integrated electives*. The first concern was apprehension
about possibly too narrow, overspecialized majors; the second was
about a potpourri approach to courses outside the student's major.
Since we were convinced that, in general, a student gains more
from a coherent, sequential group of courses in each of several
areas than from a completely random selection of unrelated
courses, we have identified and provided readily available courses
in the various programs, where a student might gain a broad understanding of the concepts, assumptions, and methods of an area
outside his major.

These concerns led to the third component, the requirement that
students' programs include at least one of the following:

- One or more "three-course sequences" in the liberal
  arts. The college has identified a number of sequences
  of courses sharing a common methodology or disciplinary approach. These courses are sometimes offered by

one academic program, other times by two programs jointly, or sometimes by combining courses from several programs. For example, a student might take the following three-course sequence in anthropology: "Introduction to Society," "Foundations of Modern Anthroplogy," "Methodologies of Anthropology," all of which may not necessarily be offered by a single program. Students proceed from introductory level courses to those that are more advanced. The lowest level courses in the sequence only assume proficiency in communicative and computational skills. The more advanced are junior or senior level. In this alternative, depth is seen as central: only at a certain level of knowledge and experience of a subject and a discipline can a student start to "see" or "think" in terms of the disciplines being developed. And learning to "see" or "think" in this way is considered central to the more general development in the student of critical and analytical skills.

- A second alternative toward fulfilling the "integrated electives" component is to include two or three "intellectual foundations" courses, for example, "Intellectual Foundations of Sociology" or "Intellectual Foundations of Modern Science." Each of these is an intermediate-level course, with no specific program prerequisites (except for skills proficiency). They seek to elucidate and critically analyze the assumptions, theoretical approaches, modes of perception, concepts, and methodologies of a particular intellectual approach to knowledge. The approach can be that of a traditional discipline or that of a closely related group of disciplines (for example, natural sciences) or that of a particular well-defined interdisciplinary approach to knowledge (for example, political economy).

- A third alternative to this component is a sequence or group of three courses dealing with a single subject, issue, or theme, from the perspective of several different disciplines. For instance, the following grouping is offered in labor studies: "Introduction to Labor Studies," "The Sociology of Work and Industry," "Labor Economics." To take another example, a grouping of three courses addresses the institution of the family: "Marriage and Society," "The Family Before the Industrial Revolution," "The Family: Institution in Crisis." In most instances, such groups are offered cooperatively by several programs. The courses are usually all of intermediate level and taken in any order or progress from intermediate to advanced and require the student to take them in sequence. In this alternative, stress is placed on bringing a number of different disciplines and methods to bear on a single problem.

We are convinced that the goals of this fourfold curriculum[6]—intellectual skills, practical skills, knowledge in depth of an area, and a coherent understanding of several other fields—represent a sound education for any student. In fact, with larger number of students entering college underprepared, regardless of their economic backgrounds, the experience derived from teaching the disadvantaged becomes increasingly applicable to other segments of the student body.

Lessons learned in skills development[7] with the disadvantaged become pertinent to wider ranges of students presenting the same problems. Topical entry points or engaging materials by way of problems posed, the cross-cultural and interdisciplinary approaches, demanding competence in all the skills, including numeration, may prove relevant and effective for other students as well. The curriculum for the disadvantaged may thus point the way to a curriculum for everyone.

The education of the disadvantaged does require special commitment and special resources. It is a scandal and a shame to undertake this effort without the resources—and they are substantial—required to achieve the task. In recent years, we have seen not only the nationwide elimination of special resources and programs for the disadvantaged but also the retrenchment of regular college resources in essential areas of advising, counseling, and tutoring. Good intentions and faculty willingness alone are not enough. Supplementary resources are required. In viewing the current national posture toward the education of the disadvantaged, one is reminded of Hemingway's sardonic comment in a rare venture into verse: "The world insisted that we sing, and then cut out our tongues!" Means simply must be found if such ventures are to succeed.

Recent studies on the impact of undergraduate curricula on students lead me to one final point. The studies confirm that, although students' attitudes generally become more open and liberal during the college years, their behavior after college does not become more oriented toward social action or "altruistic." A curriculum that affects only attitudes and that does not promote behavioral change is, in my view, inadequate. For if social changes are not made, we shall have "the 'disadvantaged' with us always," indeed, in ever greater numbers. The ultimate measure for success of a curriculum for the disadvantaged is the extent to which its students emerge empowered to engage in the struggle toward a society in which there are fewer and fewer disadvantaged.

Notes

1. Two of the most discerning recent analyses of "The New Student," particularly disadvantaged students, are by Kathryn Cowan, Ronald Saufley, J. Herman Blake, *Through the Hourglass (Darkly): An Exploratory Analysis of 'The New Student' at a Traditional University* (n.p.: Oakes College, University of California, Santa Henry Paley), and "Characteristics of the New Student," in *Recruitment, Enrollment and Retention of New Student Groups*, a working paper for the Higher Education Long Range Planning Group, New York State Department of Education (Albany, N.Y.: May 1980), pp. 1-3.

2. The entire body of recent work on adult development from Erik Erikson to Gail Sheehy underlies this section. See especially, Daniel Levinson, *The Seasons of a Man's Life* (New York: Knopf, 1978).

3. A useful, if slightly dated discussion of these issues is included in Patricia Cross, *Beyond the Open Door: New Students to Higher Education* (San Francisco: Jossey-Bass, 1971), pp. 114-32.

4. Thomas F. Green, "Career Education and the Pathologies of Work,"

in *Essays on Career Education*, ed. Larry McClure and Carolyn Buan (Portland: Northwest Regional Educational Laboratory, 1973), pp. 207-20.

5. John A. Dunn, "Old Westbury I and Old Westbury II," in *Academic Transformation: Seventeen Institutions Under Pressure* ed. David Riesman and Verne Stadtman (New York: McGraw-Hill, 1973), pp. 199-224, and Gerald Grant and David Riesman, *The Perpetual Dream: Reform and Experiment in the American College* (Chicago: University of Chicago Press, 1978), pp. 27, 183, 293-94.

6. Old Westbury would be a paradigm institution in terms of the axioms suggested by Patricia Cross, John R. Valley, and associates, *Planning Non-Traditional Programs* (San Francisco: Jossey-Bass, 1974), pp. 95-115.

7. The principles and approaches in the "blocked program" have proven so successful that, in 1981, the college initiated a structured freshman year program for all first-time-to-college students. This freshman year curriculum builds on the principles of the blocked program and assigns new students to a particular year-long course structure based on the proficiency level of their skills.

SIX

THE INTERCONNECTEDNESS OF THE WORK WORLD AND THE LIBERAL ARTS

11

VOCATIONAL AND LIBERAL ARTS EDUCATION: IN SEARCH OF A NEW STRATEGY

MARY ANN BILLER

This essay clearly invites reflection on two components of learning that are often placed in adversarial roles: vocational education and liberal arts education. Educators are well versed in the concerns that an increasing percentage of career education has watered down the broad liberal content in college degree programs. They are familiar with the arguments that narrow professional education can restrict an individual's opportunities intellectually, personally, and even in career advancement. On the other hand, the nonspecific career orientation of the liberal arts inspires questions about whether a liberal arts education can provide anything useful to persons who must earn their living in a competitive job situation. The tightening market for academics themselves and the thinning numbers of students in some liberal arts classes also tend on some campuses to heighten the polemics. Concerns are real and legitimate.

In such a climate of confrontation, however, it is important to choose a vantage point that positions the "competitors" as allies within the broader perspective of the goals of higher education. This more philosophical viewpoint is well stated by John Dewey:

> All social institutions have a meaning, a purpose. That purpose is to set free and to develop the capacities of human

individuals without respect to race, sex, class or economic status. . . . [The] test of their value is the extent to which they educate every individual into the full stature of his possibility. Democracy has many meanings, but if it has a moral meaning, it is found in resolving that the supreme test of all . . . institutions and industrial arrangements shall be the contribution they make to the all-around growth of every member of society.[1]

Dewey's notion of educating persons toward the "full stature" of their possibilities is certainly not inimical to the root meanings of "vocational" or "liberal" arts "education." These terms connote a calling or leading forth of what is within persons. They refer to a sense of freeing, enabling, self-development. While the concepts to which they refer are idealistic, some innovations within higher education curricula have implemented programs integrating liberal arts and vocational studies to foster the fullest growth of individuals in realistic ways.

Such a curricular reorganization took place at Alverno College in Milwaukee, Wisconsin, a liberal arts institution, whose president, Sister Joel Read, emphasized that the young students who studied today at Alverno were the workers of tomorrow. While responding to the traditional ideals of a liberal arts college, she was also attuned to the other professional realities that students need in order to have wider options in life. The president challenged the institution with the following:

What kinds of questions are being asked by professionals in your field that relate to the validity of your discipline in a total college program?

How are you dealing with these new problems in your general education courses and in the work for a major in your field?

What are you teaching that is so important that students cannot afford to pass up courses in your department?[2]

The institution responded by totally reordering the curriculum, basing it on the development of competencies. Liberal learning was to assist students to develop generic abilities essential to a wide variety of careers. The focus was to develop a notion of career in students not just as a job but as the pursuit of personal, professional, and civic responsibilities. The framework was a liberal arts education that was more concerned with the *outcomes for the students* than with the input of the faculty. Paradoxically, such a concern usually requires greater input from the faculty.

The purposes of the curriculum for students have been enumerated in one of their brochures:

- to be capable of managing change successfully in their own lives.
- to become integrated, functioning humanists.
- to acquire a transdisciplinary view of a complex and rapidly changing world.
- to choose, plan, and design their own professional direction and career orientation.
- to do competently what they have learned.
- to act as effective agents of change in providing leadership in business, profession, school, community, or any organization that seeks change in any of its structures or mission.

In addition to extensive course work, the program includes off-campus experiential activities and evaluations that often involve professionals from the outside community. The students, most of whom are women who are the first in their families to aspire to careers, in general have internalized the process of integrating skills, content, and experience, and the process has in itself become a learning skill. Alverno thus has created for its students a model that has integrated liberal and career education.

Besides the students, the whole college has profited from the experience. When the president first challenged the faculty to justify its existing curriculum, the college was in serious financial difficulty. The intensive faculty development effort resulted in a college that now not only has financial stability and a national reputation but also serves its students and small metropolitan community very well.

Although Alverno demonstrates that a curriculum can integrate studies to better prepare liberally educated students for career options, other curricular innovations have utilized career goals to motivate study in the liberal arts. Learning contracts, developed for individual students at Empire State College of the State University of New York, illustrate this point.[3] For example, a student with a long work background in child care agencies had completed his concentration in human services. His prior liberal arts work had involved taking one evening course at a time in a more conventional college, where he experienced only marginal success. His attitude was rather apathetic to liberal arts, which he looked on as one might look on a medicinal requirement. At Empire State, the mentor and student designed a contract with two parts: the first was a thematic study of the orphaned and institutionalized child in English and American literature; the second was a psychological study of alienation. The study was related to his work experience and deepened his understanding of that work immensely. Suddenly, he became intellectually alive; his papers became scholarly; he was eager to meet with his mentor. A business student had been recalcitrant when the academic committee recommended various liberal arts possibilities—among them literature. Reluctantly, he contacted a literature mentor who suggested working on a contract using the theme of the business person in literature. Through a carefully structured contract that guided his reading, the student went from Shakespeare to modern and contemporary literature, enjoying it immensely. A third student used small business as the focus for a problem-oriented concentration and through that focus included studies in economics, finance, marketing, accounting, history, literature, sociology, psychology, ethics, and writing. Such curricular designs utilized what is known about student motivation and learning and transformed the study of liberal arts subjects into positive learning experiences for students already in the work world.

LaGuardia Community College in New York City has also designed a curriculum that recognizes explicitly that its student population was necessarily work oriented. Working within the reality and need, LaGuardia found a point of departure for another curriculum that integrated liberal and vocational learning. LaGuardia has also confirmed its belief that people are better equipped when they have greater or more accurate information on career options.

LaGuardia students come from an industrialized section filled with factories and warehouses. The people who live in the residential ring around these work places had little education, but their value systems were strongly oriented toward work. Coming from low-income families, high school graduates from this area placed a high priority on a job after high school. Therefore, LaGuardia would obviously attract students only if it had a strong work-related program. What emerged was a co-op educational institution that is viewed as an apprenticeship program serving not the needs of industry but rather the developmental needs of the student. Again, the focus was to educate more broadly than would be necessary to prepare for a specific job.

The close integration of liberal arts education and career education at LaGuardia was described by Harry Heinemann, dean of cooperative education:

> Cooperative education has traditionally been understood as a way to reinforce technical and other career-related studies for the student who is a recent high school graduate and attends college full time during the day. LaGuardia interprets co-op more broadly and sees it having particular relevance in the liberal arts and for the adult student. LaGuardia sees co-op as a way for students to observe that "reality" from which theoretical principles of political science, psychology, economics, etc., are derived. More broadly, we see co-op as a way for students to begin to internalize for themselves the way of functioning which marks an educated person: integrating theory and practice, reflection and action.
>
> In order to offer a program that systematically provides these outcomes, more is needed than simply an impressive array of internships; what is needed is a total learning scheme —a kind of "co-op curriculum."[4]

One of the keys to integrating liberal learning and cooperative education at LaGuardia was the Introduction to Philosophy course. Abstract conceptions of freedom and human nature, developed by a professor who taught an introductory philosophy course, were later realistically evaluated by the students against their actual working experiences in subsequent seminars. It also was a prerequisite to philosophy co-op seminars that focused on linking questions about work and freedom.

Students appeared well served by the program. They learned to narrow their job expectations, not lower them. They made useful contacts in their internships, and on graduation, many were hired by their former employers. The money earned in co-op education was an added inducement to stay in school. Many students came into the college with initial career decisions that had been made on incomplete information or because of a poor self-image, but the LaGuardia staff has worked to alter some of these factors.

The New Models for Career Education Program, created at the Lower Hudson Center of Empire State College, substituted a different approach for LaGuardia's practical work experience. The majority of the students in the New Models Program were adults who often had been working, sometimes for as many as ten, twenty, even forty years. Here again, within the framework and requirements of a liberal arts college, student-centered individualized curricula expanded student career options by focusing on the development of intellectual skills.

One way that this integration was achieved was the *bridging contract*. This had as its purpose the connection of previously acquired knowledge and skills (sometimes acquired in different careers or through life experience) with some new endeavor. Not only was knowledge expanded, but students gained in self-confidence since they became aware of the possession of a core of knowledge and skills that was applicable in other career areas. For example, a woman who had almost completed a degree in sociology when she came to the New Models Program wanted to build on her experience as a volunteer worker in hospital settings and to prepare for the role of a patient representative/ombudsperson. In her first contract, she did a major study of the American health care system, an in-depth study that would readily have been accepted on a graduate level. In this first contract, the study was concerned with all aspects of the health care system. This led to greater understanding and knowledge, enabling the student to assume the role of an ombudsperson with security and competence. She rounded out her studies by doing fieldwork as a patient representative.

Another method developed by the New Models faculty to achieve these goals was the *career lattice*. In an attempt to develop structures to guide students in developing their degree programs, the faculty realized that there were certain competencies that crossed a number of career fields. The New Models Program shifted from the standard notion of developing career ladders to one of developing career lattices. Ladders connote a certain rigidity of structure while lattices imply an open framework made of interwoven stripes and patterned spaces. The Empire State program demonstrated the richness of a lattice pattern, which can achieve a variety of combinations—the possibility of an overlay of equivocal but complementary "core competencies."

In the New Models Program, "core curriculum" came to have a meaning different from its more traditional definition as a necessary common group of studies on which specialization could be built. The differences in the understanding of "core" were fruitfully expanded to provide new educational horizons. Persons interested in career education and advancement usually needed clusters of "core curricula." They needed to be skilled in at least one career area, but this was hardly a sufficient "career core" for mobility. Those interested in career advancement often needed development in interpersonal competencies,[5] in supervision and management, in political systems. Another possible overlay of competencies was some development in an auxiliary career field or even in a disparate area. The use of experiential learning in the development of their degree programs also had particular value. Learners were guided to an awareness that certain competencies in their background, sometimes coupled with additional learnings, enabled them to branch out into other career paths. This life-long learning skill freed the learner to see and to plan a variety of career possibilities, as subsequent examples will demonstrate.

To illustrate, a human services student began as a volunteer worker for a community agency, followed by a paid work experience in which she developed an expertise in graphics. This gave her entry into a public relations position for the Day Care and

Child Development Council. Eventually, with experience and additional study in aspects of administration, communications, writing, and social systems, she was able to advance to the directorship of the council.

In the following group of degree programs, which were developed for allied health students, career lattices are also clearly indicated. Four of the five students whose degree programs are represented had some prior education in health areas. Three were registered nurses who prepared for (1) community health, (2) school-nurse teacher, and (3) nursing and patient education; another student with an AAS in Medical Technology (4) prepared for laboratory management; and (5) a student with 159 credits in general studies and twenty-six years of experience concentrated in the area of health care administration. *Particularly interesting in the program are the alternative and latent careers that are possible for these students in their degree programs.* Comparisons are also made with undergraduate programs, where they exist. The degree program in laboratory management is compared with a similar graduate program. In the area of health care administration, there are few undergraduate programs. In this program, as well as the ones in nursing and patient education and laboratory management, intellectual and career competencies were used in the development/ evaluation of the programs. Table 2 summarizes the programs.

These cases highlight some principles of adult learning that must be understood by career educators of adults: (1) adults come from a heterogeneous background of skills and knowledge that can easily make single-route career education a frustrating and repetitive experience—educators skilled in lattice planning are helpful; (2) adults often have specific goals that should be included in the degree-planning process; and (3) the experience of adults provides already developed abilities that career education can extend, enabling students to reflect on knowledge and skills, to determine educational lacunae that obstruct attainment of career goals, and to combine existing and planned knowledge and skills in creative combinations leading to greater career flexibility. Such expansion of options supports the goals of liberal learning described earlier. Such reflection also employs and develops a number of cognitive

TABLE 2

STUDENT	PRIOR FORMAL DEGREE	NEW MODELS BACCALAUREATE CONCENTRATION	ALTERNATIVE CAREER POSSIBILITIES	COMPARATIVE DATA
1. M.K.	RN	Community Health	In-Service Education in Nursing	Comparison with BSN skills
2. M.N.	RN	Health Care and Educational Studies K-12 grade School Nurse Teacher	Health Education and Care in Community Health Programs	Requirements for Provisional Certification
3. R.C.	RN	Nursing and Patient Education	Enterostomal Therapy Administration of Health Care Services In-service Education in Nursing	Comparison with Competencies for the Clinical Health Educator Developed by Zimering and McTerman, SUNY (Stony Brook).
4. E.N.	AAS Medical Technology	Laboratory Management	Management of Physician's Office, Small Health Maintenance Office, or Community Health Agency Also possible with additional study: Lab Technology	Based on Competencies Comparison with Graduate Program
5. A.R.	159 credits + twenty-six years	Health Care Administration	Medical Lab Technician Technologist Administration	Competencies Few undergraduate programs available

Compiled by Lois Muzio, Allied Health Mentor, New Models in Career Education Program, Empire State College, Lower Hudson Center.

skills: analysis, research, reflection, synthesis, evaluation, and planning.

George O. Klemp's research is useful in showing how a carefully conceived liberal education that focuses on cognitive skills can be helpful in career development.[6] Klemp set out to identify such useful skills by discovering which ones were important to individuals successful in a variety of occupations and professions. Among the cognitive skills he found most frequently applicable for success was the ability to conceptualize. His definition of conceptualization goes beyond simply organizing information. These conceptual skills enabled persons to bring some thematic order to the barrage of information that often surrounded them. Over and above an ability to analyze, these skills involved an ability to apply information from a prior analysis to present problems, to see thematic consistencies in seeming diversity, and to communicate these perceptions through creative solutions. Often viewed as "intuitive" problem solvers, in truth, they achieved success by their ability to conceptualize, organize, and communicate complex information thematically and logically.

Another cognitive skill for success in work was the ability to appreciate a variety of points of view. This implies another characteristic of liberal learning—tolerance for ambiguity. For example, persons involved in negotiations need to be able to live with apparent contradictions while sorting out and delineating the basic issues and the different views of them. Less conceptual thinkers often appeared more dogmatic in their stands. They were unable to admit the validity of other viewpoints or what, in fact, some of these opposing positions had in common with their own. Another cognitive skill found by Klemp in the successful worker was the ability to learn from experience. This ability was found particularly among the most effective process consultants and workers in human service areas, especially counselors. They were able to distill their observations and analysis of behaviors into theories that generated alternative actions.

The examples above indicate the many ways in which liberal arts and career education can interrelate and enrich each other. Narrow career training may help a student achieve an entry-level job, but cognitive skills, often related to liberal arts education, are documented to be more than helpful for career advancement. If the purpose of learning is to liberate, then the use of cognitive skills in discovering and planning a variety of career options contributes to that overall notion of liberation and self-development repeatedly mentioned throughout this essay as a framework for learning. Vocational interests have also been shown to provide transitions and motivations for liberal arts studies. Many of the most complex and problemmatic areas that liberal arts faculty can address are those that arise from the world of work—human service delivery systems, health planning, international business, economic systems, resource allocation. One of the finest contributions to a career education or liberal arts curriculum would be the development of courses, contracts, seminars on the philosophy of work. These contributions, together with those explored earlier, are promising strategies for gaining a more binding integration of vocational and liberal arts education.

The work presented by the challenge of such integration is not meant for faculty members, whether in professional or in liberal arts areas, who are content to remain undisturbed within relatively fixed parameters of their disciplines. It is not for the educator who seeks the least amount of resistance, the least amount of time on campus, or the least interest in student learning. It is for educators who are continuously challenged by their work; by their profession; by developments in other fields; by their dedication to the development of a kind of learning that really enables the students in whom it occurs to fulfill their individual potential.

Notes

1. John Dewey, *Reconstruction in Philosophy* (New York: New American Library, 1950), p. 147. Dewey's notion that institutions contribute to people's growth is in many respects amplified and superseded by Paulo Friere's concept of "conscientization," a dialogic process in which persons are not seen as recipients but as knowing subjects who are not viewed as tabula rasa. They have potential to achieve a deepening awareness both of the sociocultural economic reality that shapes their lives and of their capacity to transform that reality. Paulo Friere, "Conscientization: Cultural Action for Freedom," *Harvard Educational Review*, 40, nos. 2

and 3 (May and August 1970). Also Paulo Friere, *Pedagogy of the Oppressed* (New York: Herder and Herder, 1971).

2. National Advisory Council for Career Education, *Master of Reality: Certificate or Performance?* ed. Paul Rosen (Washington, D.C.: National Student Education Fund, 1977). See also, in this publication, section on the New Models Program of Empire State College.

3. *The Second Annual Report to the Kellogg Foundation: The New Models for Career Education Program*, ed. Mary Ann Biller (Saratoga Springs, N.Y.: Empire State College, 1975).

4. Harry Heinemann, LaGuardia Community College Proposal to U.S. Office of Education (n.p.: National Advisory Council for Career Education, n.d.), p. LG-7.

5. For an interpersonal skills inventory developed for persons in the human services/allied health professions by mentors Myra Fooden and Lois Muzio of Empire State College, see *The Third Annual Report to the Kellogg Foundation: New Models in Career Education*, ed. Mary Ann Biller (Saratoga Springs, N.Y.: Empire State College, 1976), Appendix F.

6. George O. Klemp, Jr., "Three Factors of Success," in *Relating Work and Education* (San Francisco: Jossey-Bass, 1977), pp. 104-5.

SEVEN

CRITICAL ISSUES OF CURRICULAR REFORM

12

THE NEW TWO-TRACK SYSTEM OF HIGHER EDUCATION

WARREN BRYAN MARTIN

Varying self-interest groups define institutions of higher learning according to their self-promulgating political views. Some see the university as a center for freedom of expression that through its intellectual influence can affect social change in some distant political arena. Others more cynically see the same institutions as perpetuating a power elite that will not brook any publicly supported institution of learning to act as agents for the overthrow of established authority. Such are some of the diverse opinions within university walls. By contrast, society in general expects these institutions to provide civil, orderly settings where students and faculty can gain the tranquility to study the human condition in the abstract, divorced from political action. Such expectations implicitly are committed to preserving a conservative, historically buttressed status quo. According to such views, institutions of higher education should allow a few extremists, liberals or Marxists, as long as they do not incite subversive action that corrodes the mission defined not only by the power elite but also by the majority. By example, one politically conservative foundation executive welcomed Marxists into his teaching fellowship program because he is confident that the system will bring these political deviants to accommodation. He has been correct. When the teaching fellows with radical rhetoric become managers of the system, they seek reforms that improve the system. But the co-option can work both ways. Some fellows attend university, proceed to graduate work, carry out the motions of the tutelary professional relationship—fully intent on co-opting the system from within. They believe that their ideology will not just reform but will transform.

Today, in the emergence of a two-track educational system, we are seeing the results of both conservative and liberal thinking. When we speak of the traditional and the nontraditional systems, es-tablished educators and unconventional newcomers, we are alluding to enduring differences. The plurality and diversity of postsecondary education long claimed by educational rhetoric are now being realized as never before. Yet some fear that the present changes will disappear in the dominance by traditional educational forms; that the nontraditional will be discredited, and that the commitment to quality will lead to the surrendering of a commit-ment to equality. Although easy to draw, these conclusions are erroneous because the changes effected in higher education since World War II are probably irreversible, especially the change from education for the privileged to that for the general populace. The number of people served, the money spent, and the political commitment at the federal levels are pushing America away from narrowly academic colleges and universities and toward broadly educational institutions.

What evidence supports this assertion that the broadly educa-tional institutions will survive with permanent significance? First, demographic data show that in the future fewer people will cus-tomarily go to traditional colleges and more will likely attend nontraditional, broadly educational institutions. Despite educators' rhetoric about a meritocratic elite student body, a definite correlation still exists between social class and the type of institution attended. Narrowly academic institutions draw their students mostly from the affluent, white middle class, where the population decline has had its chief affect. To be sure, the selective, narrowly academic institutions have recruited from racial and ethnic minorities as well as from blue-collar homes, but the overall minority representation in such places is still embarassingly small. The best hope for the vast majority of blue-collar and minority students is with the broadly educational colleges and universities.[1]

Other demographic developments also support the survival of the broadly educational institutions. In the 1970s alone, the number of Americans in the fifty to fifty-nine age bracket rose by 17 percent. Persons over sixty increased by 35 percent. Approximately one-third of all college students were twenty-five years of age or older, and nearly 50 percent attended part time.[2] These part-time and older college students were mainly candidates for nontraditional education. Other social developments strengthened prospects for the continued presence of the atraditional approach. In 1976, 11.6 million students attended colleges and universities, while 17 million adults engaged in adult education courses outside the traditional setting. Correspondence schools, vocational schools (proprietary), and other noncollegiate postsecondary activity claimed about 2 million additional students. What educators refer to as the academy's "periphery," meaning those unaccredited institutions that educate those past traditional school age, actually became mainstream organizations. These unrecognized institutions and their student enrollments had been supporting the nontraditional method. And American industry has been heading the same way. The nation's largest companies have been spending more than $1.6 billion annually for the in-house education of employees. This figure does not include the $220 million used for tuition-refund programs and the $180 million for other outside courses taken by employees. In time, educational benefits will be made available to workers within the firm rather than as outside services for which the firm pays. The educational programs that industry evolves will be classified nontraditional.[3]

So, too, those large and effective career-oriented instruction programs offered by the military will qualify for nontraditional classification. Similarly, more and more universities—traditional and nontraditional—are offering courses in off-campus locations in student-contracted programs. All these factors enhance the movement toward nontraditional, broad-based, postsecondary education. Other evidence that the alternative educational approach can be expected to carry increased traffic is shown by the fact that most sources of federal funding are friendly to programs and institutions in the broadly educational, nontraditional sector. The record of grants from the Fund for the Improvement of Postsecondary Education and the pronouncements and policy statements from leaders in the Department of Education and in the National Endowment for the Humanities—all document this support. Among Washington-based associations, the success of the Council for the Advancement of Small Colleges in getting federal money for various projects suggests the clout that the nontraditional possesses. The national program committee of the American Association for Higher Education has for several years selected nontraditional conference themes for reasons of appeal as well as of policy.

Given these data and developments, it is worth remembering that traditional academic colleges and universities have been hesitant to offer adult education for credit, to move classes and programs to off-campus sites, or to recognize the importance and legitimacy of the so-called new clientele. Therefore, it is unlikely that the traditionalists will be restored to their former position of power. Despite current curiosity among traditionalists about lifelong learning as well as signs of nationwide sociopolitical conservatism, it is more likely that these traditionalists will be pushed into ivied, but isolated, enclaves while the nontraditionalists surround them. At a time when American institutions of higher learning seem locked into place by fiscal stringencies, competing priorities for tax dollars, and uncertain enrollments, a profoundly important change is nevertheless taking place. At a time when the forces of conservatism, even of reaction, seem to be gaining the upper hand and reasserting the old order's authority, social developments make it extremely unlikely that we will see, in fact, the restoration of the old order.

Instead, we will see a new two-track system established in American higher education, and its influence on the future of this country may be as great as that of the mid-nineteenth-century decision to lay the nation's train tracks along an east-west rather than a north-south axis. The engineering decision helped to reinforce an abiding regional division and an escalating hostility that contributed to the outbreak of the Civil War. Today's educational decision, although unlikely to result in bloodshed, could create social divisions just as crippling and just as enduring.

The two-track educational system emerging should not be confused with the familiar division between two-year and four-year colleges, nor with the recognized differences between the single-purpose college and the multipurpose university, nor with the distinction between the public and the private sectors. The developing division only partially relates to the one existing between institutions committed to liberal learning and those committed to professional training. What is the division, then? The two tracks of academe are occupied, on the one hand, by institutions that are narrowly academic and, on the other, by institutions described as broadly educational. As the two tracks diverge, the diversity and pluralism long espoused by educational rhetoric will be ensured.

Yet diversity has become addictive. No matter how diverse colleges become, further diversity is called for, and while many have been busy extending the definition of pluralism, too few have been defining its limits. Consequently, a new effort is being made to reorder priorities. The limits of our tolerance for diversity have been reached, at least among many parents and students, faculty and governing bodies. But it is the substance, not just the magnitude, of the changes that have attended educational reform that are questioned by many in the academic world. The concern for social justice expressed in the equal access doctrine has had its expected effects, as well as some that were unintended. The status of accreditation in the United States uniquely reveals how unintended negative consequences have attended intentional positive commitments. Accrediting bodies, in general, are the guardians of tradition. They monitor institutional behavior from the perspective of established practice. That which is new can best prove its worth by being tested against that which is old.

In the late 1960s, in California, the Senior Commission of the Western Association of Schools and Colleges sought to accommodate innovation—meant here as new means to establish agreed ends. It never occurred to the commissioners that they would have to deal with radical institutional experimentation—meant here as new means to new or unknown ends. Soon, however—certainly by the 1970s—it became apparent that institutions that would not before have applied for accreditation were doing so, especially when federal funds were tied to accreditation. The Senior Commission tried to handle these cases individually, and slowly, it was drawn into a more open, flexible stance toward nontraditional institutions.

Reaction soon followed. As the commission tried to remain open-minded about innovation and experimentation, it was sorely disappointed several times. Outcries of dismay and anger arose from the defenders of traditionalism—particularly from those institutions that were newer members of the establishment. Meanwhile, some of the smaller institutions that were innovative concluded that the accrediting commission expected much more of them, in terms of reports and documentation and site visits, than was expected of the older, conventional institutions. They charged the commission with obstructionism, clubbiness, and regressive tendencies.

These developments are not reported here in order to elicit sympathy for the commissioners, nor to show that the fate of a centrist is to be pulled by centrifugal forces. The point, rather, is to show that a body of earnest, hard-working persons shared in the breakdown of the social consensus about the purposes and proper organization of higher education, about the rationale for the enterprise, about the ways of measuring its successes and failures and that this body gave evidence of that breakdown in its actions. Commissioners have long espoused the notion of pluralist ideals and organizational diversity. An institution is free, they have said, to set its own purposes within the broad framework of higher education, and each institution can expect to be assessed on its performance in light of its intentions. But few commissioners foresaw a day when education's vaunted diversity, heterogeneity, and pluralism would become so varied, so differentiated; that the differences would be not only substantive but also mutually contradictory.

In America, educators have arrived at a place they cannot inhabit. Their differences in educational philosophy, in methods of teaching, in standards and criteria, in modes of measurement, and in judging the meaning of what is measured are so great now, and the consequences of their commitments so profound, that now—at least for the time being—we are separating into a two-track system. Under the new arrangement, there will be less effort to blur distinctions and more acknowledgment of their significance. We will have the traditional places and the nontraditional; we will have places for the "knowledge elite" and for the "social egalitarians." These divisions have less to do with ethnicity or race than with social class or caste. Individual preference for learning environment familiar to that of one's social standing is difficult to overthrow.

A final comment on the great continuing social experiment in education: thus far, we have achieved one basic goal—equality of access. A student who wants to go to college in America can find a place that calls itself a college. A second major goal—equality of opportunity—has not yet been achieved, but definite progress is being made. Students who get into college are increasingly getting fair treatment. The third fundamental goal—quality education for a significantly larger portion of the populace and educational excellence in the offerings of institutions and in the achievements of individuals—has eluded us. Its attainment now is our greatest challenge.

It may be a good sign that Americans are adopting a new strategy in this quest for quality education. We seem ready to stop acting as though nothing can be done or as though everything has been done. A heavy burden is on the broadly educational institution—to define standards appropriate to their purpose and then to work out the means for achieving those standards.

The narrowly academic institutions have a great responsibility, too. Their task is that of educating the meritocratic elite for leadership characterized by its determination to achieve social justice. To these efforts, we will couple the hope that, in the future, the unintended consequences will be more positive than negative and that the final outcome—the one now deferred—will be a higher educational system involving many types of colleges and universities, most of them successful in achieving both quality and equality.

Notes

1. U.S. Department of Education, National Center for Education Statistics, Office of Educational Research and Improvement, *The Condition of Education*, 1981 ed. (Washington, D.C.: GPO, 1981), p. 165.

2. Patricia Cross, *The Adult Learner* (San Francisco: Jossey-Bass, 1981), pp. 3-13.

3. U.S. Department of Education, National Center for Education Statistics, Office of Educational Research and Improvement, *Digest of Education Statistics*, 1980 ed. (Washington, D.C.: GPO, 1980), pp. 167-68. As a general reference, also see U.S. Department of Education, National Center for Education Statistics, Office of Educational Research and Improvement, *Projections of Education Statistics to 1988-89* (Washington, D.C.: GPO, 1980).

13

"THE MOST IMPORTANT QUESTIONS"

MARTIN KAPLAN

The most thorough investigation of education of any type, in any nation, and at any time in history was conducted in the United States beginning in 1967. The Carnegie Commission on Higher Education, chaired by Clark Kerr, the former president of the University of California, spent six and one-half years and $6 million sponsoring dozens of conferences and scores of published research reports. In the process, it also produced a shelf of more than twenty fat and impressive volumes of conclusions. That the commission's reports and recommendations aroused some criticism was a predictable and welcome event; after all, educational policy alternatives aimed at changing current practices deserve to be greeted with arched eyebrows and vigorous debate. But no attacks on the commission's five-foot shelf were so virulent or revealed so much about the spiritual and intellectual climate of the emergent 1970s than those that accused it of one colossal, cardinal sin of omission.

Sidney Hook, for example, admitted of the Carnegie Commission that "there is hardly a facet of the mechanics and organization

---

of higher education that it does not treat, exhaustively and objectively.'' But he went on: "What it does *not* do is address itself to the most important questions that can be asked about higher education: What should its content be? What should we educate for, and why? What constitutes a meaningful liberal education in modern times, as distinct from mere training for a vocation?'' Although Hook was ready to acknowledge the merit of the work the commission did accomplish, still he finds it puzzling that "the most important questions'' have not been asked, that "there has been no corresponding effort to explore what the curriculum of higher education should be in our modern age.''[1]

The same issue was joined in a 1973 *Center Magazine* essay by Donald McDonald called "A Six Million Dollar Misunderstanding.'' Kerr and the commission, McDonald wrote, "decided to do a strictly social science job on higher education—they climbed all over it, counting, measuring, describing, gauging, and projecting enrollment trends, demographic patterns, financing practices, student and alumni attitudes, governance procedures, and community relations. In short the Commission spent most of its energy and attention on the arrangements and circumstances of higher education rather than on the education itself.'' By neglecting the curriculum, McDonald charged, the work of the commission, "no matter how detailed and massive,'' amounted to "a waste of time on a scale of monumental proportions.''[2]

The exasperation with the work of the commission—McDonald's distress with a social science job—can of course be pragmatically countered without much difficulty. Even had the commission plunged into the cauldron of values, learning, and curriculum, wrote George Bonham in response to McDonald:

> I doubt that the results would have been worth the candle, any more than Presidential commissions on national purpose have ever come even close to a consensus opinion on what the country is all about. Surely Mr. McDonald with his sense of fairness can tell the difference between Alfred North Whitehead's *The Aims of Education* and the working papers of a mammoth commission. . . . In point of fact college presidents these days worry precisely about the issues with which

the Carnegie Commission has come to grips. The heads of our institutions of learning are largely no intellectual giants, but for the most part well-intentioned and hard-pressed men of practical affairs. They worry about planning, constituencies, students, and—always—money, money, money. . . . Mr. McDonald's spitballs are largely misdirected, for the Commission dealt with matters as they *are* rather than as they ought to be.[3]

I am not exhuming these attacks and defenses of the Carnegie Commission to decide whether the goals of the multimillion dollar effort were so radically misconceived as to make junking the entire shelf necessary. Rather, what gives this dispute a continuing urgency is the paradox at its root. On the one hand, few people doubt that the financial and administrative health of higher education today suffers grievously or that institutional remedies need thoughtful articulation and swift implementation. Nor would many deny, on the other hand, that the purpose of these troubled institutions is to provide education and that the most important questions to which such institutions can address themselves are those ultimate ones that concern the content and goals of education. To secure the health of institutions, commissions and panels can convene and study and recommend, and policymakers and administrators and—in the best of all worlds—taxpayers can in turn consider and respond. But even policy successes of utopian dimensions can only provide the setting for education, an activity whose goals and content . seem insusceptible to the "national commission" approach and, alas, chronically distressed.

That the purposes of contemporary education are on the whole sloppy and muddled is apparent, whether one listens to critics or simply examines curricular structures. McDonald cites Martin Trow, who says we have witnessed a "complete collapse of any generally shared conception of what students ought to learn,"[4] and Eric Ashby, who writes:

How can the nation be asked to raise enrollments to nine million, when there is no longer any consensus about what ought to be taught to candidates for bachelor's degrees. . . ?

Put bluntly, there is no convincing defensible strategy behind the undergraduate curriculum, and the more intelligent students and the more self-critical faculty knows this. We ought to be disturbed that the pundits of higher education cannot themselves agree what constitutes a liberal college education. . . . The gravest single problem facing American higher education is this alarming disintegration of consensus about purpose.[5]

Twenty years ago, a "defensible strategy" might have been apparent at countless institutions, at least in name and rule. The old Harvard/Chicago/Columbia models had percolated into the mainstream. There were broad distribution requirements in areas like the humanities, the social sciences, and the natural sciences; there was the idea of the major ("a gentleman should know a little about everything and a lot about something"); there were great courses in topics like Western Civilization or the Modern Tradition. But a look at undergraduate course offerings and regulations today confirms the disintegration of consensus. Now it is a rare institution that rules anyone's curricular desires out of order or that views course requirements—beyond those of sheer quantity—as plausibly imposed degree prerequisites. How is it that the strategy behind the curriculum and its enforcement has so precipitantly surrendered?

To hear some tell it, the real lingering catastrophe left by the 1960s—the time of "the troubles," of "the student riots"—is the collapse of authority. Student thugs succeeded in terrorizing nerveless liberal faculty members so ruthlessly that their every desire was hastily granted. Not only were campuses shut down or on strike; not only were foreign policy and corporate investments and interlocking directorates at issue. No, in this version of the 1960s, a generation of spoiled young people—fresh from permissive child-rearing strategies—had gone on a rampage, eager to escape *all* responsibility, to denounce *all* authority. Small wonder that so many faculty members, themselves confused by international events, unwisely surrendered not only to the demand to abolish campus ROTC, but also to pressures to abandon curricular distribution requirements, grading, guidelines for course legitimacy, academic standards, and political impartiality. Small wonder, say those who take this historical perspective, that the curriculum became a smorgasbord and the university a haven for the dilettante and the irresponsible. To this point of view, the educational needs of the nontraditional "new students"—adults, part-timers, mid-career changers—are receiving the legitimacy that they do have today not on their own merits but by riding the coattails of the current fiscal crises. The widely reported rabid preprofessionalism of the current crop of undergraduates simply proves the failure of the laissez-faire market economy model of the curriculum, with educational supply reflecting student demand. The humanistic beautitudes that still preface many university catalogs notwithstanding, the surge in prelaw and premedicine and the ghost-town atmosphere in humanities faculties prove that no benevolent invisible hand regulates the curricular free market.

There is also a rather different point of view from which to appraise the decline of the old general education schemes. It starts from the political reality that the last few decades have made access to education by formerly disadvantaged and excluded groups—minorities, women, the poor—a top priority. It acknowledges the grim function of education as a screening mechanism, a credential for sorting job applicants. It notes that, as more go on to postsecondary institutions, the relative economic advantage of the baccalaureate declines. Once one thinks of the educational system as serving a macroeconomic social function, an analogous mode of thinking—the laying bare of hidden agendas and premises—can also be directed to the curriculum itself. Rather than see the general education requirements that still flourished in the early 1960s as the neutral embodiments of eternal wisdom, they can also be seen as ideologies, tacit bearers of quite forceful value premises. If the social sciences that formed the core of the well-rounded student's learning experience chose to stress the merits of detachment and neutrality and quantification, then this was *politically interesting*, especially in terms of the values that good students were consequently being asked to mimic and absorb. If the humanities were offered as a list of approved great books (by white males) to be swallowed whole; if art was comfortably divided between high and low; if "human nature" was insouciantly proffered as a philosophical truism: then this, too, was interesting, particularly for its hidden lessons about the nature of change and the prescribed locale and idiom of good judgments. If the sciences stressed the virtues of insulation from society and of objective knowledge pursued for its own sake disengaged from its social implications, then the facts of massive government contracts to universities and of pervasive "I only *invent* defoliants, I don't *drop* them" attitudes become relevant to an inquiry into what universities might mean by "learning the scientific method."

If one sets aside the first version of what has happened to the curriculum, one gives up the radical thugs versus the liberal faculty cartoon. If one examines the second version with some care, then its sweeping indictments of universities are not abandoned, but qualified. The chief lesson to be drawn is the ability to extract the values that animate the facts. If we can look at the traditional general education curriculum that lasted until the day before yesterday and see the value assumptions it made, all the better. If we are restless with those value assumptions, finding them inadequate to us today, then we have taken on ourselves the responsibility to remake the curriculum in terms of values we do wish to nourish, preserve, and perhaps forge. We can never be reminded too often that the ends of education, and the institutional means and content aimed at achieving them, represent moral and political decisions. However unfashionable it may be to avow moral intent, however difficult it is to argue intelligently about values, however discreditable the idea of politics may have become—still there is no escaping the fact that educational institutions are the bearers of our value-laden social wills.

When a culture builds the content and regulations of its schools and universities, it institutionalizes and thereby legitimizes a particular myth or vision of itself and of its hope for the future. When it declares (or refrains from declaring) what it is that people ought most to know, when it defines (or shrinks from defining) basic skills and information, when it establishes (or skirts establishing) the rudiments of competence without which a person is unable to function in the society, it has simultaneously made a moral and political announcement to the world about what kind of a society it is and what it wants to become. Whether it establishes certain fields of learning and modes of inquiry, and not others, or whether it greets all comers; whether it prizes certain traits of mind and feeling, and not others; or whether it emblazons "Everything is permitted" on its shield—in all these curricular choices a culture constructs its value-table.

Should people be required to learn the scientific method? musical notation? a foreign language? computer language? Should the university offer courses in women's studies? sculpting? carpentry? astrology? Should it provide unlimited options for oral rather than written evidence of competence? independent study? course credit for "life experience"? Are there books everyone should read? thoughts they should consider, and perhaps hold? tastes they should experience, and perhaps acquire? The world has never been without a debate about the answers to questions like these. So much of the Platonic dialogs, for example, pivots on what wisdom is, who—if anyone—possesses it, through what subjects and activities it might best be acquired, and for what private and public purposes it should be pursued. Whether education—*paideia*—ought to be transmitted by the Old Homeric epics and the frenzies of lyric poetry, or through rigorous training in number and calculation, or in visionary orphic possession: whether citizenship and statecraft have curricular prerequisites: these concerns apparently exercised the same civilization from which we also pluck our modern notions of Socratic method, of sophistry, and of academy. To name the great religious traditions or the great moral thinkers who shaped the modern world—like Marx and Darwin and Freud—is concomitantly to incant the history of educational schemes.

We are a part of that history. Surely it should not come as an unpleasant surprise to discover that a culture's educational ideals for its citizens, and the de facto ideals that its educational institutions carry, are the products of a vision of the good society, of what ought to be. It would be unwise for us today to presume any immunity from the same questions that have occupied every other civilization in history. If we have substituted an open curriculum free of requirements for patterned and limited options, if we promote diversity over control, then in our way we, too, have offered moral and political answers to educational—that is, moral and political—questions. Although the attention of the educational community seems today to be the exclusive captive of fiscal peril, we do ourselves a disservice by ignoring that other shudder of anxiety, the one that arises from the frightening acknowledgement that curricular decisions are value-laden. The richly instantiated moral crisis of our Western societies has of course taken its toll wherever priorities need to be identified and choices need to be made, but in the educational domain, this moral agony seems particularly excruciating because of education's function as hope-chest for the future.

Battle lines are emerging, and the temptation to draw them should be resisted *almost* successfully. When the University Centers for Rational Alternatives published the proceedings of its conference on the need for general education, the one theme that galvanized nearly all of its contributors was the question of nihilism. Repeatedly, when it was admitted that curricular decisions are normative ones, it was also acknowledged that we live in a time when no one seems willing or capable of making value choices applicable beyond the lines of his or her own stomping ground. When, for example, Gertrude Himmelfarb describes the present state of historical studies, she identifies a "nihilistic tendency . . . fed by the pervasive relativism of our culture, the prevailing conviction that anything is possible and everything is permitted, that truth and falsehood, good and bad, are all in the eyes of the beholder, that in the free and democratic marketplace of ideas, all ideas are equal—equally plausible, equally valid, equally true." When M. H. Abrams sketches the state of the humanities, he admits that many see the denial of certainty entailed by the epistemology of humanistic studies as the prologue to "radical skepticism and relativism." When Gerald Holton looks at the sciences, he sees scientists caught between the anvil of "the New Dionysians" (the antirationalists) and the hammer of "the New Apollonians" (the neopositivist quantifiers). Indeed, the very last essay in the proceedings reiterates the threatening and ineluctable presence of the moral question. Reuben Abel writes, "A specter is haunting this discussion of the philosophy of the curriculum—the specter of nihilism. We humanists are forever embarrassed at the uncertainty of our conclusions, whereas the logicians and the mathematicians can define precisely the validity of their inferences. We can never, alas, determine absolutely the truth or falsity of any proposition about history, nor of any interpretation of literature, nor of any evaluation of art. Therefore (it is implied), anything goes! No indubitable judgments can be made in the humanities. Every man can be his own historian. Any one criticism of poetry is valid as any other."[6]

Although reactionary thinkers enjoyed something of a renaissance in the austere 1970s, and although quite an attempt is now being mounted to throw out the baby of the 1960s—its moral and critical awakening—with the bathwater, the absolutists have yet to enlist many allies in their attempts at curricular planning. To the question, "What is an educated person?" really very few individuals are prepared to give a blunt declarative answer. "An educated person is . . ." followed by a list of qualities, a set of required courses, a catalog of information and competencies, a sketch of values and attitudes: this is the least likely response.

And yet without some category that functions as an absolute, without some grounds for saying that one reading of a poem is better than another, we would seem to be lost, and not only in the literature classroom but also in the university—and society—at large. "One has to make some decisions about *transcendent* human qualities," said Jerome Kagan at an Aspen Institute conference on the educated person, "and that, in large part, is what education is for."[7] At the same meeting, Lionel Trilling said that he was not at all sure that it would be wrong for a conference on the educated person to discuss what an approach to excellence in an individual human being might be. He thought it was well worth considering what the ideal is and then to see if it could be extended in point of numbers. How, he asked, if one had one's own children to think about, would one want them trained—in college, in the secondary school, and in the primary school, too? What do we really think the educated person should be like, and how do we expect him to behave? As he wrote in a background essay for the Aspen Institute conference:

The humanistic ideal insisted in the traditional humanistic way that the best citizen is the person who has learned from the great minds and souls of the past how beautiful reason and virtue are, and how difficult to attain. . . . If we consider that the word *initiation* carries archaic and "primitive" overtones, bringing to mind tribal procedures and mystery cults, we may suppose that a great deal of what we will say at our meetings here will disclose our assumption that the educated person is exactly an initiate who began as a postulant, passed to a higher level of experience, and became worthy of admission into the company of those who are thought to have transcended the mental darkness and inertia in which they were previously immersed. This assumption has always existed somewhere in the traditional humanistic ideal of education.[8]

The case for excellence, for the "higher level," is also the case for the *possibility* of answering the question: "What is an educated person?" It suggests that despite local differences in aspirations and interests, despite the claims of diversity, there is a goal toward which all education strives: a high quality of attainment based on shared criteria. There is, *must* be, a standard of achievement that can be used to measure and compare the goals even of diverse educational schemes. And there are, this case would claim, some skills, values, and a body of knowledge that all people—no matter what their autonomy and particular interests—ought to acquire, if they are to be considered educated. The problem, of course, involves *whose* notions of excellence it is that get incorporated into curricular rules. Our skirmish with the 1960s—when putatively transcendent educational schemes were laid bare as the institutionalized forms of particular cultural values, particular economic structures, particular class perceptions—makes us uneasy with the very transcendent values we need if we are ever to say what an educated person is. Even discounting the usual inadequacies of conferences and making allowances for the genteel demurring that is the hallmark of self-respecting intellectuals at their gatherings, the number of participants was strikingly large who expressed their sense that the Aspen Institute discussions had fallen drastically short of defining the educated person in the contemporary world. Yet in so many ways, this sense of failure comments not so much on the merit of the Aspen colloquies, as on the moral temper of the time, on the difficulty of coming to terms today with a genuinely normative ideal.

The opposite extreme—saying, in effect, that *no one* has the right to define an educational ideal, nor to institutionalize such a decision—is a relativism that slides quite effortlessly into nihilism. To abandon all curricular choices because they inevitably reflect values and ideologies is a great temptation; in this light, the market economy model with which one is then left takes on its peculiarly *practical* attractiveness. But few are so blunt as to say that universities should provide whatever kind of education that people—the "clientele"—claim to want. Although this arrangement may indeed obtain at many institutions, far more common is an appeal to the ideal of pluralism. If no constituency is willing to design educational ideals admitting that they flow from ideologies, then at least there are many groups in the society whose several needs can be severally served. Steven Weinberg stated this pluralistic ideal at the Aspen Institute conference cited earlier. "We should work for a balance in which we maintain the diversity that has always characterized the West and try to keep a balance between different models of the educated person. We should glory in the diversity of models." Or as Mortimer Adler put it at the same conference: "Each educated person should get the full exertion of his mind, the full discipline of his mind, up to his capacity." According to the pluralistic model of the educational ideal, there are many different groups in society, each of which holds distinct goals, aspirations, and requirements. Consequently, there are as many valid answers to the question "What is an educated person?" as there are communities of values and interests. What emerges as the responsibility of the educational enterprise in democratic societies is to serve the needs expressed by those communities.

It is the "essential pluralism in the humanistic pursuits" that Abrams invokes when he says that one can steer "between the rocks of nihilism and the whirlpool of fanatacism." It is pluralism that Abel offers to avoid the "false model of our situation . . . the alternative of *aut Caesar aut nullus*—either absolutism or nihilism."⁹ But what are the real differences between a university that is all things to all comers and one that is nothing at all? It is no large step from the right of any subcommunity to assert its educational values to the absence of any values larger than a subcommunity; there is hardly a boundary between the diversity of pluralism and the anarchy of "your own thing." What starts as the freedom of self-expression finishes as the abandonment of all transcendent standards, without which a normative purpose for education seems hardly susceptible of definition. If an ideology can be said to underline the contemporary curricular chaos, it is pluralism, a commitment to diversity prompted not solely by the drive to open access to education to the many and their claims, but rather—and more fundamentally—by the horror of making moral and political choices one believes in.

Attend any policy planning meeting, any convention of plumbers, any freshman poetry class. The conflict among opposed points of view will be chalked up to the different premises from which arguments proceed. If decisions need to be made, if criteria need to be advanced that transcend the boundary lines drawn by the disputants, nervousness and embarrassment stalk the group, as if there were something deeply suspicious, fundamentally illegitimate, about making hard moral choices. Far easier to present an array than to force a commitment, to settle for a plural embrace of many positions—even at the risk of thereby denaturing and defusing the often mutually hostile and contradictory premises of the stances so embraced—than to choose among them. Curricular planners are caught between a rock and a hard place, between a pluralism that amounts to the same empty relativism that prompts one to ask with such urgency, "Well, what *is* an educated person?" and the prison-house of one's own inevitably culture-bound and value-laden ideologies. Unwilling to surrender to the nihilism and relativistic anarchy they see lurking behind pluralism, educators do maintain that universities have purposes and priorities, serve an ideal, and set their goals above the contingencies of the consumer marketplace. Unable to agree even among themselves on what constitutes that ideal, burdened by the reductionist insight that translates their ideals into the expressions of particular moral and political interests, they retreat to the smorgasbord strategy.

There is, of course, a way to approach "the most important questions" that avoids the moral abnegation entailed by pluralistic pablum and yet also refuses to traffic with absolutism. Such an approach—for which "cultural dialectics" is perhaps as good a name as any—maintains that there are no eternal verities toward which education strives, or ought to strive, nor is there such a thing as a timeless essential core of learning to be passed on. Instead, ideals of educational attainment are intrinsically *historical* expressions of certain interests held by certain groups in society. This is not catastrophic or even unfortunate; it is how the world is. The localization of models of the educated person within cultures or subcultures is not an invitation to relativism; rather, it is the acknowledgement that such ideas are conventional and made, rather than natural or given. If institutions and their ends are made by societies to reflect values and commitments and ideas about how the world works, so, too, can they be unmade by societies to reflect *changed* epistemologies and changed sensibilities. The concept of the educated person must be dynamic, reflecting the history and struggle of cultural communities and their often conflicting and changing aspirations. "To my mind," Asa Briggs commented at one point at the Aspen Institute conference, "any conception of an educational model, if it is really going to be dynamic, must contain the possibility of protest, of getting out of it, while at the same time retaining something which is there."

The making of curriculum, then, is coextensive with the making of history, whose present tense is politics. The answering of "What is an educated person?" then, is a way of defining the content of what a group momentarily sees as the keystones of its culture, while at the same time being an investigation of the *limits* of that process of definition. Education teaches not only continuities but also— and at best—the way to disobey, to reject extant models and values, to denounce ossified conventional ideals whose social times have passed. Some curricular planners want "stable frameworks" that organize the content of learning; when the quest for the stable framework itself becomes questionable, when stability can be seen as the potential tool both of order and of repression, then extant ideals of educated persons take on meaning *within* history, rather than beyond it.

Sometimes our hostages choose us as cannily as we pick them. If the curriculum has recently become such a hot topic among educators, it may have something to do with financial distress, administrative burdens, preprofessionalism, declining enrollments, and humanities faculties languishing on the vine. But I suspect that we wage the battle for a new ideal of the educated person not in the educational arena alone, not solely for mechanical and fiscal reasons. We are mesmerized by the curriculum in chaos because— like the crisis in corporate and government ethics, like engagement with foreign powers we regard as malevolent, like the trade-offs in energy and environment, in knowledge and national security— these practical questions inevitably draw us into asking ultimate questions about the good life and the good society. They attract us as powerfully as they resist solution. Their surfaces are pragmatic, but the politics and decisionmaking that they require of us are as rooted in ancient moral agons as they are in our need to get through the day. To answer "What is an educated person?" is to speak of process, of consensus and alliance and politics. It is to inquire into the nature of changing values and of ideologies in conflict. Such inquiries and conflicts may be painful, but in the most radical sense, they are also good for us.

Notes

1. *The Philosophy of the Curriculum: The Need for General Education*, Proceedings of a conference by the University Centers for Rational Alternatives, ed. Sidney Hook, Paul Kurtz, Miro Todorovich (Buffalo, N.Y.: University Centers for Rational Alternatives, 1975), p. xi.

2. Donald McDonald, "A Six Million Dollar Misunderstanding," *The Center Magazine*, September/October 1973, pp. 33-34.

3. George Bonham, "Follow Up/The Carnegie Report," *The Center Magazine*, November/December 1973, p. 51.

4. McDonald, "A Six Million Dollar Misunderstanding," pp. 33-34.

5. Sir Eric Ashby's Carnegie Commission essay *Any Person, Any Study* is cited in McDonald, "A Six Million Dollar Misunderstanding," p. 35.

6. Citations are to Hook et al., *The Philosophy of the Curriculum,* p. 84 (Himmelfarb); p. 90 (Abrams); pp. 101-18 (Holton); and p. 275 (Abel).

7. "The Educated Person in the Contemporary World," Conference cosponsored by the Aspen Institute for Humanistic Studies and the National Endowment for the Humanities, 28 July-11 August 1974, Aspen, Colorado.

8. Lionel Trilling, "The Uncertain Future of the Humanistic Educational Ideal," *The American Scholar* 44, no. 1 (Winter 1974/75): 56, 61.

9. Citations are to Hook et al., *The Philosophy of the Curriculum*, p. 93 (Abrams), and p. 275 (Abel).

EIGHT

CONCLUSIONS

14

A MODEL COLLEGE EDUCATION: FROM AN ATRADITIONAL VIEWPOINT

JAMES W. HALL WITH BARBARA L. KEVLES

In this volume, we have presented points of view that challenge in a variety of ways the current efforts to restore the fixed core and distribution requirements in the baccalaureate college curriculum. *In Opposition to Core Curriculum*, however, is not an effort in iconoclasm. Rather, our writers have offered constructive alternatives that take as their unifying theme the fundamental questions raised in Martin Kaplan's essay, "The Most Important Questions," namely "What is an educated person?" "What should we educate for?" Each author in this collection meets Kaplan's provocations differently. And some press further to ask "How should undergraduate curricula and faculty be organized to achieve these goals?" In these conclusions, we will address these essential questions. In doing so, we will offer a renewed definition of the purpose, structure, and implementation of college curricula. Such a revitalization is imperative if higher education is to effectively educate widely diverse students and to regain the confidence and support of the broad American public.

Ideally, educators have expected four years of baccalaureate work to transform the college freshman into a well-educated person.[1] By this, they mean not only a graduate who has learned a body of knowledge and grown significantly as a person but, more particularly, someone who has honed the intellectual capabilities to think and to judge. Unfortunately, these goals are not achieved by many students. Even in the most successful colleges, only a small portion of students attain all three goals by graduation. While the acquisition of knowledge may be adequately achieved, the personal growth of students is haphazardly addressed, if at all. And student attainment of the highest goal, the development of strong intellectual and judgmental faculties, is a rare by-product of a college education. So while most educators share similar aims for the highest of personal and intellectual achievements for college students, in practice few professors move students beyond the level of the acquisition of knowledge to cultivate the desired maturation and conceptual abilities in their undergraduates.

Frustrated in finding ways to help students achieve the broader educational goals, educators have tended to debate the part of the curriculum with which they have been the most successful and over which they exercise the most control—the specific content of the knowledge that is to be transmitted. Such discussions are not wrong. In fact, they are a necessary part of the continuous review of all college offerings. Many writers in this volume express some view regarding the specific knowledge the ideal college graduate should possess. For Martin Kaplan, the college curriculum encompasses "a body of knowledge that all people—no matter what their autonomy and particular interests—ought to acquire, if they are to be considered educated." For Ernest Lynton, this expansive curricular definition results in "an educated person [able] to place issues and events and individuals in a historical as well as a contemporary context." Charles Muscatine aptly describes this curricular information as the resource for solving "the major future problems of human civilization." For the disadvantaged student, John Maguire believes that the civic content of a curriculum will unlock "the riddle of human justice." Warren Bryan Martin implies all these approaches in such organizing curricular themes as "the common fate," "the common tools," "the common ground," and "the uncommon individual."

But most of our writers also recognize the limits inherent in a purely substantive, content approach to a college education. In such a curricular approach, the educational process degenerates into decisions about the best combination of knowledge appropriate for a degree and the correct course sequence to convey it. Intensive arguments can center on whether the well-educated person will emerge from the proper blending of math, drawing, experimental psych, or computer science. In our view, these narrowly focused discussions cast a myopic shadow over the perspective of faculty curricular committees such that they lose sight of the three-tiered aims of a college education—knowledge, personal growth, and intellectual capability. And they limit the curriculum's potential for transforming undergraduates into truly educated persons.

As a consequence, the curricular structure in most American colleges adequately supports only a one-dimensional goal for a college education. The single-goal, substantive approach formulates a curriculum composed of so many disciplines comprised of courses grouped like numerous discreet islands unto themselves. Ultimately, a student signs up for some thirty-two to forty individual courses that introduce him or her to a smattering of subject areas and one major discipline in depth. And typically, if the college curriculum is centered on the acquisition of knowledge, then the undergraduate college will be organized by academic departments according to discipline.

Existing distribution requirements in many colleges reinforce this restrictive, departmentalized, curricular structure. After all, distribution requirements mandate that freshmen and sophomores have a superficial acquaintance with a breadth of knowledge divided by disciplines that are drawn from the social and natural sciences, the humanities, or the arts. More often than not, however, these surveys only introduce students into the specialized jargon of a single field.[2] But if a student fulfills a social science requirement with an entry level course in psychology, he or she never is exposed, because of the course's single-discipline orientations, to the complex interrelationships of ideas drawn from anthropology or sociology.

Whether or not students required to meet such distribution requirements can achieve any sharpening of their mental faculties or personal maturation depends on the teachers' abilities to interrelate the concepts ·of their disciplines with similar conceptual developments in related fields and periods and in the history of ideas at large. We have jaundiced hopes for such courses accomplishing much in the way of personal or intellectual development for students beyond fact-oriented memorization and examination recall.

Admittedly, core requirements differ from distribution requirements. A carefully planned and implemented core curriculum could overcome many limitations of a highly jargon-filled, single-discipline orientation. Ideally, such core courses developed by an interdisciplinary faculty committee could help the student cultivate the intellectual acumen of analysis, synthesis, and application of judgment by linking knowledge from several disciplines to address significant interrelated issues. A course on the City in America that ties together into one skein history, anthropology, social services, city politics, commerce, and cultural life could truly call itself a core course. The Program Seminar at the Federated Learning Communities at Stony Brook, which employs a professorial discussion leader and the same reading list as three other FLC courses, is another type core course. In effect, as the intellectual binding among the three other FLC courses, the Program Seminar provides the stimulating interconnective tissues that could foster students' intellectual development.

However, a core curriculum has certain built-in hazards. Debates about the content of such a requirement suggest that a core curriculum represents the particular slice of the entire body of knowledge that defines most essentially the educated person. On the contrary, no argument could illustrate more forcefully, we believe, why an entirely new curricular approach is needed at this time.

It is presumptuous to argue that a specific and highly limited set of courses can or should be an adequate prescription for the educated person. The baccalaureate education ought not to be an identical educational experience that typifies college graduates from one end of this nation to the other. Possibly such a curricular requirement is appropriate for the high school diploma. This diploma ought to represent the working series of cultural assumptions and knowledge or practical skills that unify people and enable them to communicate and function within a society. Although many current holders of high school diplomas are unable to do these things, it is, nonetheless, at the high school level that the common or core education ought to be addressed.[3]

The single definition of the educated person grounded on a knowledge-based core curriculum is simply too restrictive for the majority of college campuses. Yet at the most homogeneous small liberal arts college, such a fixed core requirement may apply. However, if we purpose to achieve educated people in the broadest sense, how can a singular approach to course work apply to the many different types of students with varied backgrounds, levels of preparation, and career aspirations who fill out college applications today? In such a richly diverse society, there ought to be dozens of ways for people to demonstrate their educated capacities. The low correlations among major fields, grades, and professional success seem ample proof that completion of a particular core curriculum is far too restrictive a definition of the educated person. The knowledge imparted by a core curriculum is far too unimaginative and inflexible a standard by which to assess the real talents and potential of a chronologically, economically, racially, educationally diverse college student population.

Moreover, the rationale of the core curriculum falls apart for even yet more diverse *adult* students. What are the odds that a required core introductory course will intersect with the interests or sophistication of an adult student who has been in the work world and probably has significant other responsibilities? When teachers devise courses, they make certain assumptions about the knowledge of their students and must direct the level of instruction to a particular group. If a residential college draws students with 550-600 verbal aptitude scores from small- to medium-size towns in the Midwest, the teacher can make certain secure assumptions about what a freshman- or sophomore-level core course should contain and the attainable goals of that class. Contrast these expectations with those of a teacher of part-time adult students whose ages range from twenty-five to sixty-three. How could a core course possibly intersect with the median or upper level of student interest? How could it possibly deliver for such diverse students what a course at a small residential campus might deliver as a college education?

Most important, we oppose a core curriculum because such curricular requirements prevent students from achieving the highest intellectual and personal maturation attainable through a college education by denying them significant involvement in formulating or choosing their own curriculum. Earlier, we said in our chapter, "The Social Imperatives for Curricular Change in Higher Education":

> The extent to which a preselected curriculum that purposes to socialize by inculcating a common core of knowledge does not allow students to confront their own career goals and make choices is the extent to which students are not helped to mature as decisionmaking, choice-making, judgmental adults. . . . Such a fixed, regimented curricular approach does not stimulate students to want to learn and become educated but inculcates the value of wanting to be knowledgeable or trained.

The single-discipline college major further narrows a student's options for mental growth. Although an undergraduate who says "I'm majoring in history" is not a historian and one who announces "I'm in psychology" is not a psychologist, the stress of this discipline-oriented major forces students into particular ways of thinking akin to vocational fields. Although students within the prevocational major may not have made a professional commitment to the subject, it will be taught as though the only thing that matters in a person's way of thinking is that subject. Thus, the emphasis on a single-discipline major within the curricular structure forces students to approach their college education through the rigid professional filter of the major discipline rather than through the broader, more analytical, individualistic prisms of the varied spectra of knowledge.

When the student has accumulated a sufficient number of courses in his or her department major and has fulfilled broad course requirements, those courses will yield a college degree or, in other words, will certify the student as an educated person. Today, in most American colleges, this is the dominant curricular system—based on the acquisition of knowledge through completion of distribution and core requirements and a discipline-oriented major.

Within this prevalent, discipline-organized curricular approach, faculty will sometimes develop courses that contradict the departmental view of knowledge. John Maguire reports the existence of a thematic major at SUNY's Old Westbury campus, where the "effort goes into tracing out . . . a cultivated commitment to social justice and social responsibility." Ernest Lynton hypothesizes a similar program under the title of "extended major," in which a French literature major would be enriched by cross-cultural and comparative courses. Whether such interdisciplinary programs are intact or imagined, faculty efforts to overstep departmental boundaries are usually doomed. In the majority of cases, what emerges is a pieced-together course that instructs by lumping surveys of various disciplines rather than by devising a truly integrated interdisciplinary approach to a particular subject or thematic problem. In short, the pervasive process for educating college students, which is measured by the number of subjects completed, usually predestines such laudable educational deviations from the "standard" curriculum to failure.

Despite its limited educational goals, some arguments support this knowledge-oriented curricular structure. A subject-based curriculum is easy to administer. It is a convenient method for establishing transferable credits. As Charles Muscatine says, "A unit earned in Maine has . . . currency in California." The system resonates with American industry's value of mass production and the interchangeability of parts. Muscatine points out how well the college degree translates into saleable credits in the job market:

The present system guarantees that the graduate has spent four years doing a variety of arbitrarily assigned jobs with a certain minimum of efficiency and reliability. The graduate has kept up to 1,800 scheduled appointments in class, or done work (or created the appearance of having done work) equivalent to 60 percent of that required in class. The graduate has been trained to anticipate the wishes of superiors, to memorize their views, and to be able to repeat them on short notice. College has taught toleration of boredom and, through the examination system, acceptance of periodic crisis.

The system is beneficial training for the job market not only outside academia but within as well. At a deeper level, the discipline-oriented curriculum is a highly efficient way to organize knowledge and to conduct research into new knowledge. Finally, it is the most uniform way to maintain certifiable academic standards for the hiring of faculty and criteria for their performance. These are powerful reasons to support the standardized curricular system. Clearly, a subject or discipline categorized curriculum has important advantages for college administrators, potential employers of college graduates, and professional academics.

But is the subject-based curriculum best for the undergraduate student? Or is the discipline-divided curriculum more appropriate for the graduate school, which purposes to train future experts in various disciplines?

If colleges are duty-bound to do more than mass produce graduates equipped with a patchwork of time-honored knowledge and an introduction to an academic discipline, then we must try to answer Martin Kaplan's question, "What is an educated person" after four years of undergraduate education? In a most general sense, an educated person is an individual who is prepared to perform in society as a thinking, discerning human being. Such traits ought to be the outcome of a college education. Since they do not depend on specific course content, our definition of the educated person demands that a curricular strategy produce demonstrable outcomes. This entire volume points to the rightness of curricular approaches that conceive the educated person not merely as a well-informed reader of *Time* magazine but also in terms of competencies effective today and in tomorrow's world.

For our discussion, it will be useful to posit a particular educational model that describes specific expectations that we associate with the educated person. Many such models have been created, and we make no claim that this one is unique.[4] The model shown in Figure 4 is shaped in a broad pyramid divided into three levels. Each level is reduced to its essential functional elements.

The first level represents the fundamental ingredients of every educated person through two equally important divisions. The first division is comprised of the competency to communicate that describes the ability to read, to write prose, and to use such non-verbal symbols as algebra, music, or computer language. Equal in importance to the first, the second division denotes the attainment of specific knowledge. As a result of the many courses pursued, college students should achieve specific knowledge in several broad areas, such as the humanities, the social sciences, the physical sciences, and the fine arts. In addition, students should gain greater depth in a particular academic field, such as literature, psychology or music, or in some career field like nursing, business, or engineering. As a result of their four years of study, many, but not all, college graduates demonstrate significantly broader knowledge and improved ability to communicate as educated persons commensurate with the goals of the model's first level.

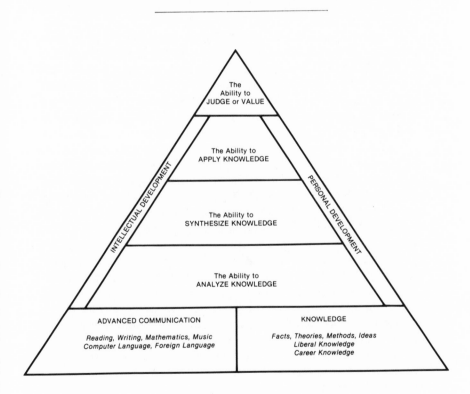

FIGURE 4
The Pyramid of the Educated Person

The second level of the model, which builds firmly on the first, represents a set of skills that begin to define the fully educated person's intellectual and personal development.[5] The first skill applicable to both areas is the analytic skill. In intellectual development, this skill is defined as the ability to examine a thing, a problem, an organization; to divide it into its parts; and to see clearly the discrete elements of the whole. In personal development, the analytic skill means the increasing capacity to perceive oneself; to understand one's physical, psychological, social, and spiritual dimensions as parts of a complex whole human being.

When the analytic skill is achieved in both areas, the higher skill of synthesis becomes increasingly important. For intellectual development, synthesis is the ability to integrate dissected parts within an entire functioning system. It is the recognition that a change in one facet will have an impact on every other aspect of an organism or a society. In personal development, the individual comes to realize his or her place as part of a larger community and to develop increased personal understanding of the relationships among the self, the society, and the planet earth.

But for the educated person, analysis and synthesis must lead to yet a higher skill: the ability to apply one's education and its intellectual and personal dimensions to contributions to society. For intellectual development, such application implies the capacity to identify and creatively solve new problems. For the careerists, application means to work creatively in a profession. For the elected, it is to successfully function as representatives of the people. In personal development, application represents the integration of one's personality so that a fully functioning, confident, compassionate human being emerges.

It is important to note that as the level and achievement of these personal and intellectual skills improve, the pyramid thins, representing the decreasing number of college-educated individuals who fully achieve these capacities *and* the decreasing number of college faculty who are professionally capable of eliciting these capabilities from their students.

At the apex of the pyramid is the level that we call judgement, that rare but learned capacity to distinguish between what is good and less good or to decide on a value. The achievement of this ability represents, in truth, the full meaning of the educated person. Pinpointed by the narrowest point of the pyramid, Figure 4 clearly indicates that few students achieve this level during their college careers and relatively few achieve it even in a lifetime.

This model of the educated person, simply and directly put, is not markedly different from the ideal goal that has attended education at all times. But it represents a goal and model that have been significantly eroded, even forgotten, in recent decades as our educational institutions have proliferated and enrollments have grown. It is again by such a model that we must now consider alternative curricular designs that promise to strengthen the capacity of our undergraduate educational institutions to more fully achieve these purposes for which colleges exist.

How should we devise curricula that enable students to achieve more consistently the educational aims of our model? We have already indicated that a purely knowledge-oriented approach to curriculum falls short in achieving these goals. At the same time, we want to stress that alternative approaches must build on a base of knowledge, as indicated in the first level of our curricular model. If a curriculum is intended to enhance a student's personal and intellectual development, then the acquisition of knowledge and facts is a necessary step to gain the raw material out of which can emerge the larger conceptual powers and maturation of the educated person. Such higher skills cannot be developed in the abstract nor in the absence of a discipline-informed content. Such a situation would be analogous to trying to learn to type by reading a book and never touching a typewriter. In the same vein, certain courses of study have a greater capacity to cultivate the student's abilities than others. The study of logic, for example, has significantly greater possibility for promoting the intellectual and personal skills of analysis and synthesis than courses in business correspondence, filing, or typing, which do not generate the facilities we are promoting as the purpose of college-level work.

We stress that we are not trying to discourage the teaching of traditional academic disciplines in American colleges. However, if courses, particularly at the elementary level, are simply used to inculcate information, they will fall short of our model's educational aims. If the teacher and student understand that the information is to be used to increase intellectual and personal development, then the results will differ from courses in which both parties understand the purpose is simply to master knowledge to be spewed back upon examination. In the latter case, knowledge is learned for its own sake; in the former, it is the use of knowledge for education's sake that is the course's desired aim.

Realistically, institutions of higher education will not change in a single stroke and pursue this curricular approach on a widespread basis as long as undergraduate faculty qualify for their jobs by being recognized specialists in a very narrow topic, are promoted by a publish-or-perish yardstick, and instruct to inform rather than to inculcate personal and intellectual maturation. As Ernest Lynton and Charles Muscatine suggest, the key to fundamental change in curricular structure is new measurements for faculty qualifications, performance, and roles.

Yet as Lynton emphasizes, faculty would agree to participate in these revised curricular and faculty systems only if salary increments, promotions to tenured rank, and other perquisites were given as rewards. Without these tangible faculty incentives, the curricular and classroom innovations required to achieve our educational model's objectives for the well-educated person would soon be extinguished.

How might faculty qualify for positions in a college with restructured curricular objectives? We caution against hiring the research-oriented specialist for undergraduate work. In Chapter 2, "The Social Imperatives for Curricular Change in Higher Education," we describe how the rapid growth of graduate programs spearheaded by massive federal support of the sciences in the mid to late 1950s introduced narrow values into undergraduate education. These discipline-based values fostered by the graduate school orientation demolished the undergraduate's options by forcing premature overspecialization. Thus, colleges can overcome this constriction of undergraduate objectives by employing faculty who not only are broadly knowledgeable in one discipline or in more than one area of study but also are equipped to subtly inculcate these essential skills of analysis, synthesis, application, and judgment leading to full personal and intellectual development. This means the *primary* goal of an undergraduate teacher would be not to help students master the knowledge of a discipline but to help them develop the requisite mental and personal capabilities through classroom lectures, seminars, individual discussions, and assignments.

Clearly, achievement of these model undergraduate goals compels a renewed emphasis on certain standards of good teaching. The best teachers, regardless of their disciplines, have always known that they had to nurture this mental and personal growth in students. But too few professional educators have adequately developed their teaching skills to inculcate these goals.

We would like to demonstrate the types of teaching bred by learning for education's sake versus learning for knowledge's sake to compare the worth of their outcomes. In a rather typical, knowledge-oriented class, a history professor would transmit by lecture the substance by which students gain a basic factual acquaintance, say, with Napoleonic Europe. In the exams, the students who knew what facts were expected in order to gain a good grade in this discrete course would respond correctly to more than 90 percent of the questions. Such a course would most likely not lead students to deal with a range of interconnecting knowledge found in other disciplines. While the best teachers would probably consider the rise of Napoleon in relationship, for example, to the Industrial Revolution or to the characteristics of mass culture, the conventional lecturer would not typically require this kind of broader exploration.

Our ideal teacher, intent on helping the student develop certain personal and intellectual competencies, would deal with the same course content—Napoleonic Europe—but would enable the students to pursue this subject from multiple perspectives. On a primary level, the professor would work to see how well the student could articulate the basic factual material. At the next higher level, the professor would test how well the student could analyze various social forces and conditions and how well the student could understand, on still a higher level how these constructs could be integrated into a social theory. On the highest level of thought, the professor would expect the student to make judgments about the impact of Napoleon on Europe, the flow of history, and the relevance of these issues to the present. Then, which student would be judged the better educated person—the student familiar with the comprehensive, factually detailed knowledge of the Napoleonic era or the student who could synthesize the historical, political, and sociological trends of that era and use them for comparative judgments about his or her own times?

We want to stress that in seminar and lecture discussions our ideal teacher would teach students not only to think but also to *decide* whether something is good or less good—in short, to make informed judgments about themselves and their world. We concur with Dee G. Appley, who writes:

> . . . moral development—the development of a capacity to judge what is right—is an essential aspect of human development and is therefore an essential aim of education, including higher education.
>
> I am proposing, then, that we accept human development as an aim of education and recognize our responsibilities as educators for providing for the development of students' socioemotional and moral, as well as cognitive capacities.

We, too, believe that a college curriculum purposes to fully develop the whole person, for premature specialization can only lead to an underdeveloped human being. Unless courses seek to nurture the whole person, teachers will discover that underdeveloped students lack the capacity to understand or make the necessary judgmental distinctions that are germane to the highest aims of education at the apex of our model.

It follows that a faculty with such model standards of teaching should not be based in departments organized according to single academic disciplines. The traditional single, departmental structure inhibits creative teaching and encourages knowledge-based, subject specialization leading to a departmental major. New organizational structures are needed to positively encourage collaborative teaching in support of interdisciplinary instruction. The older divisional structure, while containing the potential for our model's intellectual goals, seldom offered more than an amalgam of disciplines. Structural experiments at Santa Cruz, Old Westbury, Evergreen State College, and Empire State College suggest exemplary innovations that have proven successful in advancing our model's curricular goals.

Since our educational approach is sometimes more easily achieved at a small liberal arts college, some observers have asked whether this approach can realistically be a policy at universities with 10,000 enrolled students. How can large institutions with massive student populations possibly encourage and manage a flexible, personalized curricular approach that emphasizes intellectual and emotional development? This is a question less of enrollment numbers than of instructional means and pedagogical attitudes. Where faculty are forced because of class enrollments to limit teaching to the lecture hall, these educational aims have little hope of being attained. But if these teaching methods can be combined with a variety of alternative, more personalized strategies, then the institution's goal to help each of its students develop his or her own full potential will not be sacrificed for enrollment numbers and tuition receipts.

In addition to requiring interdisciplinary knowledge for faculty hiring and an interdisciplinary, developmental approach to classroom teaching, our ideal higher educational aims must rest on a more systemized, interdisciplinary approach to student advisement. Faculty advisement at most colleges is woefully inadequate, or even nonexistent, especially for evening or off-campus programs. Most often in a departmentally organized college, a student sits down with an adviser once a semester. The adviser points to the courses recommended in the catalog and assigns them routinely to the student almost without thoughtful regard for the student's interests or motivation. Then the student's course schedule bearing the adviser's signature is transmitted to the registrar for enrollment. Faculty members view such advisory work as a formal chore to be endured rather than a creative act of education, and no wonder. It is the exception when any truly substantive exploration of student goals is carried out by the faculty member and the student in concert.

In some colleges, the advisement structure is even less well off. The advisory duties have been relegated to a cadre of professional counselors affiliated with either the student personnel office or, occasionally, with the academic dean's staff. Although willing in spirit, these counselors are limited to how much time they can give any of the hundreds of students assigned to them in a single term. More often than not, they are crucially unprepared to deal with substantive academic questions best handled by the faculty.

To fundamentally improve the effectiveness of institutions of higher learning, faculty roles will have to be substantially modified to allow faculty to engage seriously in curricular advisement as *an educative act.*[6] The barnacled blinders of the single-discipline major or the departmental structure that inhibit intellectual development can be dissolved if teachers change their role from commander to collaborator in helping students devise their course schedules. The faculty should be less the uninvolved expert dictating a predesigned course pablum and more the guide, eliciting from the student the interests and motivations best implemented in a meaningful, individually designed academic program.

Clearly, this collaboration between faculty and student does not lead to a "do-your-own-thing" curriculum. An individually planned curriculum is not synonymous with student fancies, incoherence, superficiality, and chaos. This curricular system is prevented from giving way to meaningless student whims by a strong, well-structured faculty support system. A competent faculty member not only would monitor the student's curricular choices but also would constantly check that the student's coursework offers a sufficiently solid base of information from which to operate. A knowledgeable and sympathetic faculty adviser will ask the right questions and encourage the student to explore his or her curricular options in an ever-widening, interlocking view of the world.

We would like to give a true-to-life example to demonstrate how a more flexible, student-oriented advisement program can transform a student's motivation to learn a vocation into an ever-widening ring of substantive career explorations, which heighten a student's intellectual capacities and work opportunities. A weaver, we shall call her Greta, came to Empire State College wanting to develop a degree program around her interest in her craft. She had considered other colleges and had been repelled by the predetermined and unexplainable requirements that seemed to hamper the pursuit of her vocational interest. At other colleges, she needed to take Western civilization, freshman composition, calculus, physical education, and a social science. Perhaps the conventional student with less individuality unquestioningly would have squeezed into that pattern. Greta feared that those required courses would leave her no time to weave. The prestructured academic setting would stifle her very reason for attending college.

Yet given our student-focused curricular structure, and, with careful faculty advisement, we were able to help her build a coherent, comprehensive, in-depth curriculum. Capitalizing on her interest in her craft, Greta evolved a curriculum of interrelating, outwardly branching courses to an ever-enlarging world. Through mastering weaving techniques, she became fascinated with the structure of different textile fibers. In a surprisingly short time, this interest diverged into two study areas. The first concerned the technological aspects of the weaving process which reached back to the structure of looms, the invention of the flying shuttle and the Industrial Revolution, and the problems of using energy sources like water power or steam. For example, one study unit focused on an eighteenth-century mill town in the English Cotswolds. The second direction of study led to a comparative study of natural and synthetic fibers broken down by their chemical attributes and other physical characteristics. Once Greta completed these technological and scientific studies, she developed an interest in textile design that quickly merged into a study of tapestry, medieval art, and a paper on the Bayeux tapestries. She also decided to do an independent project on the philosophy of aesthetics. At a later stage, her proficiency at weaving so increased that her work was sold and accepted as art. Then she chose to broaden her vocational competency so that she could work with others, using her weaving as a medium for therapy and teaching.

What did this alternative advisement approach accomplish for that atraditional vocational college student? The faculty adviser could not have known at the start which avenues of study would interest Greta. The curriculum design truly evolved out of the student's specific vocational interests. Yet most academics would agree that this program fulfilled the best characteristics of an undergraduate curriculum from the criteria of depth and breadth. Her curriculum was not narrowly vocational or purely academic but combined the two areas of liberal arts and vocational learning to cultivate the mental and personal competencies that are the aims of higher education. The curriculum related the weaver's spontaneous interest in one specific substantive area to an ever-enlarging world that included science, technology, history, and aesthetics, ultimately enabling her to use her craft as an occupational therapist and artist of substantially priced works.

Yet because of our three-level goals for students, we expect curriculum and advisement to do more than interrelate the spheres of knowledge of her employment and her art. We also expect a vocational curriculum to cultivate the higher level competencies cited in our educational model. Greta was allowed to discover her own intellectual capability through a curriculum that permitted her mind to shape her own coursework so that her personal interests could grow, expand, and explore. She learned to acquire and communicate knowledge, which gave her the confidence to work independently on intellectual projects. Because of the natural links between her self-routed courses, she learned how to analyze, compare, synthesize, and make critical judgments of the work of medieval craftsmen and of her own achievements. That same educational process increased her understanding of her particular, discrete capabilities and inspired her to apply them in working with others who could creatively gain from her experience. So the curriculum taught her knowledge, communication, the thinking processes, self-awareness, confidence, and how to contribute to others through her talents and experience and better abide by her own rational judgments.

With strong faculty advisement and the possibility of an individually planned curricular structure, students have a much greater opportunity to achieve both their own personal goals for college and the basic educational goals espoused by our pyramidal model. If Greta had enrolled in a traditional college curriculum—where her weaving would have been subordinate to a predetermined curriculum, where each department would have used its distribution requirements to pretend to describe the whole universe and thus indoctrinate or seduce freshmen into seeing the world through its prisms—Greta might have floundered, developed less quickly, or found difficulty becoming what she wished. Ultimately, the college would not have provided the ambience for her fullest realizations or achieved the broadest and richest development of her mental and personal competencies. Clearly, a strong faculty based advisory system can help to free undergraduate learning from the yoke of the prevocational departmental structure.

If a college is to respond sensitively and directly to individual students, an advisory system such as we have described is essential. However, we do not advocate student-initiated curricula as appropriate for all students. For example, we recognize that for the lower income, minority student the individualized curricular orientation relies on basic skills, which, as John Stevenson and co-author Barbara Kevles point out, conflict with the community values of the disadvantaged student's background. Stevenson and Kevles say:

> In Bed-Stuy, survival requires cooperation, collaboration, and a communication style that is highly verbal and group oriented. By contrast, Empire State is a highly individualistic place, stressing self-determination and self-definition and relying on highly articulate written communications to conduct its business. Empire State's academic values contrast dramatically with how people conduct business in Bed-Stuy.

Should the curriculum, as Stevenson and Kevles imply, separate disadvantaged students from their verbally oriented collaborative ethic and help them achieve success in a literate-oriented society? Should the curriculum help the minority, lower income students to adjust their past cultural values in order to succeed in the larger world? Another writer, John Maguire, forcefully answers:

> . . . when colleges refuse to acknowledge the disadvantaged student's deficiency in basic skills and take steps to remedy this deficiency at the *outset* of the college experience, these students are sentenced to academic failure or to only minimal academic achievement.

We concur with Maguire but acknowledge Stevenson and Kevles' insight into the background of the minority student. Thus, an individualized curriculum for the minority student should blend elements of the literate and oral traditions, thereby increasing the probability of success of a student with low literate background in the postcollege world. To be sure, this is an arduous developmental process of acculturation, one that cannot be achieved in six months or in a single remedial year; rather it has to be integrated throughout a minority student's college life.

Educational critics invariably denigrate curricular approaches that overstep departmental lines to respond innovatively to individual student needs and to social imperatives of the times. Such critics have worried that these new curricular systems are capitulating to consumer demands. We disagree. Outright consumerism does exist in education; it means the selling of degrees and academic credentials to those who will pay tuition with little concern for student performance or course substance in a gross violation of educational integrity. Marketing of degrees flourishes in many traditional as well as atraditional colleges. In these institutions, a student cannot fail short of disappearing from campus or failing to mail in an exam. No educational philosophy can be found, save an interest in tuition revenue.[7]

Then what, educators ask, is the difference between a consumerist curriculum and one designed to meet society's needs as expressed through the aims of those students which a college admits? It is probably inevitable that a curriculum that is responsive to student interests is especially vulnerable to the charge of selling out to what the public wants. Yet an educational system that is responsive to its students' needs cannot be indicted or maligned on that basis alone.

In contrast to this consumerist trend, we are proposing a *student-oriented* education that, although not determined by seasonal trends, does regularly update its curriculum to meet students' preparations, interests, and motivations for a college education. Institutions whose approach to curriculum is student-oriented do not provide the college's clientele with a curriculum designed on the principle of the best-seller mentality. Such institutions are not slavishly giving students knowledge students want to meet the current fad. Such colleges are trying to capitalize on the students' motivations and interests to help them achieve the highest goals for undergraduate education. A curriculum devoted to these goals has no chance of ever becoming commercially consumer oriented. The consumerist curriculum is devoid of these educational and philosophical pyramidal goals that the educator with integrity inculcates as the objectives of curricular design.

We favor student-oriented curricular approaches that allow students to set reasonable expectations for their coursework with regard to content, process, and educational objectives. What is wrong with the numerous alternative curricular approaches targeted for specific constitutencies that meet standards of academic quality and depth? What is inherently unrespectable about curricula based on individualized student interests coherently organized with strong faculty advisement, or with curricula grounded on principles that interrelate vocational and liberal learning, or with curricula reponsive to a minority, lower socioeconomic experience, or with curricula directed by academic-moral-personal development?

We uphold the student's right to expect that a college's services will move them toward their career goals, give them a real opportunity to become an educated person, and enable them to adapt with certain intellectual and personal skills to a changing world. Such responsible responsiveness to student interest and demand can hardly be defined as consumerism.

Recommendations

In summary, we assume that in the 1980s colleges and universities should continue to serve increasing numbers of atraditional students—adults, part-timers, working people—as well as increasingly well-informed, often street-wise traditional campus students. Effectively serving these diverse students while avoiding the consumerist, marketplace heresy will require new educational and philosophic approaches to departmental organization, to curricular design, and to faculty role. The following recommendations codify some new approaches that we believe are necessary:

1. Student curricula will be designed and implemented to encourage students not only to gain communication skills and broad knowledge but also to develop sig-

nificant intellectual and personal capacities leading to the ability to make independent and moral judgments.

2. In order to achieve this student goal, significant changes in college structure and pedagogical role will be required. The organization of the undergraduate curriculum by a departmental, discipline-based structure should be abolished in favor of a structure that positively encourages faculty to support strong interdisciplinary and collaborative teaching with rigorous intellectual and developmental goals for undergraduates.

3. Distribution and core requirements would be assigned to the secondary school curriculum and would be replaced in colleges and universities by truly inter-disciplinary core *elective* courses designed around contemporary problems or issues or around broad cultural ideas and themes. Such courses would be responsive to the social imperatives of the times and to the student's interests, motivations, and life requirements. Serious academic advisement and student curricular planning would play significant roles at the beginning and end of each academic term and would be central responsibilities of each faculty member.

4. A major redefinition of the role, function, and qualifications of faculty would be required to effect such an educational approach. Faculty members would be hired not only because of their reputations as specialists in one field, but also because of their broad-based proficiency in such wide areas as the humanities, social sciences, or physical sciences. A redefined faculty role would emphasize classroom performance that stressed the development of students' powers of analysis, synthesis, and judgment and their personal maturation.

5. Student evaluation will be based on a demonstration of those highly prized intellectual and personal skills described in our educational model rather than only on

their memorization and recall of a fixed body of knowledge.

6. A faculty reward system of salary increases, promotions, and other perquisities would recompense participation in these revised curricular aims, structure, and academic support system.

If such curricular restructuring, faculty redefinition, and refocused educational aims become the norm rather than the exception, then an American college education would have sharply increased meaning and relevance to the many different constituencies institutions of higher learning serve today. By devising curricular approaches that enable students to gain the mental and personal capabilities with which they can affect their individual futures and adapt to a changing world, colleges will have quit the nineteenth-century world of the restricted, elitist germanic university and responded to the social and individual imperatives necessary for successful undergraduate learning in the 1980s and beyond.

Notes

1. A historic summary of past efforts to define curriculum may be found in Arthur Levine, *Handbook on Undergraduate Curriculum: Report for the Carnegie Council on Policy Studies in Higher Education* (San Francisco: Jossey-Bass, 1978), pp. 329-417.

2. For further discussion of this point, see John C. Sawhill, "Higher Education in the 80's: Beyond Retrenchment," in *Current Issues: New Models for General Education* (Washington, D.C.: American Association for Higher Education, 1980), pp. 13-22.

3. Ernest L. Boyer, "Bridging the Gap Between High School and College," in *Current Issues: New Models for General Education* (Washington, D.C.: American Association for Higher Education, 1980), pp. 6-12, builds a strong argument for the development of a core of common study at the high school level. He suggests, however, that this pattern be extended into the beginning college years.

4. A variety of purposes for undergraduate curricula are described in the chapter, "The Mission of Undergraduate Education," in *Missions of the College Curriculum*, A Commentary of the Carnegie Foundation for the

Advancement of Teaching (San Francisco: Jossey-Bass, 1977), pp. 150-63.

5. These skills and others are described in a full taxonomy in B. S. Bloom et al., *Cognitive Domain*. Handbook 1 of *Taxonomy of Educational Objectives* (New York: Longmans, Green, 1956).

6. Alexander Astin in "When Does a College Deserve To Be Called 'High Quality'?" in *Current Issues: Improving Teaching and Institutional Quality* (Washington, D.C.: American Association for Higher Education, 1980), p. 5, reminds us that much research "shows that students learn best when they have knowledge of the results of their learning efforts and when they invest time and energy in the learning task."

7. In describing the 1960s and 1970s in higher education, *Missions of the College Curriculum* (1977) sees this period as one of "greatly increased attention to consumer choice and to direct consumer influence. . . . New types of students, more of them part-time and more of them adults, came to campus to pick and choose what they wanted to take—and they rejected the 'tie-in sales' of requirements." The Carnegie commentary stresses that, in the absence of faculty convictions about "what is right and proper," market forces will determine curriculum. "What is offered is what is desired—or can be sold."

BIBLIOGRAPHY

Adler, Mortimer J., and M. Mayer. *The Revolution in Education.* Chicago: University of Chicago Press, 1958.

Appley, Dee G. "Anxiety and the Human Condition." *Journal of Canadian Association of University Student Services* 1, no. 1 (1966): 23-31.

_____. "Human Development and Higher Education." Unpublished conference paper. Conference on Coherence and Curriculum: Alternatives for the Future. Sponsored by Empire State College, The Danforth Foundation, and the Society for Values in Higher Education, Rensselaerville, New York. 12-14 April 1978.

_____, and Alvin E. Winder. *T-Groups and Therapy Groups in a Changing Society.* San Francisco: Jossey-Bass, 1973.

_____. "An Evolving Definition of Collaboration and Some Implications for the Work Setting." *Journal of Applied Behavioral Science* 13, no. 3 (August 1977): 279-91.

_____, eds. "Collaboration in Work Settings." *Journal of Applied Behavioral Science* 13, no. 3 (August 1977): 261-464.

Argyris, C. "Dangers in Applying Results from Experimental Social Psychology." *American Psychologist* 30, no. 4 (April 1975): 469-85.

Arrowsmith, William. "Thoughts on American Culture and Civilization." In *Schoolworlds '76*, p. 156.

Ashby, E. *Any Person, Any Study: An Essay on Higher Education in the United States.* New York: McGraw-Hill, 1971.

Astin, Alexander W. *Four Critical Years*. San Francisco: Jossey-Bass, 1977.

————. *Preventing Students from Dropping Out: A Longitudinal, Multi-institutional Study of College Dropouts*. San Francisco: Jossey-Bass, 1975.

————. "When Does a College Deserve To Be Called 'High Quality'?" in *Current Issues: Improving Teaching and Institutional Quality*. Washington, D.C.: American Association for Higher Education, 1980, pp. 1-9.

Bailey, S. K. *The Purposes of Education*. Bloomington, Ind.: Phi Delta Kappa Education Foundation, 1976.

Bedford Stuyvesant Unit Evaluation. Empire State College Research Series. Saratoga Springs, N.Y.: Empire State College Office of Research and Evaluation, 1977.

Belknap, Robert L., and Richard Kuhns. *Tradition and Innovation: General Education and the Reintegration of the University*. New York: Columbia University Press, 1977.

Bell, D. *The Reforming of Higher Education*. 1966. Reprint. New York: Anchor, 1968.

Berte, N. *Individualizing Education Through Contract Learning*. University, Ala.: University of Alabama Press, 1975.

Biller, Mary Ann, ed. *The Second Annual Report to the Kellogg Foundation: New Models in Career Education Program*. Saratoga Springs, N.Y.: Empire State College, 1975.

————. *The Third Annual Report to the Kellogg Foundation: New Models in Career Education Program*. Saratoga Springs, N.Y.: Empire State College, 1976.

Birnbaum, Norman. "The Arbitrary Disciplines." *Change*, July-August 1969, pp. 10-21.

Blackburn, R., E. Armstrong, C. Conrad, J. Didham, and T. McKune. *Changing Practices in Undergraduate Education*. Berkeley, Calif.: Carnegie Council on Policy Studies in Higher Education, 1976.

Blake, J. Herman, Kathryn Cowan, and Ronald Saufley. "Through the Hourglass (Darkly): An Exploratory Analysis of 'The New Student' at a Traditional University." n.p. Oakes College, University of California, Santa Cruz, Fall 1979.

Bloom, B. S., M. D. Englehart, W. H. Hill, E. J. Furst, and D. R. Krathwohl. *Cognitive Domain*. Handbook I of *Taxonomy of Educational Objectives*. New York: Longmans, Green, 1956.

Bloom, B. "Time and Learning." *American Psychologist* 29 (1974) 682-88.

Bonham, George. "Follow-up: The Carnegie Report." *The Center Magazine*, November/December 1973, p. 5.

Bouwsma, W. J. "Models of the Educated Man." *American Scholar* 44, no. 2 (1975): 195-212.

Bowen, H. R. *Investment in Learning: The Individual and Social Value of American Higher Education.* San Francisco: Jossey-Bass, 1977.

Boyer, Ernest L. "Bridging the Gap Between High School and College," in *Current Issues: New Models for General Education.* Washington, D.C.: American Association for Higher Education, 1980, pp. 6-12.

_____, and Martin Kaplan. *Educating for Survival.* New Rochelle, N.Y.: Change Magazine Press, 1977.

Brandstadter, Jochen, and Klaus A. Schneewind. "Optimal Human Development: Some Implications for Psychology." *Human Development* 20 (1977): 48-64.

Carnegie Commission on Higher Education. Following volumes:

A Chance to Learn: An Action Agenda for Equal Opportunity in Higher Education. New York: McGraw-Hill, 1970.

Less Time, More Options: Education Beyond the High School. New York: McGraw-Hill, 1971.

Reform on Campus: Changing Students, Changing Academic Programs. New York: McGraw-Hill, 1972.

Toward a Learning Society: Alternative Channels to Life, Work, And Service. New York: McGraw-Hill, 1973.

Carnegie Council on Policy Studies in Higher Education. *Three Thousand Futures: The Next Twenty Years for Higher Education.* San Francisco: Jossey-Bass, 1980.

Carnegie Foundation for the Advancement of Teaching. *Missions of the College Curriculum: A Contemporary Review with Suggestions.* San Francisco: Jossey-Bass, 1977.

Chickering, Arthur W. "Adult Development: A Workable Vision for Higher Education," in *Current Issues 1980: Integrating Adult Development Theory with Higher Education Practice.* Washington, D.C.: American Association for Higher Education, 1980.

_____. *Education and Identity.* San Francisco: Jossey-Bass, 1969.

_____. *Commuting Versus Resident Students.* San Francisco: Jossey-Bass, 1974.

_____, ed. *The Modern American College.* San Francisco: Jossey-Bass, 1981.

Cox, Harvey. *The Secular City.* New York: Macmillan, 1965.

Crittenden, K. S., J. L. Norr, and R. K. LeBailly. "Size of University Classes and Student Evaluations of Teaching." *Journal of Higher Education* 46, no. 4 (1975): pp. 461-70.

Cross, P. K. *Accent on Learning: Improving Instruction and Reshaping the Curriculum.* San Francisco: Jossey-Bass, 1976.

Cross, Patricia. *Beyond the Open Door: New Students to Higher Education.* San Francisco: Jossey-Bass, 1971.

————. *The Adult Learner.* San Francisco: Jossey-Bass, 1981.

———— et al. *Planning Non-Traditional Programs.* San Francisco: Jossey-Bass, 1974.

Dearing, B. "Abuses in Undergraduate Teaching: 1965," in *Twenty-Five Years: 1945 to 1970,* edited by G. K. Smith. San Francisco: Jossey-Bass, 1970.

Dewey, John. *Experience and Education.* New York: Collier, 1963.

————. *The Public and Its Problems.* Chicago: The Swallow Press, 1927.

————. *Reconstruction in Philosophy.* New York: New American Library, 1950.

Diversity By Design. Report of Commission on Non-Traditional Study: Samuel B. Gould, chairman. San Francisco: Jossey-Bass, 1972.

Dressel, Paul L. "Liberal Education: Developing the Characteristics of a Liberally Educated Person." *Liberal Education* 65 (1979): 313-22.

Educated Person in the Contemporary World. Proceedings of Conference cosponsored by the Aspen Institute for Humanistic Studies and the National Endowment for the Humanities. Aspen, Colo., 28 July-11 August, 1974.

Empire State College Bulletin, 1978-80. Saratoga Springs, N.Y.: SUNY/Empire State College, 1978.

Feldman, K. A., and T. M. Newcomb. *The Impact of College on Students.* Vol. 1. San Francisco: Jossey-Bass, 1969.

Frank, Austin C. *The 1975 Seniors at Berkeley.* Berkeley: University of California, Office of Student Affairs Research, 1976.

Friere, Paulo. "Conscientization: Cultural Action and Freedom." *Harvard Educational Review* 40, nos. 2 and 3 (May and August 1970).

————. *Pedagogy of the Oppressed.* New York: Herder and Herder, 1971.

Gaff, J. G. *Toward Faculty Renewal: Advances in Faculty, Instructional, and Organizational Development.* San Francisco: Jossey-Bass, 1975.

Gagne, R. M. *The Conditions of Learning,* 3rd ed. New York: Holt, Rinehart and Winston, 1977.

Gould, Samuel B., and Patricia K. Cross, eds. *Explorations in Non-Traditional Study.* San Francisco: Jossey-Bass, 1972.

Grant, Gerald, and David Riesman. *Perpetual Dream: Reform and*

Experiment in the American College. Chicago: University of Chicago Press, 1978.

Hall, James W., with Barbara L. Kevles. "Democratizing the Curriculum." *Change* 12, no. 1 (January 1980): 39-43.

Hall, James W., and Ernest G. Palola. "Curricula for Adult Learners," Paper #17, The Open University Conference on the Education of Adults at a Distance. Milton Keynes, U.K.: The British Open University, 1979.

Handlin, O., and M. F. Handlin. *The American College and American Culture—Socialization as a Function of Higher Education.* New York: McGraw-Hill, 1970.

Harris, Norman C., and John F. Grede. *Career Education in College.* San Francisco: Jossey-Bass, 1977.

Harvard Committee. *General Education in a Free Society.* Cambridge: Harvard University Press, 1945.

Heath, D. H. *Growing Up in College: Liberal Education and Maturity.* San Francisco: Jossey-Bass, 1968.

Hefferlin, J. L. *Dynamics of Academic Reform.* San Francisco: Jossey-Bass, 1969.

Heist, Paul A. *The Creative College Student: An Unmet Challenge.* San Francisco: Jossey-Bass, 1968.

Hill, Patrick J. "The Incomplete Revolution: A Reassessment of Recent Reforms in Higher Education. *Cross Currents* 24, no. 4 (Winter 1975): 423-43.

Hook, Sidney, Paul Kurtz, and Miro Todorovich, eds. *The Philosophy of the Curriculum: The Need for General Education.* Proceedings of a Conference by the University Centers for Rational Alternatives, Buffalo, N.Y., 1975.

Howard, Jan M., and Robert H. Somers. "Resisting Institutional Evil from Within," in *Sanctions for Evil,* ed. Nevitt Sanford and Craig Comstock. San Francisco: Jossey-Bass, 1971, pp. 264-89.

Jencks, C., and D. Riesman. *The Academic Revolution.* Garden City, N.Y.: Doubleday, 1968.

Jung, Carl. *Psychological Types.* London: Pantheon Books, 1923.

Katz, Joseph. *No Time for Youth: Growth and Constraint in College Students.* San Francisco: Jossey-Bass, 1968.

————, and Nevitt Sanford. "The Curriculum in the Perspective of the Theory of Personality Development," in *The American College,* ed. Nevitt Sanford. New York: John Wiley & Sons, 1962, pp. 418-44.

Kaysen, Carl, ed. *Content and Curriculum.* New York: McGraw-Hill 1973.

Kevles, Daniel J. *The Physicists: The History of a Scientific Commmunity in Modern America*. New York: Knopf, 1978.

Klemp, George O., Jr. *Relating Work and Education*. San Francisco: Jossey-Bass, 1977.

Knefelcamp, Lee, et al. *Applying New Developmental Findings*, no. 4. New Directions for Student Services. San Francisco: Jossey-Bass, 1978.

Kohlberg, Lawrence, and Rochelle Mayer. "Development as the Aim of Education." *Harvard Educational Review* 42, no. 4 (November 1972): 449-94.

Kolb, David A., and Ronald Fry. "Towards an Applied Theory of Experiential Learning," in *Theories of Group Processes*, ed. Cary L. Cooper. New York: John Wiley & Sons, 1975, pp. 33-58.

Laing, R. D., et al. *Interpersonal Perception*. London: Tavistock Publications, 1966.

Lasch, Christopher. *Culture of Narcissism: American Life in an Age of Diminishing Expectations*. New York: Warner, 1979.

Levine, Arthur. *Handbook on Undergraduate Curriculum*. San Francisco: Jossey-Bass, 1978.

_____ and J. Weingart, *Reform of Undergraduate Education*. San Francisco: Jossey-Bass, 1973.

Levinson, Daniel. *The Seasons of a Man's Life*. New York: Knopf, 1978.

Lewin, Kurt. "Group Decision and Social Change," in *Readings in Social Psychology*, ed. T. Newcomb and E. Hartley. New York: Holt, Rinehart, and Winston, 1947.

McClure, Larry, and Carolyn Buan, ed. *Essays on Career Education*. Portland: Northwest Regional Educational Laboratory, 1973.

McDermott, John. *The Culture of Experience*. New York: New York University Press, 1979.

McDonald, Donald. "A Six Million Dollar Misunderstanding." *The Center Magazine*, September/October, 1973, pp. 33-34.

McHenry, D. E. *Academic Departments: Problems, Variations, and Alternatives*. San Francisco: Jossey-Bass, 1977.

McKeachie, W. J. "Procedures and Techniques of Teaching: A Survey of Experimental Studies," in *The American College: A Psychological and Social Interpretation of the Higher Learning*, N. Sanford (Ed.) New York: John Wiley & Sons, 1962.

Maguire, John. "Can Change Be Institutionalized? How?" *Liberal Education* 63, no. 4 (December 1977).

_____, Joshua Smith, Joseph Palamountain, Henry Paley. "Recruitment, Enrollment and Retention of New Student Groups." New

York State Department of Education Long-Range Planning Working Paper. Albany, N.Y.: SED, 1980.

Marcus, Steven. "Some Questions in General Education Today," in *Parnassus: Essays in Honor of Jacques Barzun.* New York: Harper and Row, 1976, p. 100.

Maslow, A. H. *Motivation and Personality.* 2nd Ed. New York: Harper and Row, 1970.

_____. *Toward a Psychology of Being.* 2nd Ed. New York: Van Nostrand Reinhold, 1968.

Mattfeld, J. "Toward a New Synthesis in Curricular Patterns of Undergraduate Education." *Liberal Education* 61, no. 4 (1975): 531-47.

Mayeroff, M. *On Caring.* New York: Harper and Row, 1971.

Mayhew, L. B., and P. J. Ford. *Changing the Curriculum.* San Francisco: Jossey-Bass, 1971.

Medsker, L., S. Edelstein, H. Kreplin, J. Ruyle, and J. Shea. *Extending Opportunities for a College Degree: Practices, Problems, and Potentials.* Berkeley: University of California, Center for Research and Development in Higher Education, 1975.

Meeth, L. Richard. "Structuring for Change in Liberal Arts Colleges." Unpublished Paper. Washington, D.C.: Council for the Advancement of Small Colleges, August 1974.

Millard, Richard. "Vocation: Central Aim of Education." *Essays on Education,* no. 2 Iowa City: American College Testing Program, 1973.

Milton, O. *Alternatives to the Traditional: How Professors Teach and How Students Learn.* San Francisco: Jossey-Bass, 1972.

Murphy, Gardner. "Human Nature of the Future in Nunokawa," in *Human Values and Abnormal Behavior,* ed. E. Walter. Chicago: Scott, Foresman, 1965.

National Advisory Council for Career Education. *Masters of Reality: Certificate or Performance?* Washington, D.C.: National Student Education Fund, 1977.

Nyquist, Ewald Berger. "Are You Getting Your Money's Worth Out of a Liberal Arts Education?" Skidmore College Commencement, Saratoga Springs, N.Y., 1977.

O'Connell, William R. "The Curriculum Committee in the Liberal Arts College." Diss. New York: Teachers College, Columbia University, 1969.

Osipow, Samuel H. *Theories of Career Development.* 2nd Ed. Englewood Cliffs, N.J.: Prentice-Hall, 1973.

Perry, N. G., Jr. *Forms of Intellectual and Ethical Development in the*

College Years: A Scheme. New York: Holt, Rinehart and Winston, 1968.

Peterson, Richard E., and associates. *Lifelong Learning in America.* San Francisco: Jossey-Bass, 1979.

Piaget, J. *To Understand Is To Invent: The Future of Education.* New York: Grossman, 1973.

Provisional Report of the Task Force on Concentrations. Harvard College. July 1976.

Radest, Howard B. "Liberal Arts and Works." *Ramapo Papers* 1, no. 1 (1976).

Rawls, John. *A Theory of Justice.* Cambridge: Harvard University Press, 1971.

Report on Higher Education. Frank Newman, chairman, Task Force. Washington, D.C.: U.S. Government Printing Office, 1971.

Riesman, David, and Verne A. Stadtman, eds. *Academic Transformation.* New York: McGraw-Hill, 1973.

Roe, Anne. "Man's Forgotten Weapon in Nunokawa," in *Human Values and Abnormal Behavior*, ed. D. Walter. Chicago: Scott, Foresman, 1965.

Rosovsky, H. "Undergraduate Education: Defining the Issues." Excerpts from the Dean's Report 1975-76, reprinted from the *Report of the President of Harvard College and Reports of Departments, 1975-76.* Cambridge: Harvard University Press, 1976.

Rudolph, F. *Curriculum: The American Undergraduate Course of Study Since 1636.* San Francisco: Jossey-Bass, 1977.

Sawhill, John C. "Curriculum Priorities for the 80's: Beyond Retrenchment," in *Current Issues: New Models for General Education.* Washington, D.C.: American Association for Higher Education, 1980, pp. 13-22.

Schumacher, E. F. *A Guide for the Perplexed.* New York: Harper and Row, 1977.

Sennett, Richard. *The Uses of Disorder.* New York: Vintage Books, 1970.
_____. *The Fall of Public Man.* New York: Vintage Books, 1978.

Sheehy, Gail. *Passages: Predictable Crises of Adult Life.* New York: E. P. Dutton, 1976.

Simon, H. A. *Models of Man, Social and Rational: Mathematical Essays on Rational Human Behavior in a Social Setting.* New York: John Wiley & Sons, 1957.

Spurr, S. H. *Academic Degree Structures: Innovative Approaches.* New York: McGraw-Hill, 1970.

Toynbee, A. *Change and Habit: The Challenge of Our Time.* New York: Oxford University Press, n.d.

Trilling, Lionel. "The Uncertain Future of the Humanistic Educational Ideal." *The American Scholar* 44, no. 1 (Winter 1974/75): 56 and 61.

Trist, Eric. "Action Research and Adaptive Planning," in *Experimenting with Organizational Life*, ed. A. W. Clark. New York: Plenum Press, 1976.

Trow, M. "The American Academic Department as a Context for Learning." *Studies in Higher Education* 1, no. 1 (1976): 11-22.

Vermilye, D. W., ed. *Learner-Centered Reform: Current Issues in Higher Education 1975*. San Francisco: Jossey-Bass, 1975.

Vermilye, Dyckman, ed. *Relating Work and Education*. San Francisco: Jossey-Bass, 1977.

U.S. Department of Education. National Center for Education Statistics. Office of Educational Research and Improvement. *The Condition of Education*. 1981 ed. Washington, D.C.: GPO, 1981.

_____. *Digest of Education Statistics*. 1980 ed. Washington, D.C.: GPO, 1980.

_____. *Projections of Education Statistics to 1988-89*. Washington, D.C.: GPO, 1980.

Wey, Herbert W. *Alternatives in Higher Education: Innovations and Changing Practices in Selected Post-Secondary Institutions Around The World*. Boone, N.C.: Appalachian State University, 1976.

Wilson, R. C., et al. *College Professors and Their Impact on Students*. New York: John Wiley & Sons, 1975.

Wuest, Francis J. *Renewing Liberal Education: A Primer*. Kansas City, Mo.: Change in Liberal Education Network, 1979.

INDEX